THE
AMERICA'S CUP
RACES

The *America's* Cup.

THE
AMERICA'S CUP
RACES

By the Editors of Yachting

HERBERT L. STONE
WILLIAM H. TAYLOR
WILLIAM W. ROBINSON

New *York*

W · W · NORTON & COMPANY · INC ·

SBN 393 03167 5

1 2 3 4 5 6 7 8 9 0

CONTENTS

ILLUSTRATIONS

The *America's* Cup *(Frontispiece)*

THE
AMERICA'S CUP
RACES

Chapter I

IN 1851, when American clipper ships were the acknowleged queens of the world's ocean commerce, a Yankee schooner yacht sailed over to England for the express purpose of proving to British yachtsmen that American yachts were as outstanding in their way as the big cargo-carrying, square-rigged clippers were in theirs. She found the yachtsmen of England, who were generally regarded as the leaders in the sport in those days, surprisingly reluctant to take on her wide-flung challenge to meet her in match races for money or marbles. But she beat 17 of them in a race around their own stamping ground, the Isle of Wight, one fine day, and brought home a trophy that became the grail for more than a century of top-level international yachting competition, and bids fair to continue in that position for some time to come.

The *America's* Cup, named for the schooner that first won it, is the oldest trophy internationally competed for in any sport. Twenty matches—not counting the original race—have been sailed for it since it came into the possession of the New York Yacht Club as an international trophy, and at this writing the 21st match was scheduled for September, 1970. How many millions of dollars have been spent in efforts to win it, and how many millions have been spent by members of the New York Yacht Club to defend it, would be hard even to make a good guess at. But the dollars in themselves mean less than the history that has woven itself around this trophy in the century-plus of competition for it. That history is the history of the

1

whole sport. It is the history of naval architecture, as applied
to sailing craft throughout the yachting world. It is the history
of the sport's outstanding men down through the years. It is
the history of the development of sportsmanship and the ethics
of competition, from the days when some people said that "a
match should be won when its terms are made" to today's ideal
of starting the contestants off with an even break.

The Cup itself is no great beauty, by modern standards, being typical of the ornate tastes of its day. It cost 100 guineas—
in fact, was originally called the Hundred Guineas Cup. It
doesn't even have a bottom to it, so you couldn't fill it with
champagne to celebrate with if you won it. But a lot of people
have wanted it, and a lot still do.

It cannot be said that competition for this venerable silver
pitcher has always generated sweetness and light among the
nations involved. Yachtsmen, after all, are a cross-section of
the population at large, and some people are nicer than others.
There have been those among the defenders who, in arranging
terms for matches, have operated on the principle, "Never give
a challenger an even break." There have been contestants on
each side who played it a little too hard and too close—easily
the nastiest being the noble Lord Dunraven, challenger of the
1890s, a man with a chip on his shoulder and suspicion in his
heart. Even in comparatively recent matches there have been
incidents that ruffled the smooth waters of international sporting good will. But the important thing is that the quality of
the sportsmanship, like the quality of the competition, has
steadily improved over the years. The *America's* Cup has been,
in general, an instrument of international good will, just as the
America herself was intended to be.

To fully appreciate what the *America* did in that expedition
to the Solent, traditional heart and nerve center of British
yachting, in 1851, let's look at the state of the sport in the two
countries.

Yachting had been an established sport in England for a couple of centuries. There was a goodly fleet of big yachts, owned largely by the nobility and gentry, cruising and racing in British waters, and there were a number of clubs, notable among which was (and still is) The Royal Yacht Squadron, founded in 1815. England, though she originally imported yachting from the Dutch, was the outstanding yachting nation as well as Mistress of the Seas.

In America there had been some yachting—in the literal sense of the word, meaning the use of privately owned vessels for pleasure—since Colonial times, but few men had either the leisure time or the money to indulge extensively in sailing as a sport until around 1840. By then there were enough yachts and yachtsmen for yacht clubs to be formed in leading cities like New York, Boston, Charleston, S.C., New Orleans and others. Most were short-lived, but the New York Yacht Club, organized in 1844 with Col. John C. Stevens as its first commodore, survived and has been this country's most prominent club ever since.

This club's first clubhouse was a simple one-room building on the Weehawken flats on the New Jersey shore of the Hudson River. (This house, far from its birthplace, stands today in the Mystic Seaport at Mystic, Conn.) In its first year nine yachts, of 17 to 45 tons measurement, sailed its first regatta over a course starting in New York's Upper Bay, down through the Narrows and the Lower Bay, out to sea to a buoy off Sandy Hook, and back, a course that was to see a lot of action in the early matches for the *America's* Cup.

By 1850 the club had a good-sized fleet of sloops and schooners. Most of them were of the shoal-draft, centerboard type, not particularly seaworthy but fast and well suited to New York Bay's sheltered conditions and shallow waters. Others, however, were seagoing keel schooners, some of which were either converted pilot schooners or craft built as yachts but more or less on the pilot boat model, much as seagoing schooner yachts of the 1920s and '30s were to be modeled after the famous Gloucester fishing schooners.

These pilot schooners were as distinctive in their way as the great American clipper ships which in the 1840s dominated the world's ocean trade routes. They had to be able, for they cruised from Nantucket Shoals to the Delaware Capes to meet incoming cargo and packet ships, in all kinds of weather. They had to be fast, for piloting was a competitive business then and it was often a race to see which schooner could put her pilot aboard the inward-bounder. They had to be easily handled so small crews, when their pilots had all been placed on incoming ships, could bring the schooners home. So they made fine yachts.

It was largely the fame of these pilot schooners that inspired a group of members of the young New York Yacht Club to build the *America* and send her abroad. The first of the great world trade expositions was being planned in England, to be held in 1851, and it was suggested that one appropriate American product to be displayed in connection with it would be one of the American pilot schooners, whose reputations were well known abroad from reports of returning British shipmasters who had seen them in action.

There was considerable correspondence back and forth across the ocean, including a most cordial invitation from the Earl of Wilton, commodore of the Royal Yacht Squadron, extending the "civilities" of that organization. No mention of definite prizes was made, but the inference was that there would be plenty of them, not to mention large cash wagers and special matches. The latter point was a real consideration with the New Yorkers who were interested. Cash bets on match races and sweepstakes were a normal part of yacht racing a century ago, and the bets ran up into the tens of thousands of dollars. If a Yankee schooner proved as fast, compared to the British yachts, as New Yorkers felt she would, this venture could be made to pay off in important money. Alas for the best-laid plans of mice and yachtsmen!

A group of New York Yacht Club members decided to give it a try. This first "syndicate" in *America's* Cup history consisted of six men—Commodore John C. Stevens, his brother Edwin A. Stevens, George L. Schuyler, Col. James A. Hamilton, J. Beekman Finley, and Hamilton Wilkes.

The moving spirit of the enterprise was Commodore Stevens, prominent member of a famous family. The Stevens's owned much of what is now Hoboken, and among other things they founded Stevens Institute of Technology which many years later, with its ship model towing tank, was to play a major part in the design of defenders for the *America's* Cup. Commodore Stevens was a noted engineer who applied his talents to, among many other matters such as the development of the steamboat, the design and building of sailing yachts. It was reported that his cooperation and advice was an important aid to the success of George Steers, who modeled the *America* and supervised her construction.

Steers was a young designer and builder who had already made quite a reputation with the yachts and pilot boats he had turned out by the time he was 30 years old. Particularly in the pilot schooner *Mary Taylor,* which he built in 1849, he had shown progressive ideas. He discarded the conventional "cod's head and mackerel tail" model of older vessels—i.e. full, bluff bows and a long, tapering run in the afterbody—and gave her long, sharp, concave bow lines, more powerful sections aft and other features. She proved a very fast vessel and the *America's* model was an improvement on the *Taylor's*.

The syndicate made a contract with William H. Brown, by whom Steers was then employed, to build the new yacht in his yard at the foot of 12th Street on the East River. It was such a contract as a yachtsman today wouldn't believe if he saw it.

The price named was $30,000, fully equipped, with the delivery date set for April 1, 1851. She was to be tried out by the syndicate, and if she did not prove the fastest vessel in the United States, the syndicate need not accept her. Furthermore, if they took her to England and she was not successful there, they could still return her to Brown. Builders today don't have that much confidence in either their own products or their customers' racing prowess or integrity.

Of course the schooner wasn't ready on contract time. Boats never are. It was May 3rd before she was launched, and on May 24th, when she was still not ready, the syndicate offered to purchase her outright for $20,000. She was finally delivered on June 18.

The principal dimensions of the *America* were: length over all, 101 feet 9 inches; length waterline, 90 feet, 3 inches; beam, 22 feet; draft, 11 feet. Her mainmast was 81 feet long, her foremast 79 feet, 6 inches and they were stepped with a strong rake, characteristic of the pilot schooners and the old Baltimore clippers. Her bowsprit was 32 feet from tip to heel and her 53-foot main boom extended well out over the stern. She carried 5263 square feet of sail in the simplest possible schooner rig—mainsail, foresail and a single jib. The sails were made by R. H. Wilson of New York, one of whose descendants, Prescott Wilson, was to make sails for the Cup defenders of the 1930s.

Below decks her accommodations were, in general, like the pilot schooners. There was a large main saloon running from the mainmast aft, around the sides of which were six built-in berths with transom seats in front. Forward of this were four staterooms, then the galley and pantry, and a large forecastle accommodating 15 men. A bathroom and a clothes locker flanked a passage that ran aft from the main saloon to the cockpit, under which was the sail locker.

The *America* was beaten in trial races by the larger centerboard sloop *Maria,* a famous yacht in top condition and sailed

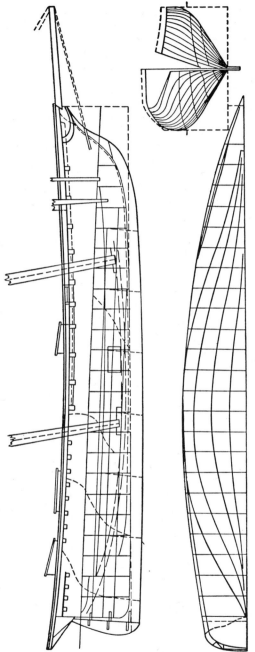

Lines of the *America* as taken off while the yacht was docked in England.

by a crew that had won many races with her. The new schooner
did, however, beat several other boats, and her owners were
far from discouraged.

On June 21, with her racing sails stowed below and a heavier
seagoing suit bent, she was towed down to Sandy Hook and

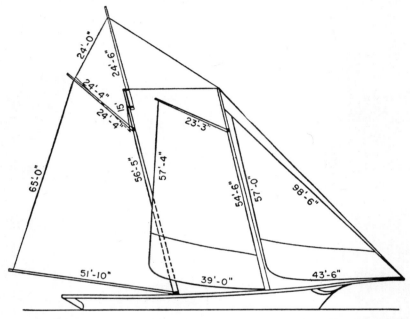

Sail plan of the *America,* taken from the original plan in Wilson's sail loft
at Port Jefferson.

took her departure, carrying with her the hopes of her owners
and a large part of the American people. She was the last word
in American shipbuilding, and she was going forth, presumably,
to meet the pick of England's yachting fleet.

Aboard her were 13 men, including George Steers, his
brother and a young nephew, Henry Steers, 15; Captain Dick
Brown, a Sandy Hook pilot, in command; Nelse Comstock,
mate; six sailors, steward and cook.

In spite of the traditionally unlucky number aboard, they

The *America* at Cowes.

The original clubhouse of the New York Yacht Club, now at Mystic Seaport, Conn.

Model of the *America*.

made a good passage of 20 days to Havre, France, which included a day's run of 284 miles and six days of over 200 miles in 24 hours. Commodore Stevens joined her at Havre, where she spent three weeks refitting and getting in racing trim for her invasion of the Solent.

Chapter II

ON JULY 31, the *America* sailed for Cowes, on the Isle of Wight, with her stores and spare gear still aboard. That night was calm, with a thick fog, and she anchored six or seven miles from Cowes. When the breeze came in the following morning and blew the fog away, the English cutter *Laverock,* one of their crack boats, ran down from Cowes to meet the stranger, and with the intention of trying her mettle then and there. She found the American boat just weighing anchor, and hung around her persistently to force her, if possible, into a trial of speed.

Commodore Stevens might have ducked an issue then; might have killed his boat so as not to show her true speed. He was looking to arrange future matches and it would have been to his advantage not to show too much speed just then. However, seeing that he could not gracefully decline a brush, he gave the orders to "let her go," and with sportsmanlike instinct tackled the *Laverock* for all there was in his boat.

It was a beat back to Cowes, and in those few miles the *America* worked out to windward surprisingly fast, finishing well ahead of the Englishman. Not many hours afterwards it was known throughout the yachting community that no English yacht was the *America's* equal in going to windward. That little brush proved unfortunate for the American hopes of putting their venture "in the black" by winning substantial bets on match races.

10

The English yachtsmen seemed impressed with *America's* speed, yet the boat made an unfavorable impression by her looks, as she was radically different from the English type, and the papers spoke of her rather slightingly at first, referring to her as "a big-boned skeleton but no phantom," and criticising

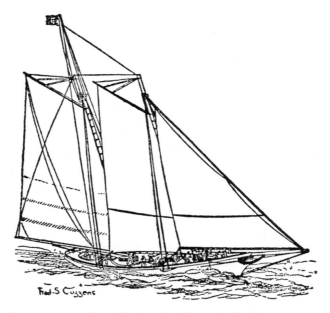

America, with her pilot-boat rig of 1851.

her long, sharp bow and heavy raking masts, and the absence of a foretopmast.

Commodore Stevens, as the representative owner, immediately set about the business of arranging matches, but for some weeks had no success at all. The Englishmen were most hospitable, but showed a strong disinclination to match their yachts against the American boat, and no effort was made on their part to arrange a special match or put up any suitable trophy to race for. Commodore Stevens first offered to sail a match against any of their schooners, and when this was not taken up he enlarged the challenge to include cutters as well.

Still meeting with no response, and thinking that if the stakes were made large enough they might prove attractive to some of the English owners, the Commodore, to quote Mr. George L. Schuyler, one of the syndicate, "with his usual promptness, and regardless of the pockets of his associates, had posted in the clubhouse at Cowes a challenge to sail the *America* a match against any British vessel whatever, for any sum from one to ten thousand guineas, merely stipulating that there should be not less than a six-knot breeze." Even this brought no response from the supposedly sport-loving English yachtsmen. Later, Mr. Robert Stephenson came forward with an offer to match his schooner *Titania* against the *America* for a race of twenty miles to windward and return, for £100. This offer was accepted, and August 28th fixed for the date of the match.

This failure of British yachtsmen to take up the gauntlet flung down by their American visitors was not viewed favorably by the English people at large, and the London "Times" commented upon it as follows:

"Most of us have seen the agitation which the appearance of a sparrow-hawk on the horizon creates among a flock of wood-pigeons or skylarks when, unsuspecting all danger and engaged in airy flights or playing about over the fallows, they all at once come down to the ground and are rendered almost motionless for fear of the disagreeable visitor. Although the gentlemen whose business is on the waters of the Solent are neither wood-pigeons nor skylarks, and although the *America* is not a sparrow-hawk, the effect produced by her apparition off West Cowes among yachtsmen seems to have been completely paralyzing. She has flung down the gauntlet to England, Ireland and Scotland, and not one has been found there to take it up."

In the meantime Commodore Stevens was notified by the Royal Yacht Squadron that there would be a regular open regatta around the Isle of Wight on August 22d, for which all of their boats would be eligible, to be sailed without time allowance, and that the *America* would be welcomed. This race was for a trophy put up by the club, valued at 100 guineas.

It was asking a good deal to have one yacht sail against a whole fleet, especially over a course that for a good part of the distance was not in open water, and where local knowledge of winds and tidal conditions counted for much. The same paper just quoted had this to say regarding the course:

"The course around the Isle of Wight is notoriously one of the most unfair to strangers that can be selected, and, indeed, does not appear a good race-ground to anyone, inasmuch as the current and tides render local knowledge of more value than swift sailing and nautical skill."

However, when the 22d came, though the wind was light, it found *America* at the line waiting for the starting signal. The fleet that the American yacht was called upon to meet was made up of seventeen British cutters and schooners. They ranged in size all the way from T. leMerchant's 47-ton cutter *Aurora* up to G. H. Acker's 392-ton, three-masted schooner *Brilliant,* with the *America's* 170 tons in the middle of the size range. It was a thoroughly representative fleet of British yachts.

In those days the start of a race was made from at anchor, instead of a sailing start as is now the custom, the boats hoisting sail and getting under way when the starting gun was fired, thus testing ability in handling.

The fleet was lined up in a double row, the cutters in the first line and the schooners some 300 yards astern of them. The preparatory signal was given at 9:55 A.M., on which the yachts made sail, and the starting gun at 10 A.M., when they were to cast off and get under way. *America* was the last of the fleet to get away. One of the most graphic accounts of the race is that of Henry Steers', nephew of the designer, who was aboard of the *America*. In describing the race at the Seawanhaka Yacht Club, in 1877, he said, in part:

"The wind was from the westward. The yachts were allowed to get up their sails after the first gun, but we found that we constantly overran our anchor and slewed around, and we had to lower our sails; and so all the yachts got off ahead of us; however, we had a large crew and got our sails up very quickly. By the time we got to the Nab (12 miles) we had walked through the whole fleet except four—*Beatrice, Aurora, Volante,* and *Arrow.* We were running wing and wing, and these boats would steer close together, so that when we tried to get through them we could not without fouling, and had to keep cutting and sheering about, very often being near gybing. From the Nab to St. Catherine's the wind was ahead (it had shifted to S. S. W. and was of variable strength), and there we left them so fast that when we got down to the Point there was not a yacht in sight. Here we caught the tide, and for a long time made little way beating against it, and the little *Aurora* came up pretty near to us, and the *Arrow* was just behind her. After getting by St. Catherine's Point we had a leading wind, and we went from there to the Needles at the rate of thirteen or fourteen knots. Off St. Catherine's we carried away our flying jibboom, and I remember that Dick Brown said he was d—d glad it was gone, as he didn't believe in carrying a flying jib to windward. We arrived at Cowes about eight o'clock."

It was 5:30 P.M. when the *America* rounded the Needles, and at that point it was estimated, by the best English authorities, she was a good eight miles ahead of the second boat, the little *Aurora,* with the rest of the squadron out of sight astern. Here the wind fell light again, with the tide ahead, and in the run up the Solent in the early evening the *Aurora* gained, being only about two miles astern at the finish. As she crossed the finish line in the darkness the Yankee yacht was timed at 8:37 P.M. and the *Aurora* at 8:55. Then came *Bacchante* at 9:30; *Eclipse,* 9:45, and the big *Brilliant* at 1:20 A.M. the following morning, the times of the other boats not being taken. Though the race was sailed without time allowance, there was but little comfort for the British yachtsmen in this fact, for by Acker's time allowance scale, then in use, the *Aurora* would still have been beaten by about two minutes had she received her allowance.

The next day the owner of the *Brilliant* protested the *America* on the ground that she had passed on the wrong side of the Nab Lightship, but as the sailing instructions given to Commodore Stevens did not specify on which side to pass it, the protest was not allowed.

Regarding the carrying away of the flying jibboom Henry Steers had the following to say:

"Some of the gentlemen of our party wanted to make their expenses after coming so far, and they went to one place and another trying to get a little money on the race, but their success was not brilliant. We were rigged pilot-boat fashion, no foretopmast and no flying jibboom, and, as we thought we could do better with a flying jib, we went to Michael Ratsey, at the Isle of Wight, to get him to make the spar, and my uncle bet him the price of that jibboom that we could beat any boat that he could name, and he named the *Beatrice*. Well, then we went to a sailmaker to have a flying jib made, and we bet the price of this sail on the race. So, after all, all that we got on the race was the price of the flying jibboom and the sail. . . .

"There was an awful crying and moaning about Cowes the night we finished. Ratsey and other builders were much chagrined, but they all said that they could build a boat that would beat the *America*. They said she was a 'mere shell,' 'a Yankee trick,' that we had exhausted ourselves and could never do it again. 'Well,' John C. Stevens said, 'what will you do?' They said, 'We will build a boat in ninety days that will beat the *America* for £500.' He said, 'Two thousand five hundred dollars won't pay us for waiting ninety days; make it £25,000

and we'll wait and sail the race.' They would not do this and
so it came to naught."

The following day Queen Victoria, who was very much
interested in the outcome of the race (so much so that an alleged
conversation between her and her signal master anent there
"being no second" to *America* has become famous), visited the
America with the Prince Consort and her suite.

The trophy won by the *America* in this race, while frequently
called the Queen's Cup, had in fact nothing to do with Queen
Victoria and was not donated by her. It was put up by the
Royal Yacht Squadron and was known as the Hundred Guinea
Cup (its cost at that time), or, later, as the *America's* Cup. It
became the permanent property of the yacht winning it, and
Commodore Stevens brought it back to America with him, as
practically the only spoils of their summer's campaign.

Chapter III

EFFECT OF THE "AMERICA" ON THE FUTURE OF YACHT DE-
SIGN, AND THE FURTHER HISTORY OF THE FAMOUS YACHT —
THE CUP DEEDED TO THE NEW YORK YACHT CLUB

THE INFLUENCE of the *America* on the future of yacht design
in the United States and abroad was immediately felt; and the
old, full, bluff bows and long run, the "cod's head and mackerel
tail" model, were doomed. In their place came the sharp, lean,
concave bow of the *America* and the other elements that her
design embodied.

In regard to sails the *America* also upset existing theories
abroad, the English yachts having at that time loosely woven
sails with a big bag, or draft, as it is called, in them, whereas
America's sails were closely woven, set much flatter, giving
greater efficiency in going to windward, and on account of their
large size had great driving power. Future yacht practice followed the *America's* lead in this matter, also.

About a week after winning the Hundred Guinea Cup, the
America sailed her match with the *Titania,* twenty miles to
windward and return, from the Nab lightship on the easterly
side of the Isle of Wight. There was a cracking good breeze, just
the kind the contestants had been hoping for. In the hard
thrash to windward the fore gaff of the *America* was carried
away, but though some time was lost in making repairs, the race
was at no time in danger and she won by 52 minutes.

Sooner than bring the *America* home, the syndicate decided
to offer her for sale in England, and she was purchased by Lord
John de Blaquiere for $25,000. On passing into the hands of
her new owner her masts were immediately cut down some

five feet—why, Heaven only knows, as she was certainly "right" as she was—iron braces were added, and she was raced in England in 1852 with only moderate success. She did not seem to be in the same trim as in the previous year (probably due to the "monkeying" that had been done on her) and her English skipper never seemed to get the hang of her and did not get the most out of her flat sails.

She cruised in the Mediterranean in 1852, where she rode out a four-day's gale without damage, and in 1853 was sold to Lord Templeton, who used her a year. After that she was hauled up in the mud at Cowes. Here she staid until sold in 1859, when she was towed to Pitcher's yard on the Thames and found to be in such bad shape inside that she had to be entirely rebuilt. This Pitcher did, wisely replacing a piece at a time, and not trying to improve upon her as many builders would have done, until she was rebuilt without in any way changing her original form.

At this time, also, the large gilt eagle resting on two crossed flags that had graced her stern since she was built was removed and placed above the door of an inn at Ryde, Isle of Wight, where it remained until it was returned many years later to the New York Yacht Club, in whose 44th Street house it may now be seen.

She was then sold to an English yachtsman, who changed her name to *Camilla* and in her made a trip to the West Indies, on his return racing her again in England. Then the Civil War broke out in the United States and a Savannah man bought her and, with a few guns mounted on her decks, she became a dispatch boat and blockade runner in the Southern cause, until she was chased up the St. John's River, Florida, by a gunboat and scuttled. At least, there she was found later by the United States ship *Ottawa,* with her masts out of water and her bottom full of auger holes. During this stage of her career she was known as the *Memphis.*

She was raised by the Federal government, repaired, and under the Stars and Stripes once more. With her original name restored, she served with the blockading fleet off Charleston, S. C., until 1864, when she was sent to Annapolis as a training ship for the midshipmen at the Naval Academy. While in the former work several captures were credited to her and her naval crew.

The old veteran was destined to appear once more in an international yacht race, and six years later she was at the line to meet *Cambria,* the first challenger for the *America's* Cup. After nineteen years of hard and varied service, she was still fast enough to trim the challenger.

After this she was sold by the United States government and was bought by General Benjamin F. Butler, of Massachusetts, in whose family she remained until 1916.

Her days of glory were over; she had lived her life and carried her message to the world, and the newer vessels, the result of years of refinement of the principle which *America,* first of all yachts, demonstrated, naturally outclassed her. Thereafter, though beaten in cruising runs or in brushes with more modern craft, she still held many years of usefulness to her owner, and wherever she appeared true sailormen gazed at her in admiration and with a feeling of reverence, nearly akin to awe, not only for what she had done, but for the idea that she stood for. Once more she was to appear on an *America's* Cup course. In 1893, during the *Vigilant-Valkyrie* match, she was off Sandy Hook, where a party from her deck watched the latest creations of the minds of yacht designers battle for the Cup she had won over forty years before.

From about 1900 to 1916, the *America* lay, sadly neglected, in a berth in Boston Harbor. In 1916, members of the Butler family were ready to accept an offer for her from a firm of Cape Verdean Portuguese who wanted to put her in the packet trade between those islands and New Bedford, but C. H. W.

Foster, of the Eastern Yacht Club saved her from that fate by buying her. She lay in the Lawley yacht basin near Boston until 1921, when a group of public-spirited yachtsmen obtained title to the old vessel, had necessary repairs made, and arranged to present her to the U. S. Naval Academy.

Her trip under tow of a Navy submarine chaser from Boston to Annapolis was a sentimental journey, with stops at many yachting centers along the way, and she was finally moored in the Academy basin on the Severn River. The Navy had no appropriation to maintain her properly, however. During World War II she was hauled out at the Annapolis Yacht Yard, to keep her from sinking in her berth, and in 1945 she was broken up. Souvenirs in the way of hardware, timber and gear were distributed among yachting organizations and individuals, and her rudder is preserved at the Mystic Seaport in Mystic, Conn., in the original 1844 clubhouse of the New York Yacht Club, which had been moved first from the Weehawken flats to the club's Glen Cove, L. I., station, and, about 1950, to Mystic.

When Commodore Stevens returned to America, the Cup he had in his possession was about the only tangible evidence of the *America's* trip to England. It was the property of the six men of the syndicate who built *America* and sent her abroad, and by their consent it remained in the custody of Commodore Stevens, where it had a place in the drawing room of his Washington Square home. It is not a particularly beautiful piece of silverware, as we judge those things to-day, and was not really a cup, but a pitcher, or ewer, rather stiff and formal in its design.

In 1857 Commodore Stevens cast about for some fitting disposition of the Cup, desiring, if it were possible, to have it stand for international competition of the highest order. To that end he and the four surviving members of the original syndicate decided to turn it over to the New York Yacht Club in trust, to be held as a permanent challenge cup, open to competition by any organized yacht club of any foreign country.

The terms of this Deed of Gift, which was really nothing more than a letter tendering the Cup to the club, were so simple, straightforward, and fair, and so devoid of an appreciation of the complexities that were to beset yacht racing, and especially international racing, forty or fifty years later, that it is worth while to give them in full.

New York, July 8, 1857

To the Secretary of the New York Yacht Club:

Sir:—The undersigned, members of the New York Yacht Club, and late owners of the schooner yacht *America,* beg leave through you to present to the Club the Cup won by the *America* at the Regatta of the Royal Yacht Squadron at Cowes, England, August 22, 1851.

This Cup was offered as a prize to be sailed for by yachts of all nations without regard to difference of tonnage, going round the Isle of Wight, the usual course for the Annual Regatta of the Royal Yacht Squadron, and was won by the *America,* beating eight cutters and seven schooner yachts which started in the race.

The Cup is offered to the New York Yacht Club, subject to the following conditions:

Any organized Yacht Club of any foreign country shall always be entitled, through any one or more of its members, to claim the right of sailing a match for this Cup with any yacht or other vessel of not less than 30 or more than 300 tons, measured by the Custom House rule of the country to which the vessel belongs.

The parties desiring to sail for the Cup may make any match with the Yacht Club in possession of the same that may be determined upon by mutual consent; but in case of disagreement as to terms, the match shall be sailed over the usual course for the Annual Regatta of the Yacht Club in possession of the Cup, and subject to its Rules and Sailing Regulations—the challenging party being bound to give six months' notice in writing, fixing the day they wish to start. This notice to embrace the length, Custom House measurement, rig, and name of the vessel.

It is to be distinctly understood that the Cup is to be the property of the Club, and not of the members thereof, or owners of the vessels winning it in a match; and that the condition of keeping it open to be sailed for by Yacht Clubs of all foreign countries, upon the

terms above laid down, shall forever attach to it, thus making it
perpetually a Challenge Cup for friendly competition between
foreign countries.

J. C. STEVENS
EDWIN A. STEVENS
HAMILTON WILKES
J. BEEKMAN FINLEY
GEORGE L. SCHUYLER

From this act has resulted some of the greatest yacht racing
the world has seen. It has been the incentive for the highest
development of yacht design, and though the terms of the
document are apparently plain, even to the layman, it has
resulted in some of the bitterest controversy that the history of
yachting has known.

Two points in the deed should be noted well, as they have
a bearing on the future history of the Cup. One is that the
terms were very elastic as regards the making of a match, as
these were to be determined entirely "by mutual consent,"
either side giving as much or as little as it saw fit; and in the
event of its being impossible for the two sides to agree on
suitable terms, the challenger had the right to a match over the
regular course used in the annual regatta of the club holding
the Cup, and subject to that club's racing rules. The other
point is that the word "match" is not defined. Strictly, it means
a specially arranged race between two boats, or with an equal
number of boats representing each side. After the first race for
the Cup, the holding club virtually conceded this point.

It will also be noticed that measurements were very elastic,
the size of a yacht eligible to compete being between 30 and
300 tons (no other restrictions), the waterline or over-all length
not being in use at that time for yacht measurement.

Chapter IV

THE FIRST CHALLENGE FOR THE CUP — RACE BETWEEN THE
"CAMBRIA" AND THE NEW YORK YACHT CLUB FLEET

THE FACT that the Hundred Guinea Cup had been offered as
a perpetual challenge trophy, open to all foreign nations, together with the terms of the Deed of Gift, was announced to all
the yacht clubs of the world by the New York Yacht Club, yet
eleven years went by before anyone challenged for it. During
that time a number of American schooner yachts had crossed
over to England, and one trans-Atlantic race of three Yankee
schooners in December, 1866, had attracted a great deal of
attention, but no move was made to send a yacht to this country.

In the first fifteen years following the *America's* invasion of
British waters, a slow but steady change was taking place in
the status of English and American shipping. At that time the
American merchant fleet was supreme upon the seas; the
American clippers were the fastest afloat. They had no trouble
in getting high freights, and insurance rates were lowest in
American bottoms.

With the passing of the Navigation Act, opening British ports
to the commerce of the world instead of limiting the carrying
between English possessions to British ships, English ship-
owners awoke to the fact that if they were to hold their mari-
time position at all they would have to have a merchant marine
that equalled or excelled that of America. So they set about
improving their sailing ships, at first having several built in
this country by the firms that built the famous American
clippers, and then building others at home from these models,
improving wherever they could. About this time iron began

to supplant wood in the construction of ships. England was the first to recognize the advantages of this building material, and with the better facilities at hand for this form of construction that country soon forged far ahead of us in shipbuilding and there followed an era of unparalleled activity in British shipping. The advent of steam for ocean-going purposes also found England prepared to profit by the change, and in this branch of building also it quickly outstripped America.

It was but natural with this advance in shipbuilding that yacht development should have kept pace with it, whereas in this country the shipping industry was on the decline, due to the Civil War and other causes, and yachting for a time languished here. We had, however, in the vicinity of New York, a fair-sized fleet of pleasure vessels, mostly schooner rigged and many of them shoal draft, centerboard boats.

The centerboard was on the high tide of its popularity in the revival of the sport following the Civil War. Not only was this due to the numerous shoals and flats around New York harbor and bay, but also to the fact that the smaller displacement of the centerboard boats and their lighter construction made them faster than the keel type, and they were unusually successful in the waters around Sandy Hook. So great was the popularity of this type that even some of the largest schooners were centerboarders.

During all these years the Cup won so decisively by the *America* in 1851 remained apparently forgotten, gathering dust in the lockers of the New York Yacht Club, until, in the fall of 1868, came a letter from Mr. James Ashbury, owner of the English schooner *Cambria,* in which he expressed a desire to race his yacht against the champion American schooner, to be selected by the New York Yacht Club; and knowing about the Cup won seventeen years before by the *America,* he suggested that that Cup be put up as a trophy.

Mr. Ashbury was evidently not a representative English

Cambria, the first challenger.

Transfilm photo

Models of *Magic* (left) and *Cambria*, winner and challenger in 1870.

yachtsman, and was not very well posted as to yachting usage and tradition, as his correspondence, carried on for the next three years, shows. He had a fast schooner, however, in which he had boundless faith.

In 1868 the large American schooner yacht *Sappho,* of 310 tons, built the year before on speculation, had crossed the Atlantic to race in England, with the expectation that she would "clean up" and could then be sold to advantage. In yacht racing, however, the unlooked for frequently happens and "no race is won till it's lost." So when *Sappho* met two English cutters and two schooners in a race around the Isle of Wight

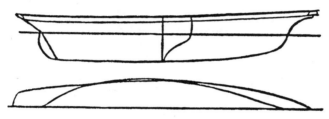

Lines of *Cambria,* the challenger of 1870.

she was badly beaten, the new schooner *Cambria* winning. There being no offer for the defeated *Sappho,* she was brought back to America and altered under the direction of Capt. "Bob" Fish, a famous yacht modeler and skipper of that day.

From the result of this race Mr. Ashbury seems to have reached the conclusion that the *Cambria* was invincible, and he was very free with his challenges. The first communication from him was more in the form of a letter of suggestion than a formal challenge for the *America's* Cup. The principal points of the proposal that he made were as follows:

Before the racing season of 1869 the New York Yacht Club was to select their fastest schooner, of a tonnage not to exceed that of the *Cambria,* which was 188 tons, Thames measurement, by more than 10 per cent. This schooner would be sent across

the Atlantic in time to take part in the English yachting season.
Then, about September 1st, this schooner and *Cambria* were
to race back across the ocean to Sandy Hook, for a piece of
silver valued at $1250; and lastly, after arriving here, these
same two vessels were to race around Long Island (a distance
of about 220 miles), two races out of three, according to Thames
Yacht Club measurement with time allowance, for the *America's* Cup. He ends this queer proposal by saying: "If I lost
I would present the N.Y.Y.C., or the owner of the successful
vessel, with a cup, value 100 guineas, or I would race any other
schooner of about my tonnage over the same course on the said

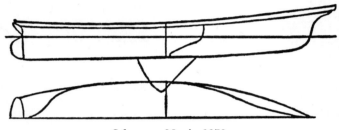

Schooner *Magic*, 1870.

conditions; the competing vessel to have been previously pronounced by the N.Y.Y.C. as the fastest vessel in America of her
size and class, and providing the said vessel had not been built
since the date of this communication, and was in all respects a
sea-going vessel, and not a *mere shell or racing machine.*"

The New York Yacht Club responded that it could only consider that portion of the letter dealing with a race for the
America's Cup, and that the club was only authorized under
the deed to accept a challenge from an organized foreign yacht
club, and not from an individual. Then followed several letters, in none of which did Mr. Ashbury comply with the terms
of the deed by which the New York Yacht Club held the Cup
in trust, until finally the New York Yacht Club cabled him in
the summer of 1869 that when he had complied with the neces-

sary preliminaries, he would, upon his arrival here, have the right, *provided no match could be agreed upon,* to sail over the annual regatta course of the New York Yacht Club, for the Cup won by the *America.*

Thus the summer of 1869 was frittered away in letter writing until, under date of November 14th of that year, Mr. Ashbury again wrote (in part) as follows:

I beg to give you six months' notice of my intention to race for the Cup on the 16th May, 1870; the course to be a triangular course from Staten Island, forty miles out to sea and back. The Cup having been won at Cowes, under the rules of the R. Y. S., it thereby follows that *no centerboard vessel* can compete against the *Cambria* in this particular race, but in all other respects I must conform to the stipulations and rules of the N.Y.Y.C. Rule 7 of the R. Y. S. states:

"No vessels which are fitted with machinery for shifting keels, or otherwise altering the form of their bottoms, shall be permitted to enter for prizes given by the Royal Yacht Squadron."

JAMES ASHBURY

This still was very wide of the conditions governing the *America's* Cup, and was likewise the first "kick" as to the form or construction of the American defenders, a point that was to be a bone of contention in many future challenges. Of course the New York Yacht Club could not agree to these terms, but they answered in a courteous and conciliatory manner, and Mr. Ashbury decided to come across the following summer.

He had also arranged for a race on the way over between the American schooner *Dauntless,* owned by the then vice-commodore of the New York Yacht Club, James Gorden Bennett, from Daunt Head, Ireland, to Sandy Hook. Owing to some delay in getting the *Dauntless* ready it was not until July 4th, 1870, that this race was started.

This ocean race attracted great interest in this country, where the *Dauntless* was considered invincible at this kind of racing. In this race she had on board Captain "Bully" Samuels, former master of the American packetship *Dreadnaught;* Martin Lyons, a well-known Sandy Hook pilot, and our old friend "Dick" Brown, an array of talent that certainly inspired confidence.

However, it was the English challenger's topsails which were first made out from the Sandy Hook lightship twenty-two days later, and as the *Cambria* swept across the finish line, *Dauntless's* sails were just lifting above the horizon astern.

The winning of this race was a great feather in the cap of

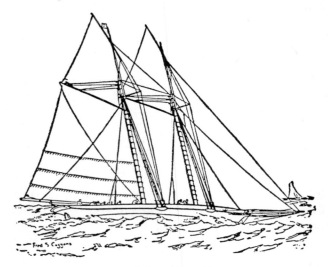

Cambria under sail.

the English schooner. A loud wail arose from the American public, and from many yachtsmen as well, that the Cup was as good as lost. They seemed to lose sight of the fact that the *Dauntless* was ahead most of the way over, and only lost by one hour and seventeen minutes on account of a shift of wind that favored the *Cambria* when within 250 miles of the finish.

Mr. Ashbury and the New York Yacht Club being still unable to get together upon the terms of the match under the "mutual consent" clause, the club gave the *Cambria's* owner the option of sailing for the *America's* Cup in one race over the club's regular course in New York Bay and against the club fleet, in

accordance with its interpretation of the deed. Though protesting at this interpretation, Mr. Ashbury decided to sail, and
August 8th was selected for the race.

The conditions, whether or not they were in accordance with
the intent of the Deed of Gift, were thus practically the same
as prevailed in England when the *America* won the Cup. There
was this important difference, however: In the race of 1851
every yacht was sailing to win a personal trophy, while in the
race of 1870 twenty-three boats were pitted against one, none
of the twenty-three having any interest in the Cup other than
to prevent its leaving this country.

Sailing against the visitor were the keel schooners *Rambler,
Dauntless, Fleetwing, America, Restless, Tarolinta,* and *Alarm,*
and the centerboarders *Phantom, Madgie, Silvie, Tidal Wave,
Madeleine, Idler, Magic, Palmer, Alice, Fleur de Lis, Era,
Josephine, Calypso, Widgeon, Halcyon,* and *Jessie.*

The *Cambria* was a keel schooner of the deep, narrow English type, stiff and weatherly, though rather heavy looking in
spite of her sharp bow. Her principal dimensions were: Length
from stem to stern post 108 feet, beam 21 feet, draft 12 feet,
and depth of hold 11 feet. The fleet lined up against her contained the pick of the American schooners, barring the old
America, which was entered by the Naval Academy in response
to strong public sentiment that she should help defend the Cup
she had won. She was fitted out by the Navy Department and
was not in the best of condition, her rigging being more suited
for a man-of-war than a yacht.

Never had public interest in a yacht race been as keen, and
a big fleet of sightseeing vessels was at the starting line, loaded
to the guards. It is even said that the exchanges closed for the
day and that Wall and Broad Streets were deserted. Mr. Ashbury was much surprised and impressed by the interest shown
by the people of this country, many of whom had never seen a
yacht race before.

The start was from anchor, that custom still prevailing, and *Cambria,* was given the windward end of the line, with the *America* next to her. The good intention went for nothing, however, as the wind shifted just before the start to southeast, and instead of the windward berth, these two yachts were at the leeward end of the line, where they were considerably bothered by the other boats in the early stages of the race.

The schooner *Magic* was first away, her crew being smart in getting the "muslin" on her. The crew of *Cambria* were also on the jump and she got a good position at the start, but the *America* was again last to get off.

The start being off the Staten Island shore in the upper bay, the course was through the Narrows, down the lower bay to the South West Spit Buoy, to Sandy Hook lightship, and return over the same course, a distance of about thirty-eight nautical miles. The wind being east of south, it was a beat down the bay to the Spit Buoy, colloquially called the "Gob" buoy by the fishermen, and the fleet was soon spread out over a long stretch of water, followed by the excursion fleet.

The little *Magic,* standing well over to the Bay Ridge shore with a strong ebb tide under her, was able, on the next tack, to lay well down through the Narrows, and she opened up a lead that it was impossible for the others to overcome, though the old *America,* coming along grandly in the stiff windward work, walked through the entire fleet to second place and was only 4 minutes and 55 seconds behind the *Magic* at the Spit Buoy.

Cambria had fallen far behind and was in twelfth position as the yachts rounded the Spit and started sheets for the reach out past the Hook. Taking a hitch to the southward when past low-lying Sandy Hook, so that they could lay the lightship, the *Idler* and *Dauntless* passed the *America* and put her back to fourth position, in which place she rounded the light vessel, the outer mark of the course. *Cambria* had improved her posi-

tion on this leg of the course, though she continued to fall
behind the flying leader. She turned the light vessel in eighth
place.

It was a broad reach back to the Spit Buoy, and the racers

Magic under sail.

were buried under clouds of canvas as they tore along at a ten-
knot clip, *Dauntless* doing the seven miles of the leg in 41
minutes. *Cambria* picked up some on this reach, but did not
alter her position in the fleet, being 23 minutes behind the
leader, *Magic,* and hopelessly beaten. As she poked her nose
inside the Hook and her crew were getting ready to jibe around
the Spit Buoy for the run home, a hard puff off the land carried
the Englishman's foretopmast with it. She kept right on going,
however, and jibed around the mark still in eighth place.

The run up the bay with a freshening wind and strong flood tide was made in fast time, though the British boat lost some four minutes more and fell back to tenth position, where she finished 27 minutes and 3 seconds, actual time, after the *Magic*. The time allowance made it 39 minutes and 12 seconds.

The times of the boats that finished:

Schooners—Start, 11:26:00 A.M.

NAME	FINISH	ELAPSED TIME	CORRECTED TIME
	H. M. S.	H. M. S.	H. M. S.
Magic	3 33 54	4 07 54	3 58 26.2
Idler	3 37 23	4 11 23	4 09 35.1
Silvie	3 55 12	4 29 12	4 23 45.3
America	3 47 54	4 21 54	4 23 51.4
Dauntless	3 35 28½	4 09 23½	4 29 19.2
Madgie	3 55 07	4 29 07	4 29 57.1
Phantom	3 55 05	4 29 05	4 30 44.5
Alice	4 18 27½	4 52 27½	4 34 15.2
Halcyon	4 03 08	4 37 08	4 35 35.9
Cambria	4 00 57	4 34 57	4 37 38.9
Calypso	4 15 29	4 49 29	4 40 21.3
Fleetwing	4 02 09½	4 36 19½	4 41 20.5
Madeleine	4 14 46	4 48 46	4 42 35.4
Tarolinta	4 10 23	4 44 23	4 47 29.2
Rambler	4 51 35½	4 51 35½	4 48 35.5

Thus the first attempt to lift the Cup failed, the faint-hearted and the doubters were silenced, and it was proved that we had not retrogressed in yacht designing and sailing, but could still hold our own with the best England could produce. The old *America*, finishing fourth in a fleet of newer boats, still beat the *Cambria* 13 minutes and 3 seconds, actual time. The practice, however, of racing a fleet against one boat is at best unfair and unsportsmanlike, and it is pleasant to chronicle that this was the last race in which a challenger was called upon to face these conditions.

Mr. Ashbury took his defeat in good part and had many

courtesies extended to him during his stay on this side. He accompanied the New York Yacht Club on its annual cruise, in the *Cambria,* and several matches were arranged off Newport between the British yacht and different American schooners, all of which were won by our yachts except one race with the *Idler.*

Cambria was taken back to England, where she was soon after sold for commercial purposes. For a long time she was engaged in the West African coasting trade.

Chapter V

MR. ASHBURY'S SECOND ATTEMPT TO WIN THE CUP — THE
"LIVONIA," "COLUMBIA," "SAPPHO" RACE

ON HIS RETURN to England Mr. Ashbury immediately set about
building a new schooner, to make another attempt for the Cup
the following year. He felt, however, though he had not made a
formal protest at the time, that it was unfair and not in accordance with the terms under which the Cup was held to require
him to sail against the whole New York Yacht Club fleet, and
he entered at once into negotiations with the club to decide
this, and some other points at issue.

There followed a heated "sea lawyers' " controversy extending
over many months. It is not necessary to go into the whole
correspondence. Summed up, it ran as follows:

The first question in dispute was whether or not the New
York Yacht Club would make him sail against a whole fleet as
before. This, he contended, was wholly against the letter and
intent of the deed, which distinctly called for a "match" race.
If, however, the New York Yacht Club still insisted on its previous interpretation, he declared he would then get as many
yacht clubs as possible in Great Britain to challenge, each naming his new vessel, the *Livonia,* as its representative, and with
this authority he would claim the right to race the New York
Yacht Club fleet in one race for each club, that he represented;
and any race which he might win should entitle him to the Cup
for the club which he happened to represent in that particular
race.

This fanciful little plan was blocked by the New York Yacht
Club finally submitting, in the spring of 1871, its position in the

matter to Mr. George L. Schuyler, the then sole surviving member of the original syndicate which presented the Cup to the club. Many yachtsmen on both sides of the water felt that the club's position was untenable; that it was asking a challenger to sail under conditions which were condemned as unfair and unsportsmanlike by the owners of *America* when they won the Cup, and that the meaning of the word "match" as applied to yacht racing was a race between two boats.

Hence Mr. Schuyler's letter to the club giving his views was gratifying to these fair-minded yachtsmen. It was as follows:

"I think any candid person will admit that when the owners of the *America* sat down to write their letter of gift to the New York Yacht Club, they could hardly be expected to dwell upon an elaborate definition of their interpretation of the word 'match,' as distinguished from a 'sweep-stakes' or a regatta; nor would he think it very likely that any contestant for the Cup, upon conditions named by them, should be subjected to a trial such as they themselves had considered unfair and unsportsmanlike. . . .

"It seems to me that the present ruling of the club renders the *America's* trophy useless as a 'Challenge Cup,' and that for all sporting purposes it might as well be laid aside as family plate. I cannot conceive of any yachtsman giving six months' notice that he will cross the ocean for the sole purpose of entering into an almost hopeless contest for the Cup, when a challenge for love or money to meet any one yacht of the New York Yacht Squadron in any fair race would give him as great a triumph, if successful, or if his challenge were not accepted, as his heart could desire. If the ownership of the *America's* Cup depended upon the result it would add greatly to the interest of the match; but the absence of that inducement would scarcely compensate for the long odds of sailing against the whole fleet. . . .

"When the word 'match' is used in horseracing or kindred

sports without any qualification, its means a contest between
two parties—and two only. If A offers to run his horse against
B's horse for $1000, and this offer is accepted, it is a 'match';
but if C desires to participate by entering his horse and by
putting up his thousand dollars, the match becomes a 'sweep-
stakes.'

"The same rule applies to yachts. The *Vesta* and *Fleetwing*
made a match for a large sum to sail across the Atlantic. When
the *Henrietta* was admitted into the contest it became 'a sweep-
stakes'."

The New York Yacht Club accepted, somewhat reluctantly,
this interpretation, but it still reserved the right to meet the
challenger with any yacht it pleased in any of the races sailed,
picking four yachts and only naming its representative on the
morning of the race. Thus, while only matching one boat in
each race against the challenger, it could pick out on the morning of the race a light weather or a heavy weather boat, as conditions warranted, or in case of accident could substitute any
one of the four it saw fit.

While agreeing to these terms, Mr. Ashbury still had two
more points he wanted settled. He desired the Americans to
meet him with a keel boat of somewhat the same type as his
new vessel, as he contended it would be unfair to race a light
displacement, centerboard yacht against a sea-going keel
schooner. This the New York Yacht Club would not agree to,
reserving the right to race with any type of boat it chose, and
Mr. Ashbury finally accepted their ruling on the point. As a
matter of fact, the New York club named as its representatives
for the race two centerboard and two keel schooners.

The other point at issue was the selection of the course. The
challenger objected to the New York Yacht Club inside course,
claiming that it was unfair for a foreign yacht, as knowledge of
local conditions played an important part in sailing it. He
asked for a series of races outside Sandy Hook, free from head-

lands. This point was finally compromised by alternating the courses between the regular New York Yacht Club course (the inside one) and one of twenty miles to windward and return outside Sandy Hook lightship.

At this stage of the negotiation the date had advanced to May, and it was then too late to give the required six months' notice of a challenge if a race was to be sailed in 1871. So on May 27, Mr. Ashbury asked the club if it would waive the six months' clause and give him a race in October, as *Livonia* could leave England September 1st. This the New York Yacht Club agreed to do.

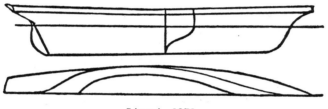

Livonia, 1871.

The waiving of the six months' notice did not at all settle the pen and ink contest, however, for on June 15th Mr. Ashbury wrote asking for a series of twelve races, and sending certificates of representation from twelve English yacht clubs naming his new boat as the challenger. The New York Yacht Club agreed to meet him in twelve races, but only to recognize the challenge of one of the clubs named, the Royal Harwich Yacht Club.

On Mr. Ashbury's arrival here negotiations were again resumed and became acrimonious. At one time it looked as if the race would fall through entirely, Mr. Ashbury still maintaining his right, under the strict terms of the deed, to sail a race for each of the clubs which he represented, and if he won any race to claim the Cup for that particular club. Finally it was agreed to sail a series of seven races, alternating the courses

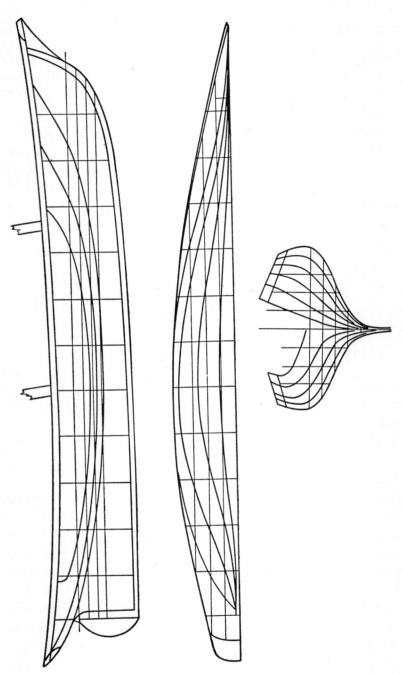

Lines of *Sappho,* one of the defenders of 1871.

between the inside one and the one off the Hook, the winner of four to take the Cup, only the Royal Harwich Yacht Club being recognized, the first race to start October 16th.

The new challenger, *Livonia*, left Cowes on September 2d and after a slow and tempestuous passage of twenty-nine days, during which she was hove to in a hurricane, and lost sails, broke her foreboom, and carried away her bowsprit, arrived at Staten Island on October 1st. She proved herself a fine, able sea boat.

She was built at Ratsey's yard at Cowes and was supposed to be a decided improvement on *Cambria*, having finer lines and a much larger sail area. Her dimensions were: Tonnage, old

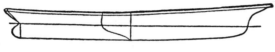

Schooner *Columbia*.

measurement, 280 tons; tonnage for racing, 264 tons; length between perpendiculars, 115 feet 2 inches; beam, 23 feet 7 inches; draft of water, 12 feet 6 inches. The length of the mainmast from hounds to deck was 68 feet, and that of the foremast 64 feet.

According to the English sporting papers of the time, her bow was very much like the old *America's*, while her midship section was a combination of *Cambria's* and that of the American schooner *Sappho*. Her forefoot was cut away considerably.

She did not create much uneasiness among American yachtsmen, and it was not considered necessary to build a new vessel to beat her. The four boats that were finally chosen by the New York Yacht Club to defend were the two centerboard schooners *Palmer* and *Columbia*, both noted as fast, light weather boats, and the keel schooners *Dauntless* and *Sappho*, the latter much improved by alterations made by "Bob" Fish after her first unsuccessful season in English waters. She was now considered a very fast boat, especially in a breeze.

On the day of the first race, October 16th, the wind was light to moderate and the committee of the New York Yacht Club chose *Columbia* as their representative. The course was the inside one, starting from anchor, and the starting signal was given at 10:40 A.M.

On the crack of the gun mooring cables were slipped, headsails sheeted home and, heeling to the northwest breeze, the two yachts were off, stretching down through the Narrows with sheets well off, and followed by the ever-present fleet of excursion vessels. As a contest the race was uninteresting. The lighter American "skimming dish," as the crew of *Livonia* styled their adversary, which drew only five feet of water while the English yacht drew 12½, slipped along so fast in the light breeze that, passing out of the Narrows, only about a mile and a half from the start, she was three minutes ahead. At the outer mark she was nearly 15 minutes ahead, and at one point of the race she had fully 40 minutes' lead on her rival. Toward the finish she was becalmed under the Staten Island bluffs at Fort Wadsworth, and *Livonia* closed up somewhat; but the *Columbia* sagged across the finish line 25 minutes and 28 seconds ahead. The times:

NAME	ELAPSED TIME	CORRECTED TIME
	H. M. S.	H. M. S.
Columbia	6 17 42	6 19 41
Livonia	6 43 00	6 46 45

Two days later the second race was started, the course being a windward and leeward one of twenty miles and return, starting at Sandy Hook lightship. Everything would have been well if the course had been laid out as called for, but with a west-northwest wind of fair strength in the early morning, the course, for some reason or other, was laid east-northeast, or fully four points off a true leeward and windward one. By the time the race started it had "piped up" to a cracking, whole sail breeze, which continued to freshen throughout the contest.

After considerable discussion in the early morning, before the breeze had stiffened, the American committee again chose *Columbia* as their representative. When sailing instructions were issued nothing was said in them about which way the outer mark was to be turned. Noting this point, the owner of *Columbia* went aboard the committee boat for fuller instructions, being told "that it could be left on either hand," a fact of which the *Livonia's* crew were in ignorance.

The *Livonia* was over the line well in advance of *Columbia*. With a quartering breeze, she hung all her kites aloft and "tore up" the twenty miles of water to the outer mark at a great rate, reaching the stake boat over two minutes ahead of her American rival. Here, owing to the lack of any instructions to the contrary, the skipper of *Livonia* jibed around so as to leave the mark on the starboard hand, that being the racing rule in England when not otherwise specified. This was a difficult thing to do in the heavy breeze that prevailed. He had a club topsail aloft and was forced to jibe "all standing," and in doing so was set well down to leeward before he could get his sheets flattened down for the close reach back.

Columbia came down on the mark, and her skipper, knowing that he could turn either way, naturally luffed around it (as the *Livonia's* skipper would have done had he known), trimming in his sheets as he turned, and thereby taking the lead.

With the wind four points on the quarter coming down, it was naturally a close reach home instead of a beat, and the leg was in no sense a windward one, not a tack being made by either boat. The wind had hardened to a moderate gale and *Columbia's* crew were obliged to shorten sail, taking in topsails and furling the foresail. Even then she had all she wanted. *Livonia* hung on to her topsails and sailed a grand race, but could not catch the flying centerboarder, *Columbia* crossing the line 5 minutes and 16 seconds ahead, and, when her time allowance was added, winning by 10 minutes 33¾ seconds.

On finishing, Mr. Ashbury immediately lodged a protest against the *Columbia* on two counts; first, that by rounding the outer mark as she did she violated the sailing regulations and thereby gained a decided advantage, and second, "in the interest of general match racing, and the danger of violating such regulations by the most obvious unfairness," quoting the exact words of the protest.

This protest was not allowed by the New York Yacht Club committee, which held that in the printed copy of the sailing rules the omission to specify which way the outer mark should be turned left the choice optional. It may be remembered that almost the same thing happened when the *America* won the Cup, the *Brilliant* protesting her for passing the wrong side of a lightship, and the English committee holding that in the lack of definite instructions she had the option of passing on either side.

Mr. Ashbury also objected to the course not being a leeward and windward one, as agreed upon, claiming that *Livonia* would have had the advantage of the centerboard boat in a hard thrash, as she undoubtedly would.

The third race was scheduled for the following day, over the inside course, and *Columbia* was again chosen as the defending boat. This did not please her crew any too well, as they claimed that they were worn out by the strain of the two previous races, a claim that could have been made with equal justice by *Livonia's* crew. There were rumors that they had been celebrating their victory too freely and were not in shape to sail.

The race was discreditable from our standpoint from the very start. In the first place, *Columbia* was late getting to the line, as her crew had not expected her to be chosen again, and it was after twelve o'clock when the race was finally started, the *Livonia* waiting until the American defender showed up. The wind was southwest, and fresh, not *Columbia* weather, but *Dauntless*, which was the committee's choice, had carried away some of her rigging, and *Sappho*, the other heavy weather boat, was not on hand.

Columbia bungled the start, *Livonia* getting away well in the lead. It is but just to say that the captain of *Columbia* had been slightly injured in the previous race, and while on board, could not steer the yacht himself. Passing out of the Narrows the Englishman was three minutes ahead, but once clear of the Staten Island hills, *Columbia* began eating up the distance that separated her from the flying leader and had almost caught her at the Spit Buoy, where they turned to go out to the lightship. At this point *Columbia's* flying jib stay parted, letting the sail stream out to leeward, and she lost some six precious minutes before they could get it in and get her on her course again.

As if this was not enough misfortune for one day, after nearly holding her own to the lightship, which she rounded about a mile astern of *Livonia*, she broke her steering gear on the way back and became unmanageable, so that the mainsail had to be taken off, and she ran up the bay under forward canvas only crossing the line 19 minutes and 33 seconds behind *Livonia*. When time allowance was applied this was reduced to 15 minutes and 10 seconds.

The count now stood two to one in favor of America, and the *Sappho* was chosen to meet the *Livonia* in the next race.

The fourth race, October 21st, was a windward and leeward one of 40 miles, starting from Sandy Hook lightship. The wind was light southerly at the start, and it looked more like *Columbia's* weather than *Sappho's*. The course was set at SSW, as the committee expected the wind to haul, which it did, making the first leg a perfect windward one.

The *Sappho's* skipper got the best of the start, putting his boat over the line 1 minute and 52 seconds ahead of the English yacht, which was sluggish in the light breeze. The yachts

tacked toward the weather mark in slow hitches, without either
gaining any decided advantage, until about three o'clock, when
the breeze hardened into a reefing breeze. *Sappho* hung on
to her topsails until she was pretty well buried, finally taking
them in. The sea was making up fast and *Sappho* gave a grand
exhibition of sailing. Buried until her lee rail was well under,
she walked out to windward in a way that made *Livonia* appear to be standing still; in an hour she had obtained a lead of
about 28 minutes and was some two miles ahead when she
turned the outer mark. She was frequently buried nearly to
her hatch coamings, and a small boat that was stowed in the
cockpit, to get it out of the way, was washed overboard and
lost. With it, it is said, went a brand new rubber suit owned
by Commodore Douglas, the yacht's owner, bought that morning and stowed away in the boat in case the weather became
"dusty."

On the run back *Sappho* was never pushed, though she averaged 12 knots for the entire leg, making the 20 miles in 1 hour
42 minutes and 14 seconds. She crossed the finish line over 33
minutes ahead of her rival, the times being:

NAME	START	FINISH	ELAPSED TIME	CORR'T'D TIME
	H. M. S.	H. M. S.	H. M. S.	H. M. S.
Sappho	12 11 00	5 44 24	5 33 24	5 36 02
Livonia	12 12 52	6 17 30	6 04 38	6 09 23

Two days later the last race was sailed over the inside course.
It was getting late in the fall for yacht racing, October 23, and
fresh breezes were looked for, so *Sappho* was again chosen,
though the *Palmer* was on hand if the committee wanted to
put in a light weather boat.

The breeze was fresh at the start, and though *Sappho* had
both working topsails aloft, the *Livonia* was content with the
main, her foretopmast being housed, a common practice of the
period when it blew so that a topsail could not be carried.

Livonia was first away and worked out a nice little lead which the *Sappho* was some time in overcoming. Going down the lower bay, the American schooner soon "found herself." In the W by S wind, making a broad reach of the first leg, she traveled like a torpedo boat, and before the outer mark was reached she had worked through *Livonia's* lee and taken the lead. On the beat back from the lightship to the Spit Buoy she again demonstrated her windward superiority and opened up a lead of 24 minutes. The *Livonia* could not gain on the run home and was 26 minutes and 36 seconds astern at the finish.

NAME	START	FINISH	ELAPSED TIME	CORR'T'D TIME
	H. M. S.	H. M. S.	H. M. S.	H. M. S.
Sappho	11 21 00	3 59 05	4 38 05	4 46 17
Livonia	11 21 00	4 25 41	5 04 41	5 11 44

This race officially ended the series, the American boats having won four races as specified in the agreement. Mr. Ashbury had other views on the matter, however, and he claimed a continuation of the series on these grounds: That his protest in the second race against *Columbia's* turning the mark the wrong way should be allowed. (He had already notified the committee that he sailed the third race without prejudice to that protest.) The third race he had already won, making two races, and that the series should be continued; in the event of his winning the sixth and seventh races he would be entitled to the Cup.

In his letter he goes on as follows: "The *Livonia* will be at her station tomorrow for race No. 6, if the committee decides to entertain my claim. If not, I hereby give you notice that I shall sail twenty miles to windward and back, or to leeward, as the case may be, and as already requested I notify you to send a member of the club on board to see that the rules of the club are complied with. If no competing yacht is at the station, the *Livonia* will sail over the course, as also on Wednesday, the 25th, at the same time."

This claim was so preposterous that the New York Yacht Club committee did not reply to it, other than to acknowledge its receipt.

The next day a private match between the *Livonia* and the *Dauntless* was arranged and sailed off the lightship, twenty miles and return, windward and leeward. *Dauntless* won, but Mr. Ashbury claimed that as this was a private match and the New York Yacht Club did not send a boat against him, *Livonia's* going over the course entitled her to the sixth race. Likewise the following day he was at the line ready to start, and no boat appearing to meet him, he claimed that race, though he did not then even go through the formality of going over the course. So by virtue of four races thus "won" he demanded the Cup. As Captain R. F. Coffin puts it, it was "something like the boarding house keeper's reckoning with the poor sailor: 'Five dollars you had, and five you didn't have, and five I ain't going to give you; an' that makes fifteen'."

The New York Yacht Club couldn't see it that way, and Mr. Ashbury went home in a rare pet, charging the club with unfair and unsportsmanlike actions, criticising its time allowance rules, and threatening if he ever came after the Cup again to bring his lawyer with him and take the decisions to the courts.

The whole series was very unsatisfactory and stirred up much bad feeling between the two countries. The people of this country were heartily tired of Mr. Ashbury and his letters, and after his departure the New York Yacht Club returned to him three cups he had presented to the club the year before.

Out of the controversy, however, some good had come, for it cleared up a number of disputed points and opened the way to better and fairer racing for the future.

Chapter VI

CANADA TRIES FOR THE CUP — THE MATCHES OF 1876 AND
1881

AFTER MR. ASHBURY, with his letter writing propensities, had departed, the New York Yacht Club came in for some pretty severe criticism in England—criticism which the facts, especially as to the last series, did not warrant. The club had conceded many points beyond those imposed under the strict wording of the deed of trust and had shown *Livonia's* owner much consideration in face of a persistent and trying controversy over details. While the odds were still largely in our favor and the terms were not entirely what we would call fair and sportsmanlike in the light of present day standards, Mr. Ashbury had accepted the conditions agreed upon before starting and should have taken his defeat in better part. Even some of the English sporting papers did not support him in many of his absurd claims.

However, the feeling engendered was sufficient to keep any other English yachtsman from attempting to lift the Cup for many years; and when the next challenge was received it was from an entirely different quarter.

Five years passed until, in the spring of 1876, a letter was received by the New York Yacht Club from the Royal Canadian Yacht Club of Toronto, challenging in behalf of Canada for a race that summer and asking the club to waive the six months' notice. The yacht named by the Canadians was the schooner *Countess of Dufferin,* owned by a syndicate headed by the vice-commodore of the club, Major Charles Gifford.

The New York Yacht Club was ready for a race and not only

waived the six months' clause, but offered a series of three races instead of one, in July, one of them to be over the inside course, one over the outside, and the third to be determined by lot. It also gave Major Gifford the privilege, if he preferred, of sailing the races in the open water off Newport after the annual cruise.

Major Gifford also wanted the New York Yacht Club to name one boat only to meet the Canadian yacht, instead of a number of boats, one of which was to be picked the day of the race. His position was that he had to name one boat which had to take all the chances as to light or heavy weather, and it was only fair that the defenders do the same.

He was asking only what would be considered today a "square deal," and though under the terms by which it held the Cup the New York Yacht Club could have refused this demand it is gratifying to note that by a vote of eleven to five it acceded to the challenger's request. Ever since then the club has followed this course and picked one boat only to meet a foreign yacht in races for the Cup, an action undoubtedly in line with the sportsmanlike spirit and intent of the original donors. There was a good deal of discussion of the matter at the time, some of the newspaper writers praising the club for its action and others blaming it, and insisting that in a yacht race it was perfectly legitimate for a club to accord to the other fellow just as little as possible, a position that is, fortunately, no longer in line with present day sporting ethics.

The *Countess of Dufferin* was designed and built by Alexander Cuthbert, a Canadian builder who had turned out a number of fast yachts. His most notable work was in the sloop *Annie Cuthbert,* which he built to beat an American designed yacht built by McGiehan of Pamrapo, N. J., which had "cleaned up" on Lake Ontario for several years. The *Annie Cuthbert* was successful and a syndicate was formed to back Cuthbert in an *America's* Cup challenger.

It has been stated that Cuthbert had no originality and merely copied the American models. It is true that the American type was followed in most of his designs. That was natural, as this was the type most frequently seen on the Lakes and the one which he was called upon to meet. Though a "rule-of-thumb" designer, he did have ideas of his own as to hull form and he possessed considerable skill; his boats undoubtedly showed the influence of the prevailing American design, but it cannot fairly be said that they were merely copies.

The *Countess of Dufferin,* and his later challenger, the *Atalanta,* were both handicapped by lack of sufficient funds, and thus suffered by being poorly rigged, equipped, and finished. It is said that funds ran short at one time during the building of the *Countess of Dufferin,* and it was proposed to finance the scheme by popular subscription, selling tickets at a low price, each ticket, or share, entitling the holder to a vote in the control of the enterprise. As far as is known, it was not necessary to resort to this expedient.

The *Countess of Dufferin* was finished in the spring of 1876 and sailed for New York by way of the St. Lawrence River and the Atlantic Ocean, arriving in New York after an ordinary passage on July 18. She was a "sizeable" schooner, being 107 feet long over all, 24 feet beam, and drawing 6½ feet (she was a centerboard vessel), with a big spread of sail. She was very sharp forward, and when she first anchored in New York harbor she attracted a great deal of attention and admiration. She was rather poorly finished, however, and when she was hauled out to have her bottom painted it was noticed that it was as rough as a down East lumber schooner. She was extensively refitted here; among other things, her sails, which fitted like a suit of sailor's dungarees, were sent to Wilson, the famous American sailmaker, to be recut.

The first chance to get a line on the abilities of the new challenger was in the Brenton Reef Cup race over an ocean course

of 275 miles, when the *Countess* started with four American
schooners (though she was not formally in the race) and was
beaten so badly that the crews of the other boats forgot that she
was on the course.

The boat which the New York Yacht Club picked to meet
the Canadian challenger was the schooner *Madeline*, owned by
John S. Dickerson, then commodore of the Brooklyn Yacht
Club. There was no question that this boat was entitled to be
called the "champion" American schooner, as she had been the
most consistent racer in the fleet since 1873, and in that year is
said to have won every regatta in which she started. She was
built in 1868, as a sloop, by David Kirby, a well-known yacht
builder of that day, and after numerous alterations, including
change of rig to a schooner, she became one of the "fliers" of an
unusually fine fleet of yachts. She was about the same size as
the *Countess of Dufferin,* having an over-all length of 106 feet
and 24 feet beam, her tonnage being a little more than that of
the Canadian, though the two boats were of the same general
type, and both were centerboarders.

After the disappointing showing made by his boat in the
Brenton Reef race, Major Gifford, her managing owner, asked
for a postponement to give him time to get some new light sails
made, and it was finally arranged to start the first race, which
was to be over the regular New York Yacht Club inside course,
on August 11th. When the two boats appeared at the line that
morning it was seen that the *Countess of Dufferin* not only had
new light sails but a new fore and mainsail of American make
as well.

The *Madeline* had towed down from Greenwich, Conn., and
was in apparently perfect condition, her coppered bottom having been scoured and burnished and given a coat of oil and
tallow to make it slippery, while her top-sides had been "potleaded" until they were as slippery as glass. She was in great
contrast to the *Countess,* which, though she had been hauled

out and had her bottom smoothed and potleaded, still looked rough and unfinished.

The start this time was a flying one, the old method of starting from anchor having been abandoned. As the two boats jockeyed for position before the starting gun, the skipper of

Madeline under sail.

the Canadian, Captain Cuthbert, threw away a splendid chance of going over first and getting his wind free, as he was coming down with a rap full and under good headway when the gun went at 11:15 A.M. But he bore off, and let *Madeline* have the windward berth, where she blanketed the *Countess*, killing her so that she was thirty-five seconds behind as well as down to leeward. The wind was ahead, making it a beat down the ship channel to the Spit. *Madeline* immediately began walking away from the challenger and at the Hook was nearly ten minutes ahead.

The breeze outside was SSE and the *Countess* tried to steal off to the southward, looking for a better slant to make up her lost ground; but the skipper of *Madeline* knew the game too well to let her go off alone and tacked after her. When they finally came about to lay the outer mark the *Madeline* overstood the lightship and lost some five minutes, the *Countess* judging the distance better and being only 4 minutes 41 seconds behind at the turn.

Both boats piled on their kites like homeward-bounders running down the trades, and, followed by a large fleet of excursion steamers and yachts, whose passengers were keyed up to see what the Canadian challenger could do in running, they tore

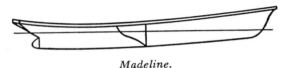

Madeline.

along at a good clip. It was seen at the Hook that *Madeline* was outrunning the other, and she continued to draw ahead, finally crossing the line 9 minutes and 58 seconds ahead, elapsed time. Those who saw the race say that this time did not represent her true lead, as she lost the wind under the Staten Island shore and the boat astern moved up on her considerably.

The official times of the race:

NAME	START	FINISH	ELAPSED TIME	CORR'T'D TIME
	H. M. S.	H. M. S.	H. M. S.	H. M. S.
Madeline	11 16 31	4 41 26	5 24 55	5 23 54
Countess of Dufferin	11 17 6	4 51 59	5 34 53	5 34 53

Madeline won by 10m. 59s.

This first race settled pretty conclusively the merits of the two boats and the second race, the following day, was chiefly interesting by reason of the presence of a third boat on the course, though, naturally, not in the contest. This was the old

America, which, in racing trim and with a full racing crew aboard, went over the line after the last boat had started and sailed over the course with the contestants.

The second race was an outside one of twenty miles to windward and back. This day the *Countess of Dufferin* was sailed by Captain Joe Ellsworth, a noted New York yacht skipper, though of course Cuthbert was on board. The breeze was light, freshening somewhat during the contest, but dying away again toward sunset, as the yachts were coming home.

The start was postponed until after noon and *Madeline* outmaneuvered the *Countess* and slipped over thirty-four seconds ahead of the latter. Right in the *Countess's* wake came the old *America,* spick and span, her crew trimming her sails as if they were after the Cup themselves and had forgotten that she was twenty-five years old with her racing career behind her.

The course was SSE and the three boats made one long tack to the eastward, holding it for about three hours in the light wind. The Canadian yacht kept sagging off to leeward, though she footed well, and when the three boats finally came about to fetch the mark she was some three-quarters of a mile astern and the *America* had slipped in between her and the *Madeline.*

The boats did not round the outer mark until after five o'clock in the afternoon, when it was seen that the *America* was only three minutes behind the *Madeline* (she had started 4½ minutes behind her) and about nine minutes ahead of the *Countess.* This was a grand showing for the old boat, when it is remembered that the weather was light and the *America* was a heavy displacement keel boat, while the others were light draft centerboarders.

The run home in the falling wind and fading light was slow and uninteresting, though picturesque, as the three boats, two of them modern racers and one an old-timer, with every rag hung aloft that would catch the faintest zephyr, stood up darkly against the western sunset and slipped almost noiselessly through the water.

It was dark before the leader, the *Madeline,* finished. Less than twelve minutes behind her came the good old *America,* and after eight o'clock, with the high hopes of her crew dashed, came the *Countess of Dufferin.* So the series came to an end.

The three yachts were timed in this race as follows, the *America's* time being shown only for comparison:

NAME	START	FINISH	ELAPSED TIME	CORR'T'D TIME
	H. M. S.	H. M. S.	H. M. S.	H. M. S.
Madeline	12 17 24	7 37 11	7 19 47	7 18 46
Countess of Dufferin	12 17 58	8 03 58	7 46 00	7 46 00
America	12 22 09	7 49 00	7 26 51	7 26 51

Madeline beats *Countess* 27m. 14s., and *America* beats *Countess* 19m. 9s.

After the race the *Countess of Dufferin* was laid up at New York, and then the financial troubles that had beset her since she was launched began to come to a head. Captain Cuthbert, who owned the largest share in her, attached her in an effort to force Major Gifford to sell his share. Cuthbert still had faith in her and it was said to be his intention to get control of her, raise enough money to alter her with a view to making her faster, and then to challenge for the Cup again. These plans fell through and she was finally sold at a sheriff's sale to satisfy some claims against her and eventually found her way back to Canada, later being sold to a Chicago yachtsman, who raced her on Lake Michigan.

While this was the end of the *Countess of Dufferin,* it was by no means the last of her designer and captain in *America's* Cup affairs. Five years went by without another challenge from any country, and during these years Cuthbert was busy turning over ways and means to have another "shy" at the famous "mug." In 1881 he had acquired sufficient backing to go ahead with a yacht from his own design, and in the spring of that year started to build a centerboard sloop, following very much the model of his successful sloop *Annie Cuthbert,* with some refinements that his observations during the years since she was built had dictated.

Cuthbert at this time was a member of a small but progressive yacht club on Lake Ontario, the Bay of Quinte Yacht Club, and on May 16th the secretary of that club sent a challenge for the Cup to the New York Yacht Club on behalf of Alexander Cuthbert, naming the new sloop, which was then on the stocks and was to be christened *Atalanta,* as the challenger. As usual, the challenge asked the New York Club to waive the required six months' notice so that the race could be sailed that autumn.

The New York Yacht Club called a meeting on receipt of this challenge and not only agreed to waive the required notice, but to sail a series of three races in September, instead of only one.

Then followed a further request from the Canadian yacht club for the New York Yacht Club to define its position on sailing one boat against the challenger or claiming the right to name any boat it saw fit for each race. To this last request the *America's* Cup committee in referring the matter to the flag officers of the New York Yacht Club said, "We do not doubt the right of the club to reserve an answer to this question, or, under the terms of the deed of gift, to take the position that it is entitled to name a boat on the morning of each race, but our judgment is that the most liberal and sportsmanlike terms should be offered to the challenging yacht. . . . We are of the opinion that we should notify the Bay of Quinte Yacht Club that the same boat will be sailed against the *Atalanta* in all three races."

In this view the officers of the club fully concurred, saying, "We sincerely trust that the interpretations of the deed of gift may be so liberal and sportsmanlike as to be beyond cavil." A

fine stand, surely, and set forth in fine words. And yet the Club
and its policy came in for a torrent of abuse, strangely, from
both sides. As showing the animus that prevailed in the minds
of some Canadian critics it is interesting to quote the following
from the Toronto *Globe,* a few days before the final decision
of the New York Yacht Club was announced:

"The New York Yacht Club is to be congratulated upon the
accommodating spirit shown in the acceptance of the challenge
of the Bay of Quinte Yacht Club, notwithstanding several in-
formalities therein. But the terms of the letter of acceptance
leave no doubt that the New York Yacht Club is again about
to resort to the discreditable tactics it has formerly adopted in
order to avoid all danger of a fair contest.

"The claim is made that there must be a series of three
matches. This is nothing but fair, as yachting is essentially a
pastime in which accident takes a great share. But the New
York Yacht Club's idea of fairness and courtesy toward any
foreign vessel that seeks to win the Cup is this:—The challenge
is considered as being directed to the club as the owner of a
great number of yachts, and in sailing the three races the club
reserves till the morning of each day's race the nomination of
the vessel which is to represent it. If there is a gale blowing
the first day, a vessel of specially seaworthy quality is desig-
nated; if there is almost a dead calm on the second day, a
'skimming-dish' is set to the work of polishing off the foreigner;
and whatever the weather may be on the third day, a vessel
exactly suited to such weather will be found on hand at the
starting point.

"It has never been open to doubt that the New York Yacht
Club has adopted this elaborate system out of a determination
to retain the Queen's Cup at all hazards. Nothing short of a
whole flotilla of yachts would stand any chance in such a skin-
game. . . .

"The New York yachtsmen protested, after she had been

beaten, that the *Countess of Dufferin* was of no account whatever against their cracks. Let them now show a practical reliance upon their own opinions and enter upon the new race with another vessel by the same builder under such conditions as the common sense of the world says are fair. The strained interpretations of a police court pettifogger ought not to prevail in a matter connected with such a noble pastime as yachting."

After reading this masterful stricture, it is pleasant to turn to an American newspaper writer's opinion of fair play and of the New York Yacht Club's announced position in this series:

"We view the making of this match to sail a single yacht against the challenger as conceding advantages to which no challenging party is entitled, either by the equities of sporting law or conditions named in the deed of trust. This historic emblem is no prize-fighter's belt. It was won by sailing against the fleet *par excellence* of the world, and the present indications are that the Canadians will make the attempt with a craft equal to any of our own; but should the challenging party to this single-handed match of 'best two in three' trials beat our craft, would this yacht show one 'jot' or 'tittle' of that superiority, naval and nautical, of which this trophy is a symbol? Certainly not. . . .

"Not for a moment do we suppose that our yachtsmen wish to 'toss a copper' for the possession of this Cup; but in what else are these single-handed matches culminating? . . . Any craft challenging for this Cup, in our opinion, should sail against all of her class that could be mustered, and therefore these single-handed matches, and also the waiving of any conditions named in the deed of trust, constitute a bad precedent. . . .

"It is an axiom in sport that 'a good match is won when made,' and really our yachting friends, guardians of the *America's* Cup, do not shine as matchmakers."

Can you beat it? Between two such antipodean viewpoints the poor *America's* Cup committee was in a bad way. However, it went on arranging matters according to its lights to bring about a fair race.

The Canadian boat was delayed in building, as yachts usually are, making a postponement of the race necessary. She was finally launched on September 17, and after a very brief try-out was made ready for the journey to New York early in October. Then it first became known that the yacht was to come to New York via the Erie Canal, instead of the St. Lawrence and ocean highway.

She was 70 feet long over all, 64 feet on the waterline, 19 feet beam, and drew 5 feet 6 inches without board, and with board down 16 feet 6 inches. She was so wide that to get her through the canal locks it was necessary to list her over on one side by shifting her ballast, and with her spars lashed on deck she was towed through the canal in this ignominious style, and did not reach New York until October 30, long after the yachting season had closed.

Meantime, the flag officers and race committee of the New York Yacht Club had not been idle. This was the first yacht of sloop rig to challenge for the Cup and the fleet of large sloops in this country did not nearly equal the schooner fleet either in size or caliber. The only large sloops in the club were the *Mischief, Gracie, Fanny, Vision,* and *Hildegard,* and it was thought best by the flag officers of the club to be on the safe side with a new boat. So they went to David Kirby, the builder of the last defender, *Madeline,* and also of the very fast sloop *Arrow,* owned outside the club. He guaranteed to build a sloop that would be faster than the *Arrow,* and though the time was short, it being then late in the spring, the boat was ready in time for the trial races in October.

This sloop, called the *Pocahontas,* was the first boat built especially to defend the Cup. Likewise this was the first year it was thought necessary to hold trial races to pick the defending yacht, and on October 13th, the Canadian yacht being still on the raging Erie Canal, these four crack sloops met in New York Bay for the first race of the trial series: *Mischief, Gracie, Pocahontas,* and *Hildegard.* It was blowing fresh and *Gracie* and *Pocahontas* lost their topmasts, *Mischief* winning. *Gracie* won the second race, beating *Mischief* nearly 4 minutes, while the new sloop was far behind. *Mischief* beat *Gracie* in the third race by 14 seconds, and the *Pocahontas,* which turned out a failure, much to the disappointment of her owners and builder, was placed out of commission.

As a result of these races the *Mischief* was chosen to represent

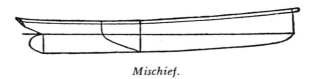

Mischief.

America in the Cup races, though the decision was not announced until the day scheduled for the first international race. This delay was due to the intense feeling that existed between the crews and partisans of the *Mischief* and *Gracie,* and because the boats were so evenly matched that it was a difficult matter to choose between them. There was sure to be criticism of the choice, no matter which was selected.

The *Mischief* was an iron sloop designed by A. Cary Smith, who was coming into prominence then as one of the new school of scientific naval architects. She was built in 1879 and showed somewhat the influence of the growing trend toward the English cutter type. She was called a "compromise sloop" at that time, though she was a centerboarder and a wide boat. Her dimensions were: Length over all, 67 feet 5 inches; waterline, 61 feet; beam, 19 feet 10 inches, and draft, 5 feet 4 inches, her rig showing some radical departures from the old American sloop type. She was a fast and an able boat and the final decision of the Cup committee was a wise one.

The first race with the Canadian challenger was fixed for November 8th, the latest date such an important event has ever been scheduled, over the club's regular inside course. Both boats were ready, but the day was foggy with no wind, and the race was postponed until November 9th.

As a contest the races were devoid of interest, the challenger being no match for the "iron pot," as the *Mischief* was frequently and endearingly called, and need only be described briefly here.

The *Atalanta* was sailed by her designer and builder, Mr.

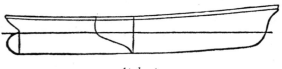

Atalanta.

Cuthbert, and her crew was largely composed of amateur sailors from Lake Ontario, who had volunteered for the race. There were a few paid hands on board, but the amateurs were largely in the majority. They had not been sufficiently drilled on board, and the *Atalanta* suffered somewhat from poor and slow handling, though even with the best of handling she could not have won, the races easily demonstrating *Mischief's* superiority.

The first race was started in a fresh SW wind, the *Atalanta* having a single reef tied down, while neither boat carried a topsail. Once outside the Narrows, where the true weight of the wind was felt, both boats set working topsails, the Canadian setting hers over her reefed main. The "iron pot" commenced to draw away from the challenger at the start, and constantly stretched out her lead, never being even threatened. On the run home the wind hardened and both boats had to stow their

topsails. *Atalanta* was by this time some half hour behind, and
the real race was between the sloop *Gracie,* which started over
the course ten minutes after the contestants for the Cup and
was courteously timed by the committee, and the *Mischief.*
The *Gracie* caught and passed the *Atalanta* before reaching the
S.W. Spit, and on the last leg to the home mark she passed
Mischief to leeward and crossed the line about a minute ahead
of her, as the following table will show:

NAME	START	FINISH	ELAPSED TIME	CORR'T'D TIME
	H. M. S.	H. M. S.	H. M. S.	H. M. S.
Mischief	11 14 50	3 31 59	4 17 09	4 17 09
Atalanta	11 15 51	4 04 15¼	4 48 24½	4 45 29¼
Gracie	11 25 00	3 30 46	4 05 46	4 10 42

  Gracie timed, but not in race.

The next race, held the following day, was even more
decisive. It was over an outside course of sixteen miles to leeward and return, the wind being W by N and fresh, though
both boats carried topsails on the run down wind. While in
the previous race there had been a good-sized excursion fleet
following the racers, on this day only one steamer was on hand
with sightseers, as the interest had waned, after the hollow
victory of the previous day.

The *Gracie* again started ten minutes late, and as she made
a pretty race with *Mischief* her time is given here with the
others. The *Atalanta* did very well on the run down the wind
in the fresh breeze, holding the *Mischief,* which got off in the
lead, and being only 2 minutes and 15 seconds astern at the
leeward mark.

As they neared the outer mark the two competitors doused
their topsails and turned in a quick reef for the hard thrash
home, and *Mischief* even set a No. 2 jib in place of her large
one. Once on the wind *Mischief* walked out to windward of
the other two boats in a way to discourage their drenched

crews. She finished over 38 minutes ahead of the *Atalanta* and 10 minutes and 5 seconds ahead of the *Gracie.* The table of actual, elapsed, and corrected times follows. On elapsed time *Mischief* and *Gracie* were very close together, though the

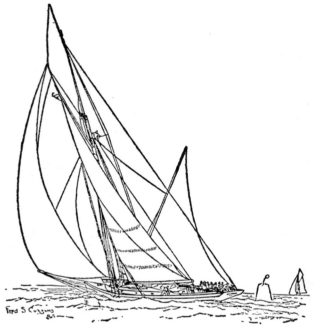

Mischief.

former won on corrected time and on the beat home gained nearly six minutes on the latter:

NAME	START	FINISH	ELAPSED TIME	CORR'T'D TIME
	H. M. S.	H. M. S.	H. M. S.	H. M. S.
Mischief	11 58 17	4 53 10	4 54 53	4 54 53
Atalanta	11 58 47	5 35 19	5 36 32	5 33 47
Gracie	12 08 30	5 03 15	4 54 45	4 59 31

As the agreement was for two races out of three, this settled the Canadian's chances and the *Atalanta* was laid up in New York.

Chapter VII

THE CONTEST with Canada in 1881 was so unsatisfactory from
every point of view that it aroused a strong feeling among the
members of the New York Yacht Club that some steps ought
to be taken to guard against such fiascos in the future. True
yachtsmen felt that the real spirit of *America's* Cup competition
had been violated in sailing against a yacht hardly finished,
poorly manned, hampered by lack of funds, and that had come
to this country by "mule power," canted on one bilge in order
to get through a canal six feet deep. They believed that the
donors of the Cup had intended it to stand as an incentive for
foreign yachts to cross the sea to race in this country and thus,
in a measure, to be a test of a yacht's seaworthiness as well as
speed.

Besides this, cup defense was getting to be an expensive
matter to the club, and the members felt that the race ought
to be worthy of the outlay. With the building of the unsuccessful defender, *Pocahontas,* the New York Yacht Club had spent
fully $20,000 on this match with the *Atalanta,* and that seemed
a goodly sum of money in those days. A lot of old time yachtsmen, including the six who bought the original *America* for
$20,000, must have done a good bit of spinning in their graves
over more recent defense costs. It is estimated to have cost
around $3,000,000 to build and campaign the four defense
candidates of 1930, for instance

This feeling came to a head in December, 1881, when at a
meeting of the New York Yacht Club it was voted to return

the Cup to the only surviving member of the *America's*
syndicate, Mr. George L. Schuyler, and practically to ask him
to draw up a new deed of gift in place of the one made in 1857.
It was necessary to have one better qualified to meet the
changed conditions of yacht racing and to cover the many
points which had caused controversy and ill feeling in the past.

The time was ripe for such a change and, realizing it, Mr.
Schuyler, then an old man, accepted the return of the Cup
and drew up a new deed of gift with which he again gave the
Cup to the New York Yacht Club. It was accepted on February
2nd, 1882. This new instrument, called the second deed of
gift, was as follows:

"Any organized Yacht Club of a foreign country, incorporated,
patented or licensed by the legislature, admiralty, or other executive department, having for its annual regatta an ocean water course
on the sea or on an arm of the sea (or one which combines both),
practicable for vessels of 300 tons, shall always be entitled, through
one or more of its members, to the right of sailing a match for this
Cup, with a yacht or other vessel propelled by sails only, and constructed in the country to which the Challenging Club belongs,
against any one yacht or vessel as aforesaid, constructed in the country of the club holding the Cup.

"The yacht or vessel to be of not less than 30 nor more than 300
tons, measured by the Custom House rule in use by the country of
the challenging party.

"The challenging party shall give six months' notice in writing,
naming the day for the proposed race, which day shall not be less
than seven months from the date of the notice.

"The parties intending to sail for the Cup may, by mutual consent, make any arrangement satisfactory to both as to the date,
course, time allowance, number of trials, rules, and sailing regulations, and any and all other conditions of the match, in which case
also the six months' notice may be waived.

"In case the parties cannot mutually agree upon the terms of a
match, then the challenging party shall have the right to contest
the Cup in one trial, sailed over the usual course of the Annual
Regatta of the club holding the Cup, subject to its rules and sailing
regulations, the challenged party not being required to name its
representative until the time agreed upon for the start.

"Accompanying the six months' notice, there must be a Custom-House certificate of the measurement, and a statement of the dimensions, rig, and name of the vessel.

"No vessel which has been defeated in a match for this Cup can be again selected by any club for its representative until after a contest for it by some other vessel has intervened, or until after the expiration of two years from the time such contest has taken place.

"Vessels intending to compete for this Cup must proceed under sail on their own bottoms to the port where the contest is to take place.

"Should the club holding the Cup be for any cause dissolved, the Cup shall be handed over to any club of the same nationality it may select which comes under the foregoing rules.

"It is to be distinctly understood that the Cup is to be the property of the club and not of the owners of the vessel winning it in a match, and that the condition of keeping it open to be sailed for by organized Yacht Clubs of all foreign countries, upon the terms above laid down, shall forever attach to it, thus making it perpetually a Challenge Cup for friendly competition between foreign countries.

GEORGE L. SCHUYLER."

The principal points of difference that are important to note between this new instrument and the old one, are, that it fixed definitely the obligation of the holding club to meet the challenger with one yacht, and one only, throughout the series of races constituting the match; that it required the challenger to proceed *under sail on her own bottom* to the port where the contest is to take place, thus eliminating towing through a canal or of shipping a boat across the ocean on the deck of a steamer, which at that time was getting to be within the bounds of possibility; the barring of a once defeated yacht from challenging again for two years; and the elimination of Canada as a factor in future races, excepting those clubs in the Dominion that were situated on the coast.

The "mutual consent" clause as to the details of the matches was left in, while the six months' notice clause was given a more prominent place in view of the necessity which might arise of having to build a boat to meet a challenger that was of different size and rig than any existing boat of the holding club.

These new conditions were something of a direct slap at the Canadian clubs on the Great Lakes and caused much bitter feeling there, which resulted in many harsh things being said of the New York Yacht Club in the Canadian papers.

Upon accepting the Cup under the new "deed" the New York Yacht Club sent a copy of the instrument to all the foreign yacht clubs, with a cordial letter expressing the hope that the Cup would still be a source of friendly strife upon the water, and tendering to any man who might challenge "a liberal, hearty welcome, and the strictest fair play."

No one seemed in a desperate hurry to challenge for the bit of silver, however, and though several rumors of a possible match were heard, it was nearly three years later, or not until December, 1884, that the gauntlet was actually taken up. A letter was received by the club from Mr. J. Beavor Webb, a British designer, giving notice that a challenge for the *America's* Cup would be forthcoming for a race in the summer of 1885, from Sir Richard Sutton, owner of the cutter *Genesta*, and from Lieutenant W. Henn, of the Royal Navy, owner of the cutter *Galatea*, then building, both boats being of Mr. Beavor Webb's design.

This letter was followed later by an official challenge proposing two matches, the first between *Genesta* and an American boat, and in the event of the New York Yacht Club retaining the Cup, then a second match between the *Galatea* and an American yacht. It was proposed that each match should consist of a series of three races, and that all of them be held outside Sandy Hook, clear of headlands.

This challenge was accepted promptly, though it meant that the New York Yacht Club had to win twice to retain the Cup, while if the Englishmen won either match the Cup would go home with them. The club offered one race over the New York

Yacht Club inside course and two outside, and suggested a seven-hour time limit on each race. It also agreed to name its representative yacht a week before the first race.

After some correspondence regarding the matter of time allowance, Beavor Webb asking that the mean of the New York Yacht Club and English allowance tables be used, the matter was left to a referee, Mr. George L. Schuyler, whose decision was that "in a race for the *America's* Cup, whatever terms may be mutually agreed upon in other respects, the time allowance should be made according to the rules of the club in possession."

Thus the terms were satisfactorily arranged and the New York Yacht Club proceeded to set about plans for defense with two races staring them in the face. This was the first time a large English cutter had challenged for the Cup, and there were not only no sloops of that size in this country, but sloop design in America was in a somewhat chaotic state owing to several causes which should be narrated briefly.

With the application of naval architecture to yacht design, there was a tendency to break away somewhat from hide-bound tradition in yacht building, and the claims of the English type of deep, narrow cutter were beginning to be heeded and its good points to be taken into consideration. About the middle of the seventies one or two small cutters had been built in America, though with some modifications of the English type. These were chiefly in respect to having more beam, the beam of the English boats being unduly narrow to give them a favorable rating under their measurement rule. One or two out-and-out cutters were built, with the cutter rig of housing bowsprit, loose-footed mainsail, double head rig, etc., but most of them were a compromise between the American centerboard sloop and the narrow English type.

Then, in 1881, a little Scotch cutter called the *Madge* was shipped to this country by her owner, a Mr. Coats, of Scotland, on the deck of a steamer. She was 46 feet long over all, had a beam of only 7 feet 9 inches, and drew nearly 8 feet of water. She was a regular "knife blade" or "plank-on-edge" cutter of the extreme type. This little boat was so uniformly successful in her races against American sloops of her size that she converted many yachtsmen to the type and the yachting world was for a time divided into two camps—the "cutter cranks," as they were called, on one side, and the adherents of the centerboard sloop on the other. From this controversy a new type of centerboard sloop was evolved, combining some of the elements of each type and being a much more wholesome, abler type of craft than the old "skimming dish" single-stickers, that were said to sail on a heavy dew.

Reports from England of *Genesta's* success abroad in 1884, her first year, where she was conceded to be the best all-round boat, convinced the officers of the club that vigorous steps had to be taken to get a suitable boat with which to defend, none of the existing ones being considered fast enough, or large enough. So the flag officers, James Gordon Bennett and William P. Douglas, decided to build a sloop and, naturally, turned to A. Cary Smith, then the most prominent yacht designer in this country, for her design. He had turned out the last successful Cup defender, *Mischief,* and many other fast boats. The centerboard type was decided on, though the new boat was to be much deeper than the prevailing centerboarders of the time, being a "compromise sloop," and she was built entirely of iron, by Harlan and Hollingsworth of Wilmington, Del. This boat was named *Priscilla,* and great things were expected of her.

At this time the waters of Massachusetts Bay had become a great yachting center and had bred some of the finest yachtsmen on the Atlantic coast, though as a rule they were small boat sailors rather than owners of large yachts. There was a strong patriotic sentiment there that Boston and its leading yacht club, the Eastern, located at Marblehead, should be represented in an international event of this kind, and a syndicate was formed, of whom the leading members were General Charles J. Paine and J. Malcolm Forbes, to build a boat to try for the honor of defending the Cup. General Paine was also a member of the New York Yacht Club, the owner of the schooner *Halcyon,* and a keen, practical yachtsman.

There was at that time a young naval architect in Boston, about thirty-six years of age, who had achieved considerable local reputation as a yacht designer, though he had only taken it up professionally about two years before. His name was Edward Burgess, and while his scientific knowledge was acquired as an amateur, he was clever, knew boats, and was a first-class yacht sailor. To him the syndicate went for the plans of the new yacht. It was an ambitious undertaking for a designer of his limited experience, for up to that time the largest boat he had turned out was only thirty-eight feet over all; and he was not only going up against the New York Yacht Club with its great prestige and resources, but he had to design a sloop larger than any at that time afloat in this country. But the members of the syndicate and his friends had faith in his abilities, and the result was the *Puritan,* launched from Lawley's yard in May, 1885, and destined to bring international fame to her designer.

While a centerboard sloop, the *Puritan* was in strong contrast to the older American boats of that rig and embodied many characteristics of the cutter type. She may fairly be called a "compromise sloop." She was built of wood and in describing her, Mr. W. P. Stephens, a well-known yachting writer, says:

"The sheer plan was that of the cutter, with plumb stem, circular sheer, and fairly high freeboard and bulwarks, and the cutter counter of the day. Her breadth was taken from the sloop, though moderate, and her depth and draft were considerably greater than in the old sloops, but less than in the cutters. Outside of the hull proper there was a clearly defined keel

some two feet deep, containing forty-eight tons of lead—the
slot for the centerboard being cut through this keel. The
greatest draft was at the sternpost, which had more rake than
the old sloops, but much less than the deep cutters. The keel
rounded up gradually, being well cut away at the forefoot."

She was a big boat and measured 81 feet 1 inch on the water,
94 feet over all, 22 feet 7 inches breadth of beam, and 8 feet
8 inches draft, which her board when down increased to 20
feet. She spread about 8000 square feet of sail.

The Cary Smith sloop *Priscilla* was 85 feet on the water, 94
feet over all, 22 feet 5 inches breadth, and 7 feet 9 inches draft.

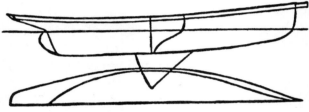

Sloop *Puritan*, 1885.

Both of these new boats were of about the same size as the first
challenger, *Genesta*, which was 90 feet over all and 81 feet on
the water. But the latter had only 15 feet of beam, while she
drew 13 feet 6 inches, and had 72 tons of lead ballast in her
deep keel. She carried less sail, however, spreading only 7150
square feet.

It will be seen from these brief descriptions that the match
was to be one of types, the narrow English cutter against the
modernized American centerboard sloop, and it was thought
that the race would settle the much discussed question of
superiority between the two types.

The members of the New York Yacht Club did not give
much consideration to the Boston boat, when word came that
one was being built, and she was referred to as the "bean boat"

and "brick sloop," the name of Burgess not being known in New York waters at that time. However, they welcomed her to the trial races, for which they had sent out a general invitation to sloops of over sixty feet waterline length, of any recognized yacht club.

The first time the two new American boats came together was in the Goelet Cup race off Newport, early in August, and to the surprise and chagrin of the New Yorkers the "bean boat" led the *Priscilla* home in a fresh breeze by over ten minutes. On the New York Yacht Club cruise that followed, *Puritan* took two more races from the New York "crack," which won only once; and when the actual trial races came off at the end of August the Boston boat won two out of the three from *Priscilla* and demonstrated beyond a doubt her superiority, especially in windward work. The other boats entered in the trials were the old sloop *Gracie* and the American cutter *Bedouin,* built in 1882. Both were badly outclassed. *Puritan* was chosen by the Cup committee as the defending boat and the announcment was made August 30th, eight days before the first international race was scheduled.

During all this racing the English challenger, *Genesta,* which had arrived in this country on July 16th after a fine passage of twenty-four days across the Atlantic, was being tuned up by her designer, Mr. Beavor Webb, and her skipper, Captain Carter. Good care was taken, by avoiding "brushes" with any of our yachts, not to let us get a line on her speed.

Earlier in the season word had been sent to the New York Yacht Club that the *Galatea* would not be brought over that year, but her challenge would be reserved for 1886. Hence the New York Yacht Club had only the one match on its hands after all, and September 7th was set for the first race.

Genesta came off the drydock September 2nd, with her coppered underbody polished by hand until one could see his face in it and with her sails in the pink of condition as the result of the attention of Lapthorn, the English sailmaker, who was brought over for the purpose. *Puritan* was hauled and had her underbody potleaded until is was as slippery as an eel, and the last touches of her grooming were finished only the day before the first race.

September 7th opened with a thick fog hanging over New York Bay, and through this the racers and a big excursion fleet, loaded to the guards with a patriotic and enthusiastic crowd of sightseers, felt their way down to the Scotland lightship off the Hook. But there was not enough breeze to get the yachts

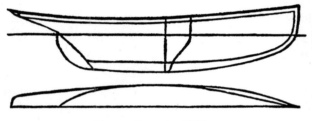

Cutter *Genesta,* 1885.

over the course, and the race was finally postponed until the next day.

The yachts were at the lightship again the following morning, and found a merry breeze ruffling the surface, giving every indication of excellent racing weather. The preparatory signal was given at 11:32 A.M. and both boats edged up near the line. As they came together, moving fast, *Puritan,* on the port tack, tried to cross *Genesta's* bows, her skipper miscalculating the distance or trying to bluff the English captain, who had the right of way, into going about. The Britishers called the bluff, however, and seeing that he could not clear the *Genesta* the *Puritan's* helmsman luffed across the *Genesta's* bow, the latter's bowsprit going through the *Puritan's* mainsail, and being snapped off short at the stem by the leach rope. Here was a pretty mess just at the start of an international race, and one

Models of *Mischief* (left) and *Atalanta,* the second Canadian challenger, in 1881.

Mayflower (left) and the 1886 challenger *Galatea*.

that might lead to all sorts of trouble. But Sir Richard Sutton, the young owner of the *Genesta,* proved himself equal to the occasion.

The committee boat went alongside the *Genesta* to find out the extent of her damage and told those on board that *Puritan* had been disqualified, as she was clearly at fault, and that if the *Genesta* sailed over the course and finished inside the seven-hour time limit, the race was hers. Mr. Roosevelt Schuyler, the American representative on board, was just asking the committee if they would give them time to rig a new bowsprit with the spinnaker boom, when Sir Richard Sutton cut in with:

"We are very much obliged, but we don't want it that way. We came over for a race, not a sailover."

This sportsmanlike spirit pleased the committee and won the owner of the *Genesta* great popularity throughout the country. He could have sailed the course and taken the race without question, *Puritan* being wholly in the wrong, but he preferred otherwise.

Time was given both boats to repair damages, and September 11th was the next time they met off the Scotland light-vessel. The course was twenty miles to windward and return, the wind light easterly, though there was considerable bobble of sea which seemed to bother *Puritan* a little. After sending them away at 11:35 the wind gradually became flatter and flatter, and it was over six hours before *Puritan* rounded the outer mark. It was then seen that the yachts could not finish in the seven-hour time limit and the race was called off, with *Genesta* about a mile astern.

These postponements were getting monotonous; but on the next race day, September 14th, there was a fair southwest breeze blowing and a race was finally sailed. This time the course was the "inside" one, starting off Owl's Head, on the Bay Ridge shore, and going out to Sandy Hook lightship and back, a distance of thirty-eight nautical miles.

The starting signal from the judges' boat, the tug *Lucken-back,* at 10:30 found the *Genesta* well to leeward of the line, where she had been set by the strong flood tide. *Puritan* crossed first, and the two boats started to beat down the bay, through the Narrows, followed by the ever-present fleet of yachts and excursion boats. *Genesta* was bothered somewhat on one tack by an incoming bark, and when they passed out by Fort Wads-worth the American boat had a lead of about seven minutes.

In the lower bay the wind was uncertain, sometimes coming in good puffs and again dying away to faint airs, and in it the boats worked down to the South West Spit, *Puritan* having a lead of three minutes at that point. Then, with sheets eased off for the reach to the lightship they traveled fast, with scuppers just awash. Off the point of the Hook the *Genesta* was crowded by the excursion fleet, which got too near in the anxiety of the captains to give their passengers a good view, and the wash undoubtedly retarded her somewhat, to the great and justified annoyance of her crew. *Puritan* rounded the lightship at 2:14:54 P.M., *Genesta* turning 4 minutes and 22 seconds behind her.

It was a close reach back to the Hook, with the wind hauling a trifle, so that a short hitch had to be taken to fetch the buoy, and then a broad reach, which *Genesta* made into a spinnaker run, back to the finish line just outside the Narrows. The wind was lightening all the time and *Genesta* kept dropping behind, so that she was about a mile astern when *Puritan* crossed at 4:38:05 P.M. in a spiritless and disappointing finish. *Puritan* allowed *Genesta* 28 seconds time over the 38-mile course, and the official figures were as follows:

NAME	START	FINISH	ELAPSED TIME	CORR'T'D TIME
	H. M. S.	H. M. S.	H. M. S.	H. M. S.
Puritan	10 32 00	4 38 05	6 06 05	6 06 05
Genesta	10 32 00	4 54 52	6 22 52	6 22 54

    Puritan won by 16m. 19s.

A day intervened before the next race was sailed, but the 16th found both boats at Scotland lightship, ready for the decisive battle of the series. There was a fresh autumn nor'-wester flecking the tops of the tumbling seas offshore, and the course was set for a twenty-mile run down wind and a beat back, with every promise of the best race of the series, which the following five hours more than fulfilled.

Mindful of his bad start in the previous race, Captain Carter, of the *Genesta*, kept his vessel near the line, so that she got the jump on *Puritan* and crossed just sixteen seconds after the whistle and forty-five seconds ahead of the American sloop. Both boats broke out immense spinnakers, but *Puritan* was not close enough to take *Genesta's* wind, and the narrow cutter slipped through the water so fast that the hopes of the patriotic aboard the excursion fleet waned as it became apparent that the Yankee sloop had met her match down the wind. Both boats were traveling at a ten-knot clip, but as they neared the outer mark the wind freshened considerably and they took in club topsails for the strenuous beat back. *Genesta* doused her spinnaker smartly and hauled sheets aft as she rounded the mark, where it was seen that she was fully an eighth of a mile ahead.

Once hauled on the wind, both boats felt the true force of the nor'wester, which was now coming in vicious puffs, while the sea was making up fast and hard. *Genesta* set a gaff topsail, which shook and slatted at a great rate, but *Puritan*, seeing that it would be too fresh to carry that sail, housed her topmast. They made a leg in under the Long Island shore, where somewhat smoother water was found, and all the time *Puritan* kept eating out to weather of the cutter, whose topsail, instead of helping her, was shaking so as to hold her back. It was the first time most of the fleet had seen a cutter in a real breeze and they were astonished at the way *Genesta* lay over in the puffs, which were now of full thirty-mile strength.

About three o'clock the boats were abeam of each other off Long Beach, but with *Puritan* some three-fourths of a mile to weather. Then the wind shifted toward the north so that they could lay the lightship, and *Puritan* wiped off on the other tack and went banging down toward the Jersey coast, followed by the cutter, both having all they could stagger under. It is the consensus of most yachtsmen that *Genesta* threw away her chances in the race by lugging her topsail, which was not drawing, instead of clewing it up and housing her topmast, as *Puritan* had done. Why Carter, who otherwise showed excellent judgment, hung on to it, is not known.

As they neared the Scotland lightship *Puritan*, being to windward and having a little to spare, started sheets and fairly tore down to the line, leaving a wake like an ocean liner, and crossed a little over two minutes ahead of *Genesta*.

The times:

NAME	START	FINISH	ELAPSED TIME	CORR'T'D TIME
	H. M. S.	H. M. S.	H. M. S.	H. M. S.
Puritan	11 06 01	4 09 15	5 03 14	5 03 14
Genesta	11 05 16	4 10 36	5 05 20	5 04 52

It was a great race, the most stirring and the closest contest for the Cup up to that time, and fortunate were those who had a chance to follow the racers over the course that blustery autumn day. As *Genesta* crossed in *Puritan's* wake, defeated but not disheartened, she luffed up alongside the winner and her crew gave three generous British cheers for the winner, which were returned as heartily with three Yankee ones from Captain Aubrey Crocker of the *Puritan* and his crew.

And so ended the most satisfactory race for the Cup that had yet been seen. *Genesta's* generous owner, Sir Richard Sutton, stayed in this country some three weeks longer, and with unbounded faith in his yacht tried to arrange another match with *Puritan*. Mr. Forbes, the latter's managing owner, would not race, however, believing that the *Puritan* had fulfilled her mission.

Genesta did not go home empty-handed, however, as she won the Bennett and Douglas prizes during the following weeks, and also the Brenton Reef and Cape May Challenge cups in two long ocean races against the schooner *Dauntless.* On October 9th she sailed for home, making a fast passage, considering the hard head winds she encountered, of 19 days 10 hours to Gosport, England. She proved herself a sturdy, able sea boat.

As for the *Puritan,* the embodiment of new ideas in yacht design that had kept the *America's* Cup in this country, she was sold at auction on September 23d, to J. Malcolm Forbes, for only $13,500. She remained his property for many years and was sailed under both sloop and schooner rig until her owner had no further use for her. Somewhere around 1905 she was sold to some Portuguese of the Cape Verde Islands, and was used as a freight and passenger packet between New Bedford, Mass., and her new owners' homes, making two trips a year across the Western ocean for many years.

Chapter VIII

THE "MAYFLOWER-GALATEA" RACE OF 1886

IF THE *Puritan-Genesta* match had been a satisfactory one, and our relations with Sir Richard Sutton pleasant, the race the following year was productive of just as good feeling; and these two matches did much to re-establish the harmony in international yachting affairs that the Ashbury incident and the *Atalanta-Mischief* race had broken.

After *Genesta's* return to England the challenge on behalf of *Galatea* was renewed by the Royal Northern Yacht Club of Scotland, and accepted by the New York Yacht Club, terms for a series of three races to be held in September, 1886, being much the same as those of the *Puritan-Genesta* match.

The *Galatea* was owned by Lieut. William Henn, an enthusiastic yachtsman who had been in the Royal Navy for fifteen years and who (while yet a young man) had retired some ten years before so that he might devote more time to his favorite pastime. As has been said, the *Galatea*, designed by Mr. Beavor Webb, was built in 1885, the year after *Genesta*, and was raced that season in English waters.

She was somewhat larger than *Genesta*, being 12 feet longer over all. Her general dimensions were: Length waterline, 86 feet 10 inches; length over all, 102 feet 7 inches; beam, 15 feet, and draft, 13 feet 6 inches, while she spread 7751 square feet of canvas, exclusive of light sails. She was a regular "lead mine" of ballast, having 81 tons run into her keel. She was built of steel, the first challenger in which this material was used, and she was jocularly referred to here as the "tin frigate."

In anticipation of *Galatea's* coming, General Paine, one of the *Puritan* syndicate, feeling sure that *Puritan* could be improved upon, which feeling was shared by the yacht's designer, placed an order with Edward Burgess for a new sloop, somewhat larger than *Puritan*, of which he was to be the sole owner.

From an unknown local designer, with a dingy back office up three flights of stairs, Burgess had taken rank among the foremost naval architects of this country and his name was known throughout the yachting world. The credit that he received was well merited, for he not only had originality but also the courage of his convictions. He had thrown traditions to the winds to take what he considered best in yacht design, no matter where it came from—which was no easy thing to do

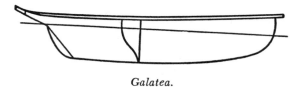

Galatea.

when nearly the whole country was convinced of the superior merits of the purely American type of shallow, flat, inside ballasted boats.

The advent of *Puritan* and of her successor, *Mayflower*, with their deeper hulls, outside lead ballast, overhanging sterns, and modified cutter rig, resulted in a great change in yacht design and brought about a vastly improved type of boat—abler, more seaworthy, and faster, except perhaps under certain conditions, than the older type of skimming dish.

Edward Burgess got to work at once on General Paine's new sloop. She was built at George Lawley's yard at City Point that winter and was launched early in May, being christened *Mayflower*. She was the biggest sloop in this country, her dimensions being: Length over all, 100 feet; waterline, 85½ feet; beam, 23½ feet; draft, 9 feet 9 inches (with centerboard down 20 feet). It is said that her sail area was 8500 square feet and

she had 37 tons of lead on her keel and 11 tons inside. Mr.
Burgess had said that stability was one of the points he aimed
at developing in the *Puritan,* and in that respect she was a
great success. She was not, however, so easy in a head sea as
could be wished, and this defect he tried to remedy in the
Mayflower. In this particular he was quite successful. The
Mayflower was a much better boat in a head sea, her forebody
being longer and her entrance, of course, being finer.

But the New York yachtsmen would not let the "down-
easters" get away with the honors without a fight. So a syndicate was formed in the Atlantic Yacht Club, then located on the
Bay Ridge shore, and Captain Philip Ellsworth, a yacht designer

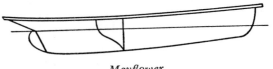

Mayflower.

and sailor of the old school, was commissioned to draw plans
for a big sloop to represent that club. The outcome of this was
the sloop *Atlantic,* slightly smaller than *Mayflower,* being 96
feet long over all, and following in general the "compromise"
model, having outside ballast through which the centerboard
worked.

The New York Yacht Club pinned its faith in this yacht and
Priscilla, which had undergone some changes under the direction of Cary Smith, her designer, with a view to lightening her
and improving her speed.

There was intense rivalry between the different camps, so
that when the *Mayflower* disappointed her followers by making
a poor showing at first, the New Yorkers saw visions of glory
returning to the metropolis. The new Boston sloop lost her
first three races to the *Puritan,* and it took a vigorous tuning up
and many changes in trim before she was "right." In fact, it
was not until the Goelet Cup races early in August that she

really came into her own and showed what she could do. On that occasion she beat *Puritan* nearly six minutes in a forty-mile race, and after that did not lose another race during the year.

On August 1st the challenger, *Galatea,* arrived at Marblehead after a leisurely and comfortable trip across of some thirty days. Her owner and his wife crossed on her, both being very fond of cruising, and she was fitted up below as a permanent home for Lieutenant Henn and his family, in which they lived the greater part of the year.

The British cutter joined the New York Yacht Club cruise at Buzzard's Bay a few days later but refrained from racing, always towing a dinghy astern when under way to show that she was not out for a test of speed. She was a handsome cutter, painted white, with a finely setting suit of sails, but neither then, nor later, when she was hauled out on drydock and her underbody disclosed, did she throw much fear into the hearts of American yachtsmen. Her owner was extremely genial and he and his wife made friends wherever they went.

The trial races to pick the defender were started on August 21st, among *Mayflower, Atlantic, Puritan,* and *Priscilla.* *Mayflower* won the first race by over 10 minutes and the second by about 4 minutes and was at once selected. She was sailed by Capt. "Hank" Haff, a skipper who was to become an international figure in *America's* Cup annals and who soon won a place in the hearts of the American public second to no other professional sailor. General Paine, her owner, was also on board in all of her races, with his thorough knowledge of racing and trim, set of sails, and the many elements that make for speed in a yacht.

After the trial races *Mayflower* received a thorough grooming for the bigger event and was at the top notch of perfection when she was towed to the line off Owl's Head, Bay Ridge, on September 7th, where she found *Galatea* waiting for her and a big fleet of yachts, steamboats, and tugs which the dull, threatening weather could not keep away. About 10 o'clock the weather began to clear and a southerly breeze came in that warranted the committee in starting the boats at 10:56, the course being the usual inside one of the New York Yacht Club.

Galatea came down on the starboard tack and in the weather berth, cleverly blanketing *Mayflower*, though the two crossed almost together. In a couple of tacks, however, the American boat worked out from her bad position and started to eat out to windward in the manner our boats usually did in these early races. As a contemporary writer put it, voicing probably the convictions of most Americans concerning the centerboard type: "As soon as the boats got on the port tack *the centerboard began to make its magic influence felt,* and the *Mayflower* outpointed the cutter, and getting the lead, kept it all day."

We can smile at the enthusiasm of the writer; but it was nevertheless true that at that time the centerboard boat was better going to windward in smooth water than the keel boat as developed in the cutter; and probably the "compromise" type of *Puritan* and *Mayflower* was superior even in rough water, when properly handled.

The race was rather devoid of interest after the beat to the Spit Buoy, where *Mayflower* was over four minutes ahead. After rounding the lightship balloon jibs were broken out, and spinnakers were set after turning the Spit Buoy on the way home. But it was only a procession, and *Mayflower* crossed the finish line 12 minutes and 40 seconds ahead of the English yacht, or 12 minutes and 2 seconds, corrected time. *Galatea* was well handled, but was outclassed in the prevailing light conditions.

On September 9th an attempt was made to sail the second race, but the wind failed.

Two days later the boats were at Sandy Hook lightship once more, with a fine northwest breeze blowing down out of the lower bay. The course was set to leeward, twenty miles and return, and the starting gun went at 11:20. Both boats were dressed in all their light canvas, spinnakers, balloon jibs, and club topsails catching all the wind there was. It took *Mayflower* over two and a half hours to run to the leeward mark, but she had gained 13 minutes and 45 seconds on the slim cutter on the slide down wind.

After turning for the beat back, the wind went flat after a sharp squall in which *Mayflower* had to get her big club topsail on deck in a hurry. Then there was a weary wait and it looked as if the time limit would again put a stop to proceedings; but, finally, a fickle breeze came off the Jersey shore, which wafted the boats along so that *Mayflower* just managed to slip over the line with 11 minutes of her seven hours to spare. *Galatea* was nearly 30 minutes behind her, and 18 minutes over the seven hours. The following table shows how close there came to being another fizzle:

NAME	START	FINISH	ELAPSED TIME	CORR'T'D TIME
	H. M. S.	H. M. S.	H. M. S.	H. M. S.
Mayflower	11 22 40	6 11 40	6 49 00	6 49 00
Galatea	11 24 10	6 42 58	7 18 48	7 18 09

Though beaten fairly, Lieutenant Henn felt that the weather was not suited to his boat and he challenged *Mayflower* to a match race off Marblehead in a real breeze. General Paine accepted and agreed to keep his boat in commission for the race until a certain date. So Lieutenant Henn sailed *Galatea* to Marblehead and there the two yachts lay for ten whole days waiting for a breeze, which, with one of those rare freaks of nature, never came in sufficient strength to allow the race to be sailed. When the agreed time was up *Mayflower* was promptly hauled out, and the very next day it "piped up" a rattling breeze fit to try the worth of both yachts.

The following spring, *Galatea* being still in this country, a race was sailed between *Mayflower* and the English cutter in a strong breeze and *Mayflower* won easily. Lieutenant Henn was then satisfied, having had the test he wanted.

Just before the races of 1886 Lieutenant Henn issued a challenge to sail any American sloop or cutter to Bermuda and back to test the real abilities of the boats, but could get no takers, and there was a lot of talk about American "racing machines" being unfit to go to sea—much of which was true, though as regards *Puritan* and *Mayflower* they would have been capable of going there easily and comfortably, and probably in a shorter time than *Galatea*.

Lieutenant Henn and his cutter remained in this country until after the races with the *Thistle* the following year, 1887, and made many friends here.

Chapter IX

THE SCOTCH CHALLENGER "THISTLE" AND HER RACE AGAINST "VOLUNTEER"

JUST AS the coming to this country of the cutter *Madge,* and the success of the *Puritan, Mayflower,* and the other "compromise" yachts, had brought about a better and abler type of boat here, so the result of these last two races had their effect on English design; and before the following year, 1887, the English modified their old measurement rule, which hampered yacht designers by its undue tax on beam, so as to give more latitude in this respect and to allow of a broader, better proportioned, and more powerful hull. Under this new rule yacht building and designing in England underwent considerable change and the sport had a period of great activity.

Shortly after the conclusion of the *Galatea-Mayflower* race a challenge was received by the New York Yacht Club from Scotland, the Royal Clyde Yacht Club sending a letter proposing a race in 1887 on behalf of Mr. James Bell, with a boat of about the size of the *Mayflower.*

Inasmuch as the prevailing deed of gift called for at least six months' notice, but *not over* seven months', this letter was not a formal challenge, but was merely a friendly communication in an effort to arrive at an amicable agreement, to be followed by the formal challenge at such time as to allow the races to be held the following September. A rather curt answer by the New York Yacht Club stated that when the challenge came "in proper form" it would be considered, and enclosed a copy of the second deed of gift.

The Scottish club still continued in trying to be forehanded

by arriving at a definite understanding as to the size of the
boats, so that neither one would be outbuilt, but getting no
satisfaction they went ahead with their plans, determined to
adhere strictly to the letter of the deed, and not to give out any
more information than was required.

So Mr. Bell formed a syndicate, of which he was the principal
member and manager, and commissioned George L. Watson,
a noted English naval architect and the designer of the *Madge,*
to get up plans for a large cutter. This boat was built in Glas-
gow that winter, and the formal challenge was sent in March,
at which time 85 feet was named as the waterline length of the
Scotch boat.

On account of the failure of the early negotiations, this boat

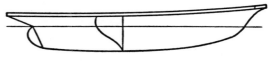

Volunteer.

was built under lock and key and no one save the designer,
builders, and members of the syndicate knew what she was to
be like until she was launched in April. Hence it was not until
the receipt of the formal challenge in March that plans could
be made for a defender. But General Charles J. Paine again
came to the front with an offer to build a sloop to meet the
Thistle, as the challenger was named, and on account of his
success in the two previous matches the matter of defense was
left to him. He went at once to Edward Burgess and placed
an order for a sloop, 85 feet 10 inches being decided upon as
the waterline length of the new boat. She was to be built of
steel and the order was placed with Pusey & Jones Co., of
Wilmington, Delaware. The yacht was built in the remarkably
short time of sixty-six days, and was launched the last day of
June, being christened *Volunteer.*

While following generally the forms of *Puritan* and *Mayflower*, she showed some marked deviation from those boats. She was narrower and deeper than either of her predecessors, had a graceful clipper bow, making her longer over all, while her keel had more curve, or "rocker," to it than the straight keels of *Puritan* and *Mayflower*. She also carried more sail, spreading 9271 square feet. On the waterline length just given she was 106 feet 3 inches long over all, with a beam of 23 feet 2 inches, and a draft, exclusive of board, of 10 feet.

Thistle's designed dimensions were 85 feet waterline, 108 feet 6 inches over all, 20 feet 3 inches beam (the widest cutter of her size built at that time in England), and 13 feet 10 inches

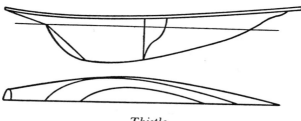

Thistle.

draft, while she spread 8968 square feet of canvas. She also had a clipper bow in contrast to the plumb stem of the older cutters, and her forefoot was cut away to give a minimum of wetted surface when sailing in a light breeze. Her bilges were also slightly harder than in the narrow, wall-sided cutters.

The English challenger was unusually successful in home waters, winning eleven first prizes, one second, and one third out of fifteen races before sailing for this country, and beating *Genesta* and *Irex,* another fast cutter, easily. So the hopes of English yachtsmen were high that she would bring home the Cup. She arrived at New York on August 16th after a fast passage across of twenty-two days, made under a moderate jury rig. After her arrival things began to happen thick and fast.

On account of the secrecy which surrounded her building

there was much speculation here as to just what form George Watson had given the new challenger, and many absurd rumors went flying around as to what the *Thistle* was like under water.

Soon after her arrival the enterprising manager of one of the New York daily papers arranged to have a diver go down some dark night and "explore" her bottom. This was done, and the result of his examination was published in a drawing of the boat's underwater form in the paper that hired him. *Thistle* must certainly have been a queer yacht if she looked anything like this drawing, and Mr. Bell, her managing owner, remarked when he saw the article in question, "The proprietor of that paper will feel like shooting that diver when the *Thistle* is docked and her real form is seen."

There was also considerable resentment in this country over the secrecy maintained about her, though the cause for it seems apparent in the attitude of the New York Yacht Club in the early correspondence. This came to a head when she was finally measured here and found to be 86.4 feet on the water instead of 85 feet as given, though it is probable that this was caused by her floating deeper than her designed waterline, as frequently happens with new yachts, and not from any intent. She paid the penalty of this in her measurement for time allowance, and as the figure sent over with the challenge was necessarily taken from the plans and not from the boat itself, no one could foretell that she would measure *exactly* this at the line of flotation.

It looked for a time as if this really slight matter, slight so far as any real advantage to the challenger was concerned, would result in a break, but the matter was adjusted amicably with the help of the old pacifier, Mr. George L. Schuyler. *Volunteer* was still the larger boat and had to allow *Thistle* time.

Volunteer's early performances were just as gratifying to us as *Thistle's* had been to the English, and in her entire first season it is said that she lost only one race. It was a foregone

Models of *Mayflower* (left) and *Galatea* show the beamy centerboarder and the deep narrow cutter.

Vigilant (left) and *Valkyrie II*, the 1893 challenger, maneuvering before the start.

conclusion that she would be chosen as the defender, and in beating to windward she was invincible against any American boat. Still there was the formality of a trial race, *Mayflower*, then owned by E. D. Morgan, of the New York Yacht Club, being the only boat to enter against *Volunteer*.

After two attempts to sail a race had to be abandoned for lack of wind, the third trial, in a fine breeze, resulted in an easy victory for *Volunteer* by 16 minutes and 2 seconds, and the new sloop was chosen without more ado.

Two out of three races were decided upon for the international series, one over the inside course, one to windward and return outside Sandy Hook, and the third, if necessary, triangular, over an outside course. The date set for the first race was September 27th.

The morning of that day broke gray and somber, with indications of fog, blown in by the fitful northeast breeze. There was no improvement as the morning wore on and the two stately racers loafed around the committee boat off Owl's Head, waiting for the starting signal, which was withheld until a real breeze should set in. In these early hours *Thistle* moved very much faster than *Volunteer* in the light air, and the English and Scottish sympathizers in the excursion fleet were jubilant and freely bet jugs of "Scotch" on the outcome.

The truth was that foxy old "Hank" Haff at the wheel of *Volunteer* was "killing" his boat in the short tacks around the line, not seeing any need of displaying her real form until after the starting gun. General Paine, with his old straw hat on as usual, was taking it easy and apparently saw little cause to worry.

It was 12:32 before the starting whistle sounded from the committee boat, and at that time there was a light SSE breeze coming in from sea. Both boats were caught some distance from the line, but *Thistle* was over first, on the port tack, nearly two minutes ahead of *Volunteer*. The wind headed both boats and they stood over for the Staten Island shore. Less than fifteen minutes after the start *Volunteer* tacked and crossed the *Thistle's* bow, having made up her early loss in this brief space, and in just the kind of airs that *Thistle* had been doing so well in before the start.

Slowly they beat down the channel, tack and tack, the wind gradually working around to southwest. At the Spit Buoy *Volunteer* was over fifteen minutes ahead and the thoughtless excursion fleet had forsaken *Thistle* for the leader, giving the latter their backwash and crowding so close to *Volunteer* on both sides that her crew hung from her quarter a big canvas sign, painted in large letters and reading "Keep Astern." They took the hint, but soon forgot themselves again and the sign had once more to be hung out.

The *Thistle* was a mile astern when *Volunteer* rounded the lightship at 3:42 P.M. The wind had freshened somewhat and gone back to south; so with no more windward work the reach and run home were a procession, *Thistle* being nearly twenty minutes astern as the *Volunteer* crossed the finish line and received the noisy demonstration of the fleet. The assurance of the Scottish and English enthusiasts was gone, and instead of drinking at the expense of their American friends, they were drowning their sorrow at their own.

The times:

NAME	START	FINISH	ELAPSED TIME	CORR'T'D TIME
	H. M. S.	H. M. S.	H. M. S.	H. M. S.
Volunteer	12 34 58¼	5 28 16¼	4 53 18	4 53 18
Thistle	12 33 06	5 45 52¾	5 12 46¾	5 12 41¾

While American yachtsmen were jubilant over the victory, *Thistle* being feared before the race on account of her radical departure from the other cutters that had come over, Mr. James Bell, the Scottish yacht's owner, was about the most disappointed man imaginable. He could not understand how his boat could have been beaten so badly and thought that something must have gotten foul of her bottom. He had *Thistle's* bottom swept before the next race, but found nothing there. The fact is that every boat seems to move fast when she is winning, but the same boat looks to be going very sluggishly when another boat near her is moving faster than she is.

Mr. Bell also criticised the inside course, saying it was the worst he had ever sailed over. While it was a poor course for an international race, with many turns, strong tides and eddies, and the true wind liable to be broken by the shores, it was no worse than many of the courses in England, which are laid out on estuaries or land-bound waters with stronger tides than we have here. As a matter of fact, this was the last race where the New York Yacht Club insisted on this inside course being used in an international event.

Although the two yachts went out to the lightship on September 29th, there was not enough wind for a race and it was postponed until the 30th, when there was a fine easterly breeze of moderate strength blowing. The course was laid dead to windward from the Scotland lightship for twenty miles and the starting gun banged at 10:40. *Thistle* was close to the line and again slipped over ahead, twenty-one seconds after the gun, though *Volunteer* luffed around the stern of the committee boat and got the windward berth. After the first fifteen minutes is was apparent that the Yankee sloop was outpointing the cutter, and on the long twenty-mile thrash she continued to eat out to windward. The breeze held true and *Volunteer* turned the outer mark fourteen minutes ahead of *Thistle*. The run home brought some solace to the canny Scots, for *Thistle* gained nearly three minutes, but not enough to bring her within striking distance, as she was over a mile and a half astern at the finish, which was represented by 11 minutes and 25 seconds actual time. The official times were:

NAME	START	FINISH	ELAPSED TIME	CORR'T'D TIME
	H. M. S.	H. M. S.	H. M. S.	H. M. S.
Volunteer	10 40 50¾	4 23 47	5 42 56¼	5 42 56¼
Thistle	10 40 21	4 35 12	5 54 51	5 54 45

This ended the affair, and though the Scotsmen were disappointed they took their defeat in a most sportsmanlike manner and the best of feeling prevailed. The *Thistle* party had no sooner gotten ashore after the last race than they sent a letter to the New York Yacht Club saying that a challenge would be forthcoming for a race the following year as soon as permitted under the terms of the deed, and naming seventy feet as the waterline length of the new yacht.

The *Thistle* sailed for home in October, and was subsequently sold to the German Emperor, who raced her for some years under the name of *Comet*. The *Volunteer* was sailed and raced for many years and was only broken up in 1911.

One thing should be mentioned in connection with this race as showing how partisanship can warp judgment. *Thistle* was sailed in her races over here by Captain John Barr, a Scotsman, who had been in this country before as skipper of the English cutter *Clara* in 1885 and was extremely successful here during three seasons. After the *Thistle* returned to Scotland the rumor spread that Captain Barr had sold out the *Thistle* to the Americans and had not raced her to win. There was absolutely nothing to support the rumor, but it fed for a time on the disappointed hopes of the Scotch partisans.

Captain Barr later settled in this country, where he had many important commands, was honored and respected, and was known as a very clever racing skipper. There was not a word of truth in the accusation.

Chapter X

THE NEW DEED OF GIFT—LORD DUNRAVEN'S TWO CHAL-
LENGES AND THE "VIGILANT-VALKYRIE" MATCH OF 1893

IN THE SIX YEARS between the *Volunteer-Thistle* race of 1887
many things happened that had a marked bearing on the future
of *America's* Cup racing, and caused a sharp controversy between the New York Yacht Club and British yachtsmen. Without going into a discussion of all the points involved, a brief
review of the whole situation is necessary for a proper understanding of the future history of the Cup races.

In October, 1887, only a few days after the last *Volunteer-
Thistle* race and of the receipt of the notice of Mr. Bell's
second challenge, the New York Yacht Club decided to ask Mr.
George L. Schuyler to draw up a new deed of gift for the
America's Cup, as it was felt that the one of 1882 was not
satisfactory, and a committee was appointed to take the matter
up. Mr. Schuyler drew up a new deed, of much greater length
and in more legal form, and sent it to the club with the Cup.
This "New Deed of Gift" was accepted by the club, and, with
minor changes, is the one at present in force. It is given here
in full.

"This deed of gift, made October 24, 1887, between George L.
Schuyler, as sole surviving owner of the Cup won by the yacht
America at Cowes, England, August 22, 1851, of the first part, and
the New York Yacht Club, of the second part, witnesseth:

"That the said party of the first part, for and in consideration of
the premises and the performance of the conditions and agreements
hereinafter set forth by the party of the second part, has granted,
bargained, sold, assigned, transferred, and set over, and by these
presents does bargain, sell, assign, transfer, and set over unto said

93

party of the second part, its successors and assigns, the Cup won by the schooner-yacht *America* at Cowes, England, upon August 22, 1851, to have and to hold the same to the said party of the second part, its successors and assigns, in trust, nevertheless, for the following uses and purposes:

"This Cup is donated upon the condition that it shall be preserved as a perpetual challenge cup for friendly competition between foreign countries. Any organized yacht club of a foreign country, incorporated, patented, or licensed by the legislature, admiralty, or other executive department, having for its annual regatta an ocean water-course on the sea, or an arm of the sea, or one which combines both, shall always be entitled to the right of sailing a match for this Cup with a yacht or vessel propelled by sails only and constructed in the country to which the challenging club belongs, against any one yacht or vessel constructed in the country of the club holding the Cup.

"The yachts or vessels, if of one mast, shall be not less than sixty-five nor more than ninety feet on the load waterline; if of more than one mast, they shall be not less than eighty feet nor more than one hundred and fifteen feet on the load waterline.

"The challenging club shall give ten months' notice in writing, naming the days for the proposed races, but no race shall be sailed on the days intervening between November 1 and May 1. Accompanying the ten months' notice of challenge there must be sent the name of the owner and a certificate of the name, rig, and following dimensions of the challenging vessel, namely: Length on load waterline, beam at load waterline, and extreme beam, and draught of water, which dimensions shall not be exceeded; and a Custom House registry of the vessel must be sent as soon as possible.

"Vessels selected to compete for this Cup must proceed under sail on their own bottoms to the port where the contest is to take place.

"Centerboard or sliding keel vessels shall always be allowed to compete in any race for this Cup, and no restriction or limitation whatever shall be placed upon the use of such centerboard or sliding keel, nor shall the centerboard or sliding keel be considered a part of the vessel for any purposes of measurement.

"The club challenging for the Cup and the club holding the same may, by mutual consent, make any arrangement satisfactory to both as to the dates, courses, number of trials, rules, and sailing regulations, and any and all other conditions of the match, in which case, also, the ten months' notice may be waived.

"In case the parties cannot mutually agree upon the terms of a match, then three races shall be sailed, and the winner of two of such races shall be entitled to the Cup. All such races shall be on ocean courses, free from headlands, as follows:

"The first race, twenty nautical miles to windward and return; the second, an equilateral triangular race of thirty-nine nautical miles, the first side of which shall be a beat to windward; the third race, if necessary, twenty nautical miles to windward and return, and one week-day shall intervene between the conclusion of one race and the starting of the next race.

"These ocean courses shall be practicable in all parts for vessels of twenty-two feet draught of water, and shall be selected by the club holding the cup; and these races shall be sailed subject to its rules and sailing regulations, so far as the same do not conflict with the provisions of this deed of gift, but without any time allowance whatever.

"The challenged club shall not be required to name its representative vessel until at the time agreed upon for the start; but the vessel when named must compete in all the races, and each of such races must be completed within seven hours.

"Should the club holding the Cup be, for any cause, dissolved, the Cup shall be transferred to some club of the same nationality eligible to challenge under this deed of gift, in trust and subject to its provisions. In the event of failure of such transfer within three months after such dissolution, said Cup shall revert to the preceding club holding the same, and under the terms of the deed of gift. It is distinctly understood that the Cup is to be the property of the club, subject to the provisions of this deed, and not the property of the owners of any vessel winning a match.

"No vessel which has been defeated in a match for this Cup can be again selected by any club as its representative until after a contest for it by some other vessel has intervened, or until after the expiration of two years from the time of such defeat. And when a challenge from a club fulfilling all the conditions required by this instrument has been received, no other challenge can be considered until the pending event has been decided.

"And the said party of the second part hereby accepts the said Cup, subject to the said trust, terms, and conditions, and hereby covenants and agrees, to and with the said party of the first part, that it will faithfully and fully see that the foregoing conditions are fully observed and complied with by any contestant for the said Cup during the holding thereof by it, and that it will assign, transfer, and deliver the said Cup to the foreign yacht club whose representative yacht shall have won the same in accordance with the foregoing terms and conditions, provided the said foreign club shall, by instrument in writing, lawfully executed, enter with the said party of the second part into the like covenants as are herein entered into by it, such instrument to contain a like provision for the successive assignees to enter into the same covenants with their respective assignors, and to be executed in duplicate, one to be retained by each club, and a copy thereof forwarded to the said party of the second part.

"In witness whereof said party of the first part has hereunto set his hand and seal, and the said party of the second part has caused its corporate seal to be affixed to these presents, and the same to be signed by its commodore and attested by its secretary, the day and year first above written.

"GEORGE L. SCHUYLER.

"THE NEW YORK YACHT CLUB.

"BY ELBRIDGE T. GERRY,

"Commodore.

"JOHN H. BIRD,

"Secretary."

When the terms of this new deed were published they provoked at once a great amount of hostile criticism abroad. The notice of challenge from Mr. Bell and his associates was withdrawn, and it was freely stated that no English yachtsmen would be found to challenge under it.

The principal clauses which caused dissatisfaction abroad and led to charges of "unfairness" may be summarized briefly: They were those in regard to the substituting of the ten months' for the six months' notice; the stipulation that the challenger must give, ten months in advance, the length on waterline, beam on waterline, beam extreme, and draft of water; the requiring of a challenger to race without time allowance in case terms cannot be agreed upon by mutual consent. Furthermore, it was said that the mutual consent clause was so ambiguous that only lawyers could decide it, and that the whole deed was too complicated to govern the sport of yacht racing satisfactorily.

Of course the principal sticking point was the giving of the exact dimensions of the challenger ten months in advance.

Strictly speaking, this in itself is hardly practicable, for it would mean that the boat would have to be designed in detail nearly a year before the first race, and that not one of these dimensions could then be exceeded, even to obtain the necessary trim by changes in or the addition of ballast that might lengthen the line of flotation. With the challenger held down to a fixed set of dimensions, the defending club could study these with a view to outbuilding, which should be easy to do if races were sailed without time allowance.

Some time later Mr. George L. Schuyler, in defense of the new deed, pointed out the reason for this clause as to dimensions, saying: "When I consented to the making of the new deed this provision was considered by me to be of minor importance. We were probably influenced by our recent experience with the dimensions of the *Thistle*. That yacht went over the dimensions sent us by her owners by about eighteen inches, load waterline measurement, but when I was called upon to decide her eligibility to race the *Volunteer*, I said I believed Mr. Bell had acted in good faith, and I consequently decided that she could sail. The main reason we ask for the load waterline length, draft of water, beam at the waterline, and extreme beam, is to know what kind of a vessel we have to meet. I believed the challenged party has a right to know what the yacht challenging is like, so that it can meet her with a yacht of her own type if it is to be desired.

"I deny most emphatically that giving the dimensions asked for will reveal the lines of a vessel, and I do not believe any yacht designer will say it will. The *Volunteer* and *Mayflower* is a case in point. The dimensions of these two yachts are almost identical, and still their lines are very different. If you give a designer these dimensions, which yacht will he produce? We never asked for the lines of a boat. We do not want them, but we do believe the challenged party has a right to know what kind of a craft it will have to contend with.

"Look at our position at present. We only have one of the recent Cup defenders—the *Volunteer*—to fall back upon, and she is for sale, and may be sold next fall. If the English gentlemen were sharp they would build a ninety-foot boat, and then tell us that they do not care to arrange a series of races by mutual consent, but will abide by the terms of the deed. The result would be races on the open sea, boat against boat, no time allowance being given, and we would be forced to build a ninety-foot boat unless we would be content to meet the challenger with a boat four feet shorter.

"The matter which I thought of greatest importance, when the new deed was drawn up, was that of courses. I wanted it so arranged that in case of a disagreement as to the conditions of races, the boats would race on the sea without time allowance, and thus avoid the possibility of a challenger being left to the mercy of a club course where she would not have an equal chance to win."

The New York Yacht Club also pointed out to the English critics that the new deed "expressly provided that the club challenging for the Cup and the club holding it, may, by *mutual* consent, make any arrangement satisfactory to both, and also any and all other conditions of the match, etc., etc."

As a matter of fact, the deed does not make it quite clear as to just how much could be conceded under this clause, and how many of the fixed terms of the deed could be waived, and this was one of the objections raised by Lord Dunraven in his first challenge. By failing to agree upon terms the challenger would be forced to the alternative of racing without time allowance, each boat would naturally be built to the limit of the deed, and, of course, the home boat could be built much lighter than one that had to sail three thousand miles of open sea.

But to get away from legal documents and back on our course again. In spite of all the hubbub over the deed, in the spring of 1889 the Royal Yacht Squadron sent a challenge for the Cup on behalf of the Earl of Dunraven, with a letter from Designer Watson saying that the challenger would not exceed seventy feet waterline length, and would be named *Valkyrie.*

The New York Yacht Club was willing to make concessions as to the dimensions furnished, and other matters could have been adjusted by mutual consent, but the negotiations finally fell through because the New York Yacht Club insisted that if the challenger won, the Cup should be held by the Royal Yacht Squadron under the full terms of the new deed of gift. This the Yacht Squadron refused to agree to, saying that it did not consider the deed fair and would not want to make other clubs race for the Cup under its terms.

Here the matter ended, with some more unimportant letter writing, and was not taken up again for nearly three years.

In the meantime Mr. George L. Schuyler died on board Commodore Gerry's steam yacht *Electra.* His death marked the passing of an important figure in *America's* Cup history. He was a fair and high-minded sportsman who always stood for the best there was in yacht racing, and he had frequently smoothed the paths that others had torn up, and poured oil on the troubled waters of international strife, to the satisfaction of both sides.

But the Earl of Dunraven was not to be balked of an attempt to win the famous Cup, deed or no deed; so, in November, 1892, after some more letter writing, a compromise was agreed upon and the Royal Yacht Squadron challenged in his behalf. The New York Yacht Club promptly accepted by a unanimous vote.

The New York Yacht Club agreed to waive the question of measurements in the ten months' notice, and to require waterline length only, with a penalty if the figure given was exceeded. In fact, the club has never since insisted on all the measurements, but has been satisfied with the length only, or in more recent years with the rating under a measurement formula.

In return, the Yacht Squadron in effect swallowed the new deed, and agreed not to refuse any challenge under its specific conditions, though it still claimed the *right* to accept a challenge under the same terms as those of the match in question, in case it won. The New York Yacht Club also agreed to Dunraven's request for a series of three out of five races rather than two out of three. Lord Dunraven named the cutter *Valkyrie II* as the challenger, with a waterline length of eighty-five feet and designed by George L. Watson.

So that stretch of broken water was safely passed, and another international race was assured. But in the six years intervening since the last race another great change had taken place in yacht designing in this country, one that had made *Volunteer,* the last defender and our only big sloop, obsolete for such an important event.

In 1891 there was launched from the shop of the Herreshoffs, at Bristol, Rhode Island, a forty-six-foot waterline sloop which was a radical departure from anything that preceded her in this country. The most noticeable things about this boat were her tremendously long overhangs, not only the stern being carried out, but the forward overhang as well. The forefoot was entirely cut away, the sweep from the stemhead to the bottom of the keel being almost a straight line. She was a keel boat, drawing ten feet, with an S form of midship section, so that she was of light displacement, yet when heeled down her long ends resting on the water gave her great additional bearing surface, and she carried 4100 feet of sail—as much as the sixty-one-foot waterline defender *Mischief.* This boat was named *Gloriana.*

She was a masterpiece of designing and technical skill, and immediately put the Herreshoffs in the foremost rank of sail yacht designers. Up to that time their reputation had been made largely in steam craft.

Gloriana had phenomenal success her first season, and she was followed in 1892 by the *Wasp,* of the same size and type, but more powerful, and, in the hands of Capt. Charles Barr, a brother of John Barr of the *Thistle,* even faster than her proto-type. Then came the eighty-four-foot sloop *Navahoe,* of the same general lines, and this hull form became the accepted one in America.

Undoubtedly many of the original features of these boats were due to the coming to this country, in 1888, of the little English cutter *Minerva,* which in the following two years was very suc-cessful, and beat all of our boats of her class. She contained, in a lesser degree, some of the elements that Herreshoff put into *Gloriana* and *Wasp,* though the American designer developed them to a much higher state.

Thus it happened that Lord Dunraven's challenge found us unprepared to meet a big boat of this design (as it was conceded that *Valkyrie* would be), and the New York Yacht Club im-mediately set about getting a defender. A syndicate of club members, which was composed of Archibald Rogers, F. W. Vanderbilt, W. K. Vanderbilt, F. A. Schermerhorn, J. P. Mor-gan, and J. E. Brooks, placed an order for an eighty-five-foot waterline sloop with Herreshoff, all the details being left to the designer. This boat was the *Colonia.* She was a keel boat, built of steel, and bore the general earmarks of *Wasp,* but on a larger scale.

Boston was not to be denied a finger in the pie, and General Paine was again in the field with a big sloop called the *Jubilee,* designed by his son, John B. Paine, and built of steel at Law-ley's yard. She was of the fin keel type, the largest boat of that type so far tried.

Edward Burgess, the young designer of the last three success-ful defenders, had died of typhoid fever in 1891, and not only Boston, but the country at large, was the loser. He was one of the foremost men of his profession, and had turned out many fine racing yachts that had usually accomplished what they had been designed to do.

Though Burgess had gone, the successors to his firm, Stewart & Binney, had a commission from another Boston syndicate for a Cup defender, and they turned out the *Pilgrim,* an extreme fin keel type of boat, with a shallow body and very little displacement.

As if these three boats were not enough, still another New York syndicate must needs come into the field, with C. Oliver Iselin as the active head, and including many prominent New York yachtsmen. They also went to Herreshoff to place their order. This boat was named *Vigilant;* and while the first Herreshoff boat, the *Colonia,* was of the keel type, *Vigilant* was a deep centerboarder, the board working through a slot in the lead keel. Furthermore, she was built of Tobin bronze plates, which were very strong and gave a smooth, slippery surface. She was the first large yacht in which this material was used.

With these four big sloops out for Cup defense honors, the best of racing was had all that summer. They created an immense amount of interest throughout the country, the daily newspapers devoting columns to their try-outs and races.

It was apparent fairly early in the season that *Vigilant* and *Colonia* were the most likely yachts. The two fin-keelers, while fast on some points, had a number of defects, which might have been expected, as they were largely in the nature of experiments, *Jubilee* not only having a fin, but two centerboards as well, one of them being small and located in the bow.

The series for the *America's* Cup was to begin October 5th, and the first trial race among these four new sloops to pick the defender was sailed on September 7th. There is not space to describe in detail this, or the two subsequent races, though they were full of interest and provided the best racing between large sloops that had ever been seen in this country. *Colonia,* with old "Hank" Haff at the wheel, won the first race, beating *Vigilant* by only six seconds, corrected time. This was in a hard breeze off the Hook. Both *Vigilant* and *Jubilee* had their topmasts housed, though Haff "cracked on" with the *Colonia* and carried a small working topsail. Both the Boston boats got into trouble. *Pilgrim* carried away the jaws of her gaff just before the start, and had to put back, while one of the peak halyard blocks on *Jubilee* gave way on the thrash to windward, and she had to retire. To show the speed of the boats, *Colonia* covered the fifteen nautical miles of the run home in 1 hour 14 minutes and 11 seconds.

All the broken gear was repaired in time for the second race, September 9th, which was sailed in light airs that hardened toward the finish. *Vigilant* won by 4 minutes 32 seconds from

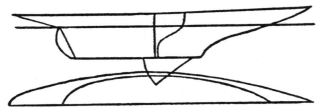

Vigilant, a deep "centerboarder."

Jubilee, Colonia being last. The third race was sailed in a strong easterly wind and rough sea. The course was fifteen miles to windward and return, and *Vigilant* again won by 6 minutes and 43 seconds from *Colonia,* the second boat. The Boston pair again had trouble with their gear and sails, and were late in starting and still later in finishing.

After seeing these three races the *America's* Cup committee unanimously chose *Vigilant* as the defender. The remaining time before the real races was spent in a thorough tuning up and in remedying such defects or weaknesses as had developed during the strenuous trials.

Before getting into the thick of the actual battle for the Cup, let us look for a moment at the two rival boats and compare them as to size and form. *Vigilant* was a big boat, 124 feet long over all, 86 feet on the waterline, with 26 feet 3 inches beam, and 14 feet draft, with a bronze centerboard, increasing this draft to 24 feet when on the wind. She spread 11,272 square feet of canvas, or over 2000 feet more than the last defender, *Volunteer.* She was very broad on deck, and this, together with the fact that she carried an abnormally large crew of about seventy men, who could lie down on the windward side and acted as so much live ballast, allowed her to carry what was then considered an enormous sail plan. Her centerboard weighed four tons.

Valkyrie II was 117 feet 3 inches long over all, 85 feet 10 inches on the water, 22 feet 4 inches beam, and drew 16 feet

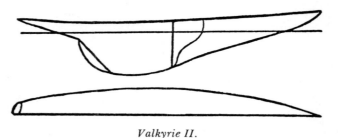

Valkyrie II.

4 inches. She carried 10,042 square feet of sail, or 1200 less than the defender. She was built of wood over steel frames, and she was commanded by Captain Cranfield, one of the foremost English professional yacht skippers.

We did not know much about the *Valkyrie's* capabilities in this country. She was said to be "good" in both a drift and a blow, and as usual there were many among the throngs that crowded the big excursion fleet who fully expected to see the Cup go back in her.

The first race of October 5th had to be called off, owing to lack of wind, after the yachts had rounded the outer mark, at which point *Valkyrie* was over twenty-six minutes ahead of *Vigilant,* due to her picking up a slant of wind that *Vigilant* missed. If the wind had held after rounding *Valkyrie* would have been a sure winner. But it flattened out to a dead calm.

On October 7th the two sloops found a soft west by north breeze coming off the land. They were sent away at 11:24, dead before the wind on a fifteen-mile leg, with a beat back. It was a one-gun start this time. That is, the starting time of the boats was counted from the minute the gun went instead of the actual time of crossing up to the expiration of a two-minute interval, as had been the custom. So every second saved at the start counted.

Valkyrie got across first, almost with the gun, and immediately set a light, snowy muslin spinnaker that caught the faintest zephyr. *Vigilant* was right after her and also hoisted light sails smartly. She was in charge of Captain William Hansen, but Nathanael G. Herreshoff, her designer, was also on board, and at the wheel a good part of the time.

They had it nip and tuck for the first half of the leg, when *Vigilant* caught a freshening breeze first and slowly passed her rival, giving the Dunraven party a capital opportunity of studying her shapely Herreshoff stern. She continued to draw ahead and was 8 minutes and 6 seconds in the lead when the outer mark was rounded.

The breeze had shifted so that the boats could lay the course home, and a little better, so they trimmed in flat and hard and "looked up" as high as possible. *Valkyrie* footed very fast on this leg, and gained perceptibly on the big *Vigilant*, which seemed to be holding rather higher than necessary. Three miles from the finish *Vigilant* started sheets, and, heading off, romped down on the finish line, which she crossed 7 minutes and 36 seconds ahead of the English cutter, or 5 minutes 48 seconds corrected time, as the table shows.

NAME	START	FINISH	ELAPSED TIME	CORR'T'D TIME
	H. M. S.	H. M. S.	H. M. S.	H. M. S.
Vigilant	11 25 00	3 30 47	4 05 47	4 05 47
Valkyrie II	11 25 00	3 38 23	4 13 23	4 11 35

According to the custom of letting a day intervene the two boats did not appear off the Hook again until October 9th. They found the wind southwest, piping a merry little breeze that gave promise of more behind it. The course this time was an equilateral triangle, ten miles to a leg, the first one being a beat to windward.

The quarterdeck gang of *Vigilant* was on the job this time, mindful of the fine work of *Valkyrie* at the start of the previous race, and got the jump on the challenger, crossing first nineteen seconds after the gun and pocketing *Valkyrie* very cleverly under their lee. Both boats made a long hitch, but Cranfield, no matter whether he sailed *Valkyrie* fine or hard full, could not squirm out of his bad position. For practically the whole first leg *Valkyrie* was right down to leeward of the American boat, and at the first turn was 4 minutes and 45 seconds behind.

It was a broad reach to the second mark, the wind increasing, and the sea getting up, but the two boats tore along at a great clip, *Vigilant* making the ten nautical miles in 50 minutes 20 seconds, or at a twelve-knot rate. They jibed around the mark, *Valkyrie* now nearly ten minutes behind, and laid a course back to the lightship, while the wind, as if still not satisfied, hardened to twenty-nine miles an hour. Lee rails were buried in suds, and *Vigilant* still kept gaining, while the mercurial beings that patronized the excursion steamers were forgetful of the unkind things they had said of "Nat" Herreshoff the first day, when *Valkyrie* was so far in the lead.

There was no chance now for the Britisher, and the black cutter trailed along in the wake, losing 3 minutes and 26 seconds more in the leg. The official figures of the race were:

NAME	START	FINISH	ELAPSED TIME	CORR'T'D TIME
	H. M. S.	H. M. S.	H. M. S.	H. M. S.
Vigilant	11 25 00	2 50 01	3 25 01	3 25 01
Valkyrie II	11 25 00	3 02 24	3 37 24	3 35 36

When it was all over it was found that *Vigilant's* bowsprit, an immense, long spar, had been sprung, and a new one had to be shipped before the next race, October 11th. This race turned out to be another fluke, due to the fickle October breezes. It was getting dark as the yachts rounded the outer mark, and the six-hour time limit expiring soon after, the disgusted crews passed towlines to waiting tugs for the journey back.

Valkyrie still had another chance to justify her long journey across the Atlantic, and it came two days later, on October 13th, a day that will be remembered always by those who went down to the old red lightship, if they were fortunate enough not to succumb to the heave of old ocean.

It was not only the 13th, but Friday also—a combination out of which most anything might come. And something came. The first thing that arrived was the breeze. It was already there when the yachts and the excursion fleet got to the line, coming from due east, with a fine jump of sea running. Storm warnings were up for a gale, but luckily it didn't come, though many of the swivel-chair fleet and the parlor yachtsmen thought it was a gale that they found outside Sandy Hook.

The first untoward happening was the carrying away of one of the *Vigilant's* throat halyard blocks shortly before the start, and the mainsail had to be taken off her to repair it. While the sail was down Captain Hansen and his crew turned in a reef, in anticipation of trouble. Captain Cranfield on the *Valkyrie*, seeing this, and also scenting a breeze, likewise lowered away and tucked in a single reef. Then both boats set working topsails above reefed mainsails.

While this was going on, the time agreed upon for the start arrived. Lord Dunraven had been very insistent upon the starting signal in all races being given at 11:25, no matter what happened; but as his boat was fully three miles from the line at that time and busy reefing, the committee very considerately waited for him, though *Vigilant* was at hand, and all ready—no, not quite ready, for her bronze centerboard was jammed, and could not be lowered. The crew finally pried it loose, and down part way, and signaled that they were ready, but it was 12:27 before the starting gun boomed over the tumbling water.

Both boats came down on the line trimmed flat for the hard fifteen-mile thrash to windward. *Vigilant* seemed to have the best position, but suddenly Cranfield jammed his helm hard up, *Valkyrie* swung around like a top, and, from a leeward berth, planted herself on the defender's weather side, where she stayed throughout the entire windward leg. It was a grand race, the seventy men on board the *Vigilant* stretched out along the weather rail to help hold her down. *Valkyrie* carried but thirty-five men.

Throughout that long, hard thrash in a heavy sea the cutter fairly outsailed the American boat, pointing higher, and for the most part footing as fast. As they rounded the outer mark after two hours of drenching work *Valkyrie* was 1 minute and 55 seconds to the good. Their elapsed times to the mark were: *Valkyrie,* 2:06:40; *Vigilant,* 2:08:35.

It was a hard task that now lay before *Vigilant*—that of making up some third of a mile in a run down the wind, with the cutter going like a scared cat and determined to hold what so few other English Cup hunters had ever won on a windward leg.

The run back resolved itself into the most spectacular race of any heretofore seen for the ancient bit of silver. As no better account of the incidents of this long stern chase has been written than the one by Mr. W. P. Stephens, in *American Yachting,* it is quoted here:

"On rounding the outer mark *Valkyrie* set her spinnaker after the English fashion. The sail, in a loose bunch, was hoisted from below deck and sheeted home as quickly as possible. In doing this it got caught on the bitts and was torn a little. Running in a sea and heavy wind this tear soon increased until the sail went into tatters. Another, a large and beautiful sail of light fabric (the famous muslin one of the first race), was set in its place, the work being done very smartly, but it was too light for such a breeze, and it soon went to pieces. Nothing daunted, the 'bowsprit spinnaker,' corresponding to the American balloon jib-topsail, but smaller, was set as the last resort.

"On board *Valkyrie* no attempt was made to shake out the reef in the mainsail or to shift topsails; but as soon as *Vigilant* was off the wind, and her spinnaker, sent up in stops in a long, compact rope, was broken out and sheeted home, the real work of the day began. Her balloon jib-topsail fouled in hoisting, and a man was sent to the topmast head, and thence down the topmast stay, to clear the sail. After this was done a man was sent along the boom, with a lifeline from the masthead about his body, cutting the reef points as he went; meanwhile a man at the topmast head was lashing the working topsail, clearing the topsail halyard, and sending it down to the deck, while another man at the gaff end was doing the same with the topsail sheet. With the working topsail still in place, the whole mainsail was shaken out, the halyards sweated up, and the small club-topsail was sent aloft. By dint of this work, such as was never before witnessed in yachting, at the imminent danger of losing the mast and the race, *Vigilant* sailed past *Valkyrie* near the finish line and led her across by 2 minutes 13 seconds, winning the race by forty seconds, corrected time."

It was an unusually fast race, as the accompanying table will show:

NAME	START	FINISH	ELAPSED TIME	CORR'T'D TIME
	H. M. S.	H. M. S.	H. M. S.	H. M. S.
Vigilant	12 27 00	3 51 39	3 24 39	3 24 39
Valkyrie II	12 27 00	3 53 52	3 26 52	3 25 19

Valkyrie had added ballast and been remeasured since the

previous race, and her allowance reduced to 1 minute and 33 seconds.

It was a close shave—the closest in any Cup contest so far. *Valkyrie* had her chance, but it was not to be. If her spinnakers had stood the strain, the story would probably have been different—but, then, yacht racing is made up of "ifs."

Lord Dunraven, on the whole, took his defeat in good part, though he complained that the first races were not true windward and leeward ones owing to the wind's shifting, which, of course, could not be helped, and, also, that *Valkyrie* was bothered considerably by excursion steamers—an evil that had grown to serious proportions since the increased interest in these matches, and one that the New York Yacht Club was called upon to take measures to abate. So, while beaten fairly, he did not think the relative merits of the two boats had been altogether decided.

Valkyrie II was laid up in New York for the winter, and did not return home until the following year, when *Vigilant,* which had been purchased by George and Howard Gould, was also sent across to race in English waters, under command of "Hank" Haff.

The two boats were not destined to decide further the question of supremacy, however, for the *Valkyrie II* was sunk on the Clyde in one of the first races of the season by the English ninety-footer *Satanita.*

Vigilant raced with indifferent success, meeting among other fast cutters the *Britannia,* owned by the Prince of Wales. In these encounters *Britannia* won twelve out of seventeen races, and although *Vigilant* was faster in a strong breeze, she was slower in light to moderate winds and was not as quick handling as the English cutter.

Vigilant was brought back to this country, where she was used as a trial horse against the *Defender,* and was subsequently turned into a yawl and saw many years of useful service.

Chapter XI

THE "DEFENDER—VALKYRIE III" RACE OF 1895. LORD DUN-
RAVEN AT ODDS WITH THE NEW YORK YACHT CLUB

THE THREE RACES between *Vigilant* and *Valkyrie II* were the
closest, as a whole, of any that had yet been sailed, and so far
from being discouraged by his failure to take home the Cup,
Lord Dunraven immediately set about another attempt to win
it. He again went to Watson for the plans, and during 1894
the famous English designer was busy evolving another boat,
better suited to American racing conditions. This time Dunraven had associated with him in the enterprise Lord Lonsdale,
Lord Wolverton, and Captain Harry LeB. McCalmont, the
latter a well known English yachtsman and sportsman.

A challenge was sent the New York Yacht Club in the
autumn of that year for a race in 1895. No difficulty was had
in arranging satisfactory terms, and a series of three races out
of five was agreed upon, the water line length of the challenger
being given as 89 feet and her rig that of a cutter. September
was the month fixed for sailing the match.

In *Valkyrie III* George Watson showed that he was not
above learning from the American designers, and he turned out
as wide a vessel as *Vigilant,* with just as large a rig as it was possible for her to carry. She was a big, powerful craft with long
ends, giving added stability as she heeled, and was very flat as
compared with the then prevailing practice. Her principal dimensions were, length over all 129 feet, waterline 88 feet 10
inches, beam 26 feet 2 inches, and draft 20 feet. Her sail area
was 13,028 feet, or 3,000 more than *Valkyrie II*—quite a jump
in one boat. She was built of wood over steel frames.

111

In this country we were not content to trust the defense to *Vigilant,* especially after her poor showing against *Britannia* in 1894, and a syndicate was formed in the New York Yacht Club (syndicates were getting to be the fashion those days, with the growing cost of building and running a defender) to build a new boat. In this syndicate were C. Oliver Ieslin, who was to manage the yacht, W. K. Vanderbilt, and E. D. Morgan. Of course the syndicate went to Herreshoff to have the boat built. The "Wizard of Bristol" as he was getting to be called, had a monopoly on Cup defense honors that year.

While Watson was following the general form of the *Vigilant,* "Nat" Herreshoff was not to be caught napping, and in *Defender,* as the new yacht was called, he made a bold move back to a narrower, deeper boat with finer lines (she was but 8 inches wider than *Valkyrie II*) and built as lightly as possible. Manganese bronze, a very expensive and strong metal, was used for bottom plating while the frames were steel and the top plating aluminum to save weight.

As a matter of fact it was thought by many that Herreshoff rather overdid this lightness, for *Defender* was structurally weak, and many stories were current as to the way she "worked" and that her mast was in danger of going through her bottom. These stories were denied, but those who were in a position to know credited them. Anyway, the structural defects were remedied, and she hung together long enough to go through the season—and also the trial races with *Columbia,* four years later.

The dimensions of the *Defender* were: length over all 123 feet, length waterline 88 feet 5 inches, beam 23 feet, and draft 19 feet, while she carried 12,602 square feet of sail, or 426 square feet less than the challenger.

In fact, the two boats were in type virtually the opposite of what had been the custom heretofore, *Defender* being practically the cutter, with her narrow beam, deep draft, fine lines, and large angle of heel, while the challenger had all the characteristics of a sloop—broad beam, shoal body, light displacement, hard bilges, and big sail spread. It was a funny switch on the part of both designers, and in the sequel we "were to see what we should see."

Defender was put in charge of the old reliable "Hank" Haff, though Mr. Iselin sailed on her in all her races as manager. For crew, it seemed fitting that we should dispense for a time with the proverbial "scowegian" or "square head" Scandinavian yacht sailor, and Captain Haff went down to Deer Isle, Maine, the home of the American fishermen, and picked up a crew from there, about which many patriotic things (and much slush) was written. But they were a good crew, and under old "Hank" they made the "brass" boat go.

Vigilant was fitted out by George J. Gould, and in charge of Captain Charles Barr, a younger brother of John, who was making his first essay in charge of a yacht in search of *America's* Cup honors, she was used as a trial horse against the new yacht. Charley Barr was always an aggressive racing skipper, and some hard and interesting scrapping was seen between the two boats throughout the season. *Defender* was picked by the *America's* Cup Committee to meet the *Valkyrie III,* which had arrived in this country August 19th.

The *Valkyrie* had made the voyage across under ketch rig in twenty-two days, a very creditable performance, though she was strained somewhat in her hull and had to be repaired at Erie Basin, where her racing spars were shipped. Before leaving England she had sailed three races against *Britannia,* winning one and losing two.

Both boats were measured by John Hyslop, the measurer of the New York Yacht Club, on the day before the first race. *Valkyrie,* rating slightly higher than the *Defender,* had to allow the American boat twenty-nine seconds over a 30-mile course.

The morning of September 7th found both racers being

towed out to the Scotland Lightship over a glassy sea, which had, however, considerable heave to it—"old sea" the sailors call it—from a previous breeze. At the lightship they found a big fleet of excursion boats, which, as the hours went by, increased to unwieldy proportions. The Coast Guard did not then patrol the course, as it has done in later years.

There was a long wait for wind and the starting signal was not given until 12:20 P.M. "Hank" Haff was first over, with sails trimmed in hard and *Valkyrie* right under his lee. The wind was east by south, and the course was fifteen miles to windward and return, with a six-hour time limit.

Valkyrie soon worked out from her bad position under *Defender's* lee, and, footing faster, drew ahead in an alarming fashion, though not pointing as high. The boats split tacks, one going off in one direction and one in the other, and when they came together again some time later, having gone about once more, the excitement was intense. As they approached each other it was seen that they were very close together, and as *Defender* finally slipped across *Valkyrie's* bow a mighty cheer broke from the crowd on the trailing fleet.

From that point *Defender* was never headed, and rounded the outer mark well in the lead. It was just "cutter" weather, a lop of sea on and a moderate breeze, and the narrower *Defender* made the better going. It seemed as if fate played a large part in the game.

On the run home the American boat continued to draw ahead and crossed the line eight minutes and twenty seconds ahead, actual time. The result:

NAME	START	ELAPSED TIME	CORR'T'D TIME
	H. M. S.	H. M. S.	H. M. S.
Defender	12 20 46	5 00 24	4 59 55
Valkyrie III	12 20 50	5 08 44	5 08 44

Defender won by 8 minutes 49 seconds.

Immediately after this race Lord Dunraven made the first step that was to lead to a serious controversy and a break of all further relations with the noble Earl. When the boats had finished Mr. Latham A. Fish, the American representative on board *Valkyrie,* went aboard the committee boat with a complaint from Dunraven that the *Defender* had had more ballast put aboard after she had been officially measured, which brought her down below her measured waterline. Dunraven asked for a remeasurement before the next race. He also complained about the crowding of the excursion steamers and claimed that *Valkyrie* had been bothered seriously by them.

In refutation of this charge, both boats were measured again the next afternoon, Sunday, and no material discrepancy was found between the two measurements, there being only one-eighth of an inch difference in *Defender's* waterline length and one-sixteenth of an inch in *Valkyrie's*. This was easily accounted for in the difference in the conditions under which they were measured. The New York Yacht Club also took steps to try to keep the course clear for the following race. Here the matter of alleged tampering with the ballast apparently ended, though it was taken up later.

The second race was sailed on September 10th, the course being triangular, ten miles to a leg. It was a quiet hazy morning with a light southerly breeze, and at 10:40 the committee set the signals for the course, the first leg of which was a beat to windward down the low-lying Jersey coast.

By the time the preparatory gun boomed at 10:50 the fleet of excursion steamers was crowding as close to the starting line as it dared. Just before the starting signal both boats were coming down on the line, close hauled, *Valkyrie* on *Defender's* weather, when the big steamer *Yorktown* blundered right across their course and separated the two boats for an instant. When they emerged on the other side of her *Valkyrie* was still on *Defender's* weather but had drawn slightly ahead. It was only a few seconds to the gun and both boats were heading up for the committee boat at the weather end of the line. Just before they reached the line Captain Sycamore, steering *Valkyrie*, swung off a trifle and bore down on *Defender*, which was under his lee.

Seeing that he could not draw clear across the American boat's bows, and that *Defender* would hit *Valkyrie* if "Hank" Haff held his course, Sycamore was forced to luff sharply, and in doing so the end of *Valkyrie's* main boom swept the deck of *Defender*, and, fetching up against the latter's starboard shrouds as *Valkyrie* swung around on her heel, the topmast stay snapped with a twang that could be heard on the committee boat.

Defender's topmast immediately sagged away off to leeward under the strain of her immense club topsail, and cracked some five feet above the lower mast head. Haff shot his boat up into the wind while sailors swarmed aloft to ascertain the amount of damage, and Mr. Iselin set a protest flag at once, which was answered from the committee boat. Seeing that the topmast was not coming down, though it hung over to leeward when on the starboard tack, Haff got his jib-topsail in, rigged a preventer or temporary topmast shroud, and kept on after the *Valkyrie*, which had not stopped to inquire as to the amount of damage she had caused. It was an unequal fight, however, as on one tack the *Defender* was badly hampered by her sagging topmast, though on the other tack she did very well.

At the first, or windward mark, *Valkyrie* was three minutes ahead. On the next leg with the wind broad off, Capt. Haff took a chance, sent up a small jib-topsail, and set sail after the flying Englishman. *Defender* moved fast and managed to hold her own with *Valkyrie* on the 10-mile leg.

Valkyrie turned the second mark well in the lead, but on the last leg, which was a reach, *Defender's* "well" side was to windward and she could carry her light sails all right. As the breeze also went lighter she immediately began to close upon *Valkyrie*.

The leg was not long enough for her to catch the leader, however, and though she got close enough to threaten *Valkyrie's* wind, Lord Dunraven's yacht crossed the finish line two minutes and eighteen seconds ahead, which, when corrected time was figured, was reduced to just forty-seven seconds.

Name	Start	Finish	Elapsed Time	Corr't'd Time
	H. M. S.	H. M. S.	H. M. S.	H. M. S.
Valkyrie III	11 00 13	2 55 22	3 55 09	3 55 09
Defender	11 01 15	2 57 40	3 56 25	3 55 56

Here was a pretty kettle of fish to add to a situation that was already very tense. The regatta committee of the New York Yacht Club, after ineffectually trying to bring about a mutual agreement between the two yachts to re-sail the race, got all the testimony together, supported by photographs of the foul, and the following day announced that they had disqualified *Valkyrie*. Their decision was worded as follows:

September 11, 1895

C. OLIVER ISELIN, ESQ.

Dear Sir:—We beg to acknowledge receipt of your letter of yesterday protesting the *Valkyrie*. We have given the matter our careful consideration and we believe that the foul occurred through a miscalculation of the distance between the two yachts at a critical moment.

From our own observation, confirmed by that of others who were in a good position to see all that occurred, we find that the *Valkyrie III*, in contravention of section eleven of racing rule sixteen, bore down upon the *Defender* and fouled her by the swing of her main boom when luffing to straighten her course. We also consider that the *Defender* left the *Valkyrie* sufficient room to windward to pass clear of the Committee boat.

Your protest is therefore sustained.

S. NICHOLSON KANE,
IRVING GRINNELL,
CHESTER GRISWOLD,
Committee.

The rule referred to says that a yacht shall not bear away to prevent another yacht from passing her to leeward.

The justice of the decision was almost universally acknowledged by yachtsmen and was in strict accord with the rules and the facts. What probably caused the foul was this: Captain Sycamore, who was steering *Valkyrie* under Capt. Cranfield, had the weather berth and did not want to relinquish it. Finding that he was a little too early for the gun, and, being close to the committee boat, he bore off to run down the line so as to kill a few seconds. As he closed in on *Defender* and saw that he could not cross her bows, and that a collision would occur unless Haff bore away also, he luffed sharply, *Defender* having the right of way under the rules. In doing so he did not allow enough room for *Valkyrie's* long main boom as the stick was 105 feet in length and projected well beyond *Valkyrie's* stern. Sycamore was used to sailing in somewhat smaller boats and probably did not quite realize that a 90-foot boat could not be handled in the same way as a 40-footer.

After the protest was decided in *Defender's* favor, Mr. Iselin immediately offered to resail the race, which he very properly would not agree to before, as he felt that a breach of the rules had caused the foul, and until it was decided which boat was at fault, he could not offer to sail the race over and thus force *Valkyrie* to jeopardize what she had already won if the committee decided in her favor. The reverse, of course, also held true. Now that it was decided against *Valkyrie,* he could be, and was, fair minded enough to offer Lord Dunraven the chance to resail it, if he wanted to.

Dunraven declined the offer in the following communications:

Dear Mr. Iselin:—I have received your note in which you express a wish that yesterday's race should be resailed.

That is a proposition to which, of course, I cannot agree. You would not have protested had you not believed that *Valkyrie* had caused a foul by committing a breach of the rules.

If she did, she must take the consequences.

The Regatta Committee has decided, for reasons according to their best judgment, but which, I confess, are beyond my comprehension, that she did break the rules. I made no protest, and because I thought the foul was probably accidental; but I consider that *Defender* caused it. You consider that *Valkyrie* was to blame. The Committee have decided that you are right and I am wrong and there the matter ends.

                        Yours very truly,

                                    DUNRAVEN.

And again, the following day:

*Dear Mr. Iselin:—*I certainly could not entertain your suggestion.

Had the Committee ordered the race to be resailed, that would have been a different matter; but how could I possibly agree to resail a race decided and given against me by the decision of the Committee?

I wrote you last night to this effect, and am sorry you did not receive my letter. I had no opportunity of communicating with you this morning; but Mr. Duryea will, I dare say, have informed you as to my views. Thanking you for your suggestion, I remain,

                        Yours very truly,

                                    DUNRAVEN.

After this second race of September 10th, Lord Dunraven wrote a letter to the Cup Committee complaining bitterly about the crowding of *Valkyrie* by the excursion fleet, and saying that in his opinion it was dangerous to try to maneuver yachts under such conditions. He made the statement that for nearly the whole distance *Valkyrie* was forced to sail in broken, tumbling water, caused by the wash of steamers, and he declined to submit to such conditions again. In another letter written the following day he receded from this position so far as to say that he would sail again "if the committee would take it upon themselves to declare the race void, if, in their judgment, either vessel was interfered with by steamers and tug boats."

These communications were purposely not brought to the attention of the Committee until after the protest regarding the foul had been decided. Indeed, the second letter did not reach the Committee until 8 A.M. of the 12th, the day of the third race.

The matter of crowding on the course, however, was discussed between the Committee and Lord Dunraven the evening of the 11th, and the Committee offered not to start the race the following day until a clear space for maneuvering was assured, though it said it could not assume the responsibility of declaring the race void if either boat suffered from the excursion fleet after the start.

While undoubtedly both boats had been interfered with to some extent by the excursion fleet, it did not seem to be intentional, and there was no evidence that *Valkyrie* was bothered more than *Defender,* though Dunraven evidently thought that she was, and even went so far as to suggest postponing the race or sailing it on a date not to be announced beforehand, so as to get rid of a large part of the excursion fleet.

The Committee did not feel that it had the power or the right to do this.

Here the matter rested, and the next day, September 12th, saw both boats at the line, *Defender* with a new topmast. This time the captains of the excursion fleet, evidently heedful of the public outcry against the crowding, kept at a respectful distance, and the two boats had all the room they wanted around the line, while the course, as far as could be seen, was clear.

Yet there was something that set all the spectators wondering as they looked at the two stately racers hanging lazily around the lightship. *Defender* had an immense club topsail set as tight as a board on her new "stick," yet, though it was getting close to the starting hour, *Valkyrie's* topsail was still tightly "stopped" at her masthead, and she did not have her staysail set.

Models of *Defender* (left) and *Valkyrie III*, 1895.

Valkyrie III (left) and *Defender* five seconds after the foul. Note *Defender's* topmast.

At last the preparatory signal went from the committee boat, the course was signalled, fifteen miles to leeward and return, and there was a nice little breeze that gave promise of a good race. Still there was no move on the part of *Valkyrie's* crew to set light sails.

The starting gun banged and *Defender* went over the line. She was followed by *Valkyrie;* but after crossing the latter immediately hauled on the wind and headed back for her anchorage. As she did this her racing flag was hauled down and the New York Yacht Club burgee sent up in its place, Dunraven being an honorary member of this club. Then it dawned on all those present that Lord Dunraven had quit and would not even finish the series.

Defender sailed over the course. As she neared the finish line Mr. Iselin hailed the Committee through a megaphone and asked if he should cross the line. The answer was "yes," so the white sloop sailed past the Committee boat, her time was taken, and the series of 1895 was over. It must be confessed that there was not much joy in the finish.

On board the Committee boat we may be pretty sure there were some hard things said about the noble Earl. They had a short forewarning of what was coming, for in Dunraven's second letter which, it will be remembered, was handed to them at 8 A.M. of the day of the race, as they were going aboard the Committee boat, he had said that if the Committee would not agree to call the race void if either boat was interfered with, he, Dunraven, would take *Valkyrie* to Sandy Hook and go over the line just to give *Defender* a start. The committee, however, hoped up to the last that Dunraven's better judgment would prevent this show of disapproval and pique.

Of course the Earl and his sporting ethics were "roasted" unmercifully in this country; but the matter finally died down to only an echo until after Dunraven's return to England the latter part of October, when he again took up the matter of tampering with *Defender's* ballast and of her re-measurement.

In an article in the London *Field* of November 9th, and again in a speech on November 21st, Dunraven specifically charged that *Defender* had surreptitiously added ballast after being measured for the series, that was sufficient to bring her down in the water three or four inches more, and that this ballast had been removed again the night after the race, before she was remeasured the following day in compliance with his complaint. He based this charge on the fact that the *Defender's* tender, the steamer *Hattie Palmer*, laid alongside the American boat the night before and the night after the race, and that her crew had been busy until late in the night carrying something from one boat to the other; furthermore he claimed that *Defender* was *visibly* deeper in the water the day of the first race than when she was measured.

This, of course, was a most serious charge, involving our national honor and sportsmanship. Mr. Iselin at once replied to it in no uncertain terms and asked the New York Yacht Club for a full investigation of the matter, placing himself and the *Defender's* skipper and crew at the Club's disposal. In his letter to the Club he said, in part:

"I was responsible for the proper officering and manning of the yacht. I personally examined the *Defender's* hold and every part of her on the morning of the 7th, immediately before the race, and I know the absolute falsity of the imputation. I consider myself therefore as standing before the world solemnly charged by Lord Dunraven with an offence as base as could possibly be imputed to a sportsman and a gentleman, and which I indignantly resent and repel; and more than that, with having betrayed the confidence of my associates in the ownership of the *Defender,* the trust placed in me by the New York Yacht Club, and the good name of my country, whose reputation for fair play was involved in the contest.

"Lord Dunraven claims to have sailed the race on Saturday, after being satisfactorily assured that he had been cheated in the fraudulent overloading of the *Defender*. He sailed the next race on the 10th, with the same conviction on his mind that on the first day's race he had been cheated. He broke off the last day's race not upon any such ground, but on the entirely distinct ground that the course would not and could not be kept clear. He went home, and after a silence of more than two months, he makes this odious charge in a communication, addressed not to me nor the owners of the *Defender*, nor to either the New York Yacht Club or the Royal Yacht Squadron, whom we respectively represented in the races for the *America's* Cup, but to a public newspaper on the other side of the Atlantic, which it would be impossible for me to read or reply to before it had already made a deep impression on the minds of his countrymen.

"Relying upon its belief in my integrity, the New York Yacht Club deemed itself justified in placing its honor and that of the country in my hands in the conduct of the race. I could not have imagined that, in assuming that trust, I should expose myself and you to such gross imputations. But now that they have been made I place myself in your hands, in order that the Club may take such steps as it sees fit, not alone to vindicate the *Defender* and the honor of her owners, but also to refute the imputation cast upon the good faith of the club and the country. I have the honor to remain,

"Very respectfully yours,

C. OLIVER ISELIN."

The New York Yacht Club immediately called a special meeting and thereat appointed a committee to go into the whole matter and sift it to the very bottom. This committee was composed of J. Pierpont Morgan, William C. Whitney, and George L. Rives, and before the inquiry began, there were added to it Captain A. T. Mahan, of the United States Navy, and the Hon. E. J. Phelps, late U. S. Minister to England, both men with a world-wide reputation.

At this meeting a letter was read from Mr. H. Maitland Kersey, Lord Dunraven's American representative, saying that while Dunraven thought it was then too late to investigate the charges, he would come over at the pleasure of the committee to testify in his own behalf.

While these charges were also mentioned in the report of Lord Dunraven to the Royal Yacht Squadron, the Squadron itself did not see fit to act, but preferred to treat the matter as a personal one between Dunraven and the New York Yacht Club. So the Earl came over in December with his testimony, and the meetings of the Committee began on December 27, and lasted five days.

It is not necessary to go into all the testimony adduced at this inquiry, which was conducted in such a way as to satisfy every fair-minded man on either side of the Atlantic. Dunraven's legal interests were looked after by George R. Askwith, a noted English Admiralty lawyer, while Joseph H. Choate took care of the New York Yacht Club's case.

Lord Dunraven failed signally to prove his charge. His case was based largely on the appearance of *Defender* in the first race, when, *to his eye,* it seemed that she was deeper than when she was measured, judging from the position of a pipe outlet in her hull, and by her bobstay bolt being nearer the water. His evidence was intangible and mostly hearsay. He claimed that he had asked the committee to place someone aboard the *Defender* after the first race until she had been remeasured, and that in failing to do this all chances of proving his charge were lost.

For *Defender,* Mr. Iselin, Captain Haff, Mr. Herreshoff her designer, the official measurer, all the amateurs aboard, and every member of *Defender's* crew, with the exception of five who were away at sea, testified.

The testimony brought out the fact that *Defender* carried eighty-five tons of fixed lead ballast in her keel, and that she did not need any more, as she was amply stiff. As *Valkyrie* did not have bulkheads and interior fittings aboard, by mutual agreement, the New York Yacht Club rule covering this point was waived and bulkheads, water tanks, and fittings were removed from *Defender.* To take the place of this weight, sixty-three pigs of lead, weighing in all three tons, were put aboard her *before* she was measured. As twenty-one of these pigs could not be properly stowed, they were taken aboard the *Hattie*

Palmer, cut in two and put back aboard the *Defender* before the first race, which was the work *Valkyrie's* crew saw going on the night of September 6.

Mr. Herreshoff and other witnesses testified that to have immersed *Defender* four inches more would have lengthened her waterline thirty-two inches, or nearly three feet.

It was apparent that Dunraven's mind had become biased before the start of the series by some remarks emanating from someone on his tender, the Steamer *City of Bridgeport,* about the alleged water ballast that had been employed in some American yachts a number of years before, and he was evidently distrustful before even starting the series.

The report of the Committee, composed of men who commanded the confidence of the public and of yachtsmen everywhere, completely exonerated Mr. Iselin and the crew of *Defender,* as is shown by the following report:

"Upon careful consideration of the whole case, the committee are unanimously of the opinion that the charge made by Lord Dunraven, and which has been the subject of this investigation, had its origin in mistake; that it is not only not sustained by evidence, but is completely disproved; and that all the circumstances indicated by him as giving rise to his suspicion, are entirely and satisfactorily explained. They deem it, therefore, but just to Mr. Iselin and the gentlemen concerned with him, as well as to the officers and crew of the *Defender,* that the committee should express emphatically their conviction that nothing whatever occurred in connection with the race in question that casts the least suspicion upon the integrity or propriety of their conduct.

"And the committee are not willing to doubt that if Lord Dunraven had remained present throughout the investigation, so as to have heard all the evidence that was introduced, he would of his own motion have withdrawn a charge that was so plainly founded upon mistakes, and that has been so unfortunate in the publicity it has attained, and the feeling to which it has given rise."

This report was signed by all the members of the Committee.

It will be noticed that the Committee, though they might have scored Dunraven, handled him with a courtesy that he hardly deserved. It was supposed after the findings of the Committee and the failure to substantiate his charges, that Lord Dunraven would apologize; yet, though the report was published January 21, up to February 13 no apology had been received, and on that date, at a meeting of the club, his resignation as an honorary member was requested. As this resignation did not come up to February 27, a resolution was offered and carried on that date expelling him from the New York Yacht Club. After this action a tardy resignation was received.

Public opinion in England did not support Dunraven in these charges. As a rule the press of that country either criticized him openly for bringing these charges, or else remained silent on the matter. Thus ended the most bitter controversy that has arisen since *America* brought the Cup to this country.

Chapter XII

AFTER THE RUMBLINGS of the Dunraven fiasco had died down English yachtsmen, though they had not supported the *Valkyrie's* owner in his position, and did not consider him a shining representative of British sportsmanship, nevertheless took but little interest in the *America's* Cup. It was felt on both sides of the water that it might be some time before another race was arranged, owing to the unpleasant incidents of the last match. There were rumors of challenges during the next two years, one of them from an Australian yachtsman, but nothing came of them.

It was with considerable gratification, then, that the New York Yacht Club, in the late summer of 1898, received a cable from the Royal Ulster Yacht Club, of Belfast, Ireland, giving notice of its intent to challenge on behalf of one of its members, Sir Thomas Lipton, and saying that a committee from the club would be sent over to arrange details.

In September, this committee of three, accompanied by William Fife, Jr., who was to design the new yacht, arrived in New York, met the cup committee appointed by the New York Yacht Club, and in less than twenty-four hours everything had been agreed upon by "mutual consent." The New York Yacht Club was anxious for a race, and did not hesitate in making terms that satisfied the Royal Ulster Yacht Club and Lipton's personal representative.

The conditions were practically the same as those that had governed the two Dunraven matches. The New York Yacht Club did not hold out for the dimensions of the challenger required under the Deed of Gift, and the waterline length only was asked for. This was given as 89.5 feet and the rig that of a cutter. The matches were to be sailed early in October, being fixed this late in the expectation of getting stronger breezes.

This challenge came somewhat as a surprise to English yachtsmen as Sir Thomas Lipton had not been particularly identified with the sport, and while the owner of a large steam yacht, he knew practically nothing about sailing yachts or racing. He was of Irish decent and had started in life as a grocer's clerk. His family was poor, but by sheer ability and perseverance he had become a successful tea merchant, and had built up a world-wide business that brought him a fortune. He was fifty-one years of age at the time of the challenge, and had already achieved considerable prominence in England, having been knighted by reason of his many philanthropies. He had many sterling qualities, was a good sportsman, and in the following thrity-two years he made five attempts "to lift the cup," as he himself expressed it, showed himself a good loser and a fair-minded gentleman.

It will be noticed, if we look at the previous three Cup races, that a change had been taking place in the general character of these contests. Instead of the challenger being a prominent yachtsman racing in some regularly established class, who had what he believed to be a boat that was fast enough to warrant a try for the Cup, he was more apt to be some rich man who could afford to build a boat especially for an *America's* Cup race and who, for some reason or other, might not be averse to the prestige that such a race would give him. In the Royal Clyde Yacht Club challenge the *Thistle* was owned by a syndicate; Dunraven was a comparatively newcomer to the sport, as was now Sir Thomas Lipton.

This was but natural, perhaps, by reason of the terms of the Deed of Gift which faced a challenger, and because of the tendency to regard the *America's* Cup as standing for speed alone, with no other qualities demanded or expected in the yachts that raced for it. It was also, in a way, unavoidable, by reason of different measurement rules in England and in America, which produced classes that did not exactly coincide.

So *America's* Cup races had come down to contests between so-called "racing machines," or yachts built only for this one event, to the extreme of lightness, with an abnormal rig, and with everything sacrificed to the one thing—speed. It was no longer a matter of types, for challenger and defender were practically alike in form, rig, etc., with only minor differences between them.

To make matters worse we were, at that time in America, sailing under a measurement rule that allowed great excesses in the way of flat bodies, long ends, etc.; and as this was the rule under which the challenger was also measured for time allowance, it was but natural that the designer of the English yacht should try to outdo us in these respects.

In any yacht the three prime factors that enter into her design as having a bearing on speed are: length, sail area (or propulsive power), and displacement, or the amount of *body* that is to be driven through the water. The rule then in force took into consideration and taxed only length of waterline when on an even keel, and sail area. With only two of the factors taxed it is natural that designers took all the liberties they could with the one that was not taxed, and they began to cut away underbodies and lengthen out the ends to give a greater waterline length when heeled than when upright, until there was produced a long, flat body, with a deep, thin keel, practically amounting to a fin, carrying at its lower end a big chunk of ballast, and with long spars of steel, trussed to give them sufficient strength to carry the tremendous sail area that was piled on them. While such machines were undoubtedly fast in smooth water, they were useless in a sea, and their

spars could not support the press of sail in a breeze in which
the older racers would have romped around the course under
lower sails, or with a single reef tucked in.

Designing a Cup racer was getting to be an engineering
problem in figuring out new forms of construction, strength
of material, rigging, etc. In these things "Nat" Herreshoff
excelled. In addition to his being one of our foremost designers
and the one with the greatest experience in large "single
stickers," the boats were constructed at his own plant.

When Lipton decided to challenge he gave designer Fife a
carte blanche order to spare no expense, but to turn out the
fastest boat that money could produce.

William Fife, Jr., was the designer of the successful cutters
Clara and *Minerva* which had raced in this country some ten
years before, and while he had been very successful in small
boats, he had only turned out two large racing yachts, neither
of which had been over successful.

In *Shamrock,* as Lipton named his challenger, Fife turned
out a boat of the extreme type. She was built by Thorneycroft
& Co., builders of torpedo boats, and lightness of construction
was demanded. She followed *Defender* somewhat in the use
of material, her bottom plating being of manganese bronze,
with aluminum topsides. This latter material had proved
unsatisfactory in *Defender,* that boat being structurally weak,
and in this country it was discarded in the construction of
large yachts. *Shamrock* was tied together with stringers, straps,
and cross braces inside to make her strong enough to stand the
ocean crossing. Her racing mast, boom, and gaff were of steel,
built up and braced, but the mast gave constant trouble by
buckling in a breeze to such an extent as to impair the efficiency of her sails, of which it is said that she had six different
suits that season.

Her principal dimensions were: length over all 128 feet,
waterline 89 feet, 8 inches, beam 25 feet, draft 20 feet, 3 inches,

and sail area 13,492 square feet. Her hull was very flat and broad, with long ends, while her keel was hardly more than a fin, being cut away forward while the rudder post had a considerable rake to it. Great secrecy was observed in building her, so the weight of the lead bulb is not known, though it was said to be in excess of seventy-five tons.

For the defense of the Cup another syndicate was formed in the New York Yacht Club. This time it was headed by J. Pierpont Morgan, and C. Oliver Iselin was again chosen as managing owner, to have charge of the new boat during the season.

Of course Herreshoff was the designer and builder. The boat was built under lock and key, and long after any need for secrecy was past the impatient public was denied any information as to what *Columbia* would be like.

When *Columbia* was launched on June 10, and measured, it was known that she was 131 feet over all; 89 feet 8 inches on the water; 24 feet beam, and 19 feet 3 inches draft; with 13,135 square feet of muslin. She was plated with manganese bronze below the water and steel above, and her spars were of steel, except her bowsprit and spinnaker boom. She carried ninety tons of lead at the bottom of her nineteen-foot fin, which exerted great leverage at that depth and allowed her to carry her sail on a fairly narrow beam. She was rather flat amidships, and in profile the challenger and the defender were very similar, though the *Shamrock* was the more powerful-looking, with greater beam and draft and slightly more freeboard.

The British boat was conceded a dangerous competitor by those who saw her, and some of her early trials in this country inspired fear for the outcome, especially when she "hit up" a thirteen-knot clip a number of times on a reach.

Shamrock left England on August 3, after a couple of inconclusive trials against the Prince of Wales' famous cutter *Britannia*. She was under a yawl rig and was convoyed by her owner's

steam yacht *Erin,* the New York Yacht Club departing so much
from the letter of the Deed as to grant permission to have the
steam yacht tow her wherever it seemed advisable. This showed
more than anything else the change that had taken place in
Cup racers. Mr. Schuyler and the members of the New York
Yacht Club had deemed it important that a yacht should
"proceed under sail on her own bottom to the port where the
contest is to take place," when they made the Second Deed of
Gift, after the Canadian challenges.

A quick and pleasant passage of 14 days and 20 hours was
made across the Atlantic, much of it at the end of a hawser
behind the *Erin;* but the racing shell arrived in good shape.

Shamrock was in charge of Captain "Archie" Hogarth, a
young man considered one of the best professional racing
skippers in England, ranking with Carter, Cranfield of the
Valkyrie III, and Parker, though much of his experience had
been in smaller boats. As "second captain" on board was
Robert Wringe, an experienced and able yacht skipper. This
position of "second captain" was an English custom that prevailed on large racing yachts, the second man being something
more than a mate, the corresponding position on American
yachts, and assisting with his advice and judgment, as well as
at the helm. During the actual races for the Cup this able
pair also had the assistance of Captain Ben Parker, skipper of
the German Emperor's schooner *Meteor II,* so that *Shamrock's*
quarter deck did not lack for talent.

When *Columbia* was launched Charles Barr was selected by
Mr. Iselin as her captain. This choice called forth much
criticism at the time, as Barr was of Scottish birth and had but
recently become a naturalized citizen, while many people felt
that an American boat should have an American skipper.
However, no better choice could have been made, and not only
did Barr prove himself one of the most wonderful skippers that
ever trod a deck, possessing all the qualities of a successful

racing man, but he later became immensely popular with the public who looked upon him as practically unbeatable.

For crew he had "Lem" Miller as mate during the series, and Deer Isle boys forward, some of *Defender's* old crew being found on *Columbia's* deck. In the early racing *Columbia* met with a number of accidents. Among others she carried away her steel mast and messed things up generally. Of course, all these were charged against Charley Barr, and he was abused pretty freely, whereas they were mostly the result of building to the extreme of lightness.

Barr first came to this country in 1885 as one of the crew of the English cutter *Clara*. In 1888, when only twenty-four years of age, he sailed the 46-foot cutter *Minerva* over, raced her in her two phenomenally successful seasons in American waters, and made an enviable name for himself. He later commanded the successful *Wasp,* sailed the unsuccessful sloop *Navahoe* in England part of the season of 1893, made a fast passage across the Atlantic in bringing *Vigilant* back in 1895, and was captain of that yacht in the trial races against *Defender* in 1895. Since that he had been in command of the big racing schooner *Colonia,* built in 1893 as a sloop for Cup defense.

For a trial horse against the *Columbia, Defender* was put into commission, under Captain Uriah Rhodes, a yacht captain of some prominence but without much experience on large racing machines. She was in charge of W. Butler Duncan, Jr., an able and resourceful amateur.

These two boats raced throughout the season, and *Columbia* showed unquestioned superiority under practically all conditions. The official trial races were held early in September, and *Columbia* beat *Defender* twice, so conclusively that further trials were deemed unnecessary. Nevertheless she was not officially named to meet the *Shamrock* until a week before the Cup race, according to the strict interpretation of the agree-

ment, in case any accident befell her in the intervening month
that might make it necessary to substitute the *Defender.*

Just before the date set for the first race, Mr. Fife, who had
been aboard *Shamrock* during practically all of her tuning-up
sails, bringing all of his experience and knowledge to bear in
getting his boat in the best possible condition, was taken ill,
and was confined to his apartments for the whole period of the
Cup races. This was doubly unfortunate, for it not only de-
prived *Shamrock's* crew of his advice and skill in those fine
points that only a boat's designer sees, but it prevented him
from making observations of inestimable value on the performance of his yacht against such a competitor as she was
bound to meet in this kind of a contest. Such first-hand knowledge would have meant much to him in the future.

October 3 found the two yachts at the line off Sandy Hook
Lightship, surrounded by the biggest excursion fleet that had
ever made the trip to the old red lightship. If Dunraven had
thought that the fleets that followed his yachts over the course
were large, he should have seen the one that was on hand to
see Sir Thomas Lipton, easily the most popular man who had
ever challenged, try to "lift the cup."

But the New York Yacht Club had taken precautions to keep
the course clear, and the Government lent its aid with a large
fleet of revenue cutters and torpedo boats, under command
of Captain Robley D. Evans, the "Fighting Bob" of Spanish-
American War fame. The excursion steamers, yachts, and tugs
were kept well away from the racers at all times; and throughout the entire series neither boat was bothered.

The first race was to be a windward and leeward one of
fifteen miles to a leg, with a time limit of five and a half hours.
The wind was light N. E. and the first leg was laid down the
Jersey beach, to leeward. Everyone was "on edge" to see what
the much talked-of challenger would do, and she showed them

quickly by beating *Columbia* over the line by 43 seconds when the starting gun banged at 11:15 A.M.

About an hour later *Columbia* got a favorable slant of wind, passed *Shamrock* and managed to round the outer mark two minutes in the lead. But the wind was light and fluky, and after a see-saw time of it the race was declared off at the expiration of the time limit, with the boats about on even terms.

This first indecisive trial was but one of many, for there followed nearly two weeks of unprecedented calm and fog, in which many attempts were made to sail a match without seeing a single finish. The tension of this delay got on the nerves of everyone, especially the crews of the two racers. It was October 16 before a race was finished.

October 16 found both yachts at the lightship, enveloped in a thin fog, but with a moderate easterly wind that gave promise of holding. The boats were sent away on the long windward leg at eleven o'clock, *Shamrock* leading over the line by three seconds. Though the wind was not of great strength and *Columbia* carried her topsail, it was noticed that Hogarth, on *Shamrock,* was content with a small one instead of the great sky-scraping "jack-yarder" she had spread in the previous trials. The reason was apparent later when the breeze freshened, and it was seen that the Lipton boat was a little tender.

Soon after crossing Barr luffed sharply, and planted his boat on *Shamrock's* weather quarter; and on the whole of that windward leg he kept the British boat under his lee, refusing to let her get out by splitting tacks. The fog was so thick on this leg that a tug was sent ahead of the racers to act as a guide boat to show them the way to the outer mark.

The short head seas bothered *Columbia* much less than the *Shamrock,* the former slipping along easily while the latter made quite a fuss in getting through the water. It took nearly three hours to beat to the outer mark, which *Columbia* rounded 9 minutes and 49 seconds ahead of her opponent.

The run home, dead before the wind, was uninteresting, as the result was a foregone conclusion, barring accidents. *Columbia* gained 22 seconds more on this leg, and crossed the finish line 10 minutes, 11 seconds ahead of *Shamrock*.

The official times:

NAME	START	FINISH	ELAPSED TIME	CORR'T'D TIME
	H. M. S.	H. M. S.	H. M. S.	H. M. S.
Columbia	11 01 06	3 54 59	4 53 53	4 53 53
Shamrock	11 01 03	4 05 10	5 04 07	5 04 01

Columbia allowed *Shamrock* six seconds, and therefore won by 10 minutes 8 seconds, after allowance was made for the difference in starting time.

Next day they found the wind in the same old quarter, east, and quite a lump of sea on, though the fog had taken wings. The starting gun banged at eleven o'clock, and the boats were sent away on a triangular course of ten miles to a leg, the first leg being dead to windward. There was more good jockeying, and though *Shamrock* got over first by two seconds, the boats were lapped, with *Columbia* to windward.

Finding that *Columbia* was taking his wind, Hogarth slammed *Shamrock* about soon after the start. *Columbia* followed, and the two boats were having a grand thrash to windward in a twelve-knot breeze, with every sheet and halyard as taut as an iron bar. *Columbia* did not draw away as fast as on the previous day, and it was anybody's race twenty-five minutes after the start, when suddenly *Shamrock's* club topsail collapsed to leeward, the topmast having snapped clean off just above the masthead. The huge topsail hung down in the lee of the mainsail and *Shamrock* was put on the other tack, while her crew swarmed aloft to get the mess cleared away. This, of course, put her out of the race. Luckily, no one was hurt, and *Shamrock* was taken in tow back to the city.

Columbia kept on, though she took in her jibtopsail after

Shamrock I in 1899 leading *Columbia*.

Shamrock III (right) and *Reliance* maneuvering for a start in 1903.

the accident to her opponent, sailed over the course in the excellent time of 3 hours and 37 minutes, and was declared the winner. She was forced to do this by an ironbound agreement between the owners of the two yachts, which read as follows:

"Inasmuch as we are of the opinion that *America's* Cup races are no less a test of the construction of the competing vessels than of their sailing qualities, and it is deemed advisable to avoid the embarrassment in which a vessel finds herself when called upon to decide whether to withdraw from a race upon the occurrence of an accident disabling her competitor, it is agreed that, in the races between the *Shamrock* and the *Columbia,* each yacht shall stand by the consequences of any accident happening to her, and that the uninjured vessel shall sail out of the race."

On the following day *Shamrock* had a new topmast sent up— a fine stick, fifty-six feet long. She also took aboard four tons of additional ballast to stiffen her somewhat. She was re-measured after this, with the result that she had now to allow *Columbia* sixteen seconds.

Both boats were at the line again on October 19, but the wind went flat and there was another heart-beaking postponement.

The series had now dragged on for eighteen days and the excursion fleet had melted away like fog before a west wind, though there was a fair-sized fleet on hand October 20 in the expectation of seeing the ending of the series. It was a fine day for a race, with a brisk northerly wind that whipped the tops off the tumbling seas and gave the two "mug hunters" all they wanted. *Shamrock* had only a working topsail up instead of her big "jack-yarder," and *Columbia,* though the abler boat, was content with none at all.

The course was a leeward and windward one again, the first leg being south by west down the Jersey beach, and the starting gun was fired promptly at eleven o'clock. It was the day of days for the *Shamrock* to distinguish herself, and she proceeded to get the jump on *Columbia* by crossing the line one minute and one second ahead of her; but as times were taken from the actual crossing and *Columbia* was in a position to blanket *Shamrock,* this was a doubtful advantage.

As they crossed the crew of *Columbia* broke out a big spinnaker, and for the next three-quarters of an hour they had all sorts of fun with that piece of canvas. First it "ballooned," then it collapsed and filled again, buckling the long spinnaker boom in an alarming fashion, making it soar skyward and drop again. It performed all manner of "stunts" and took charge of the ship generally, until everyone expected momentarily to see it burst. Finally it was put on its good behavior. While this was still going on Barr set his gaff topsail, and just before the mark was reached, *Columbia* had the satisfaction of passing her rival. As soon as she had done so Barr took in his topsail, evidently not wanting to take any chances on carrying away something on the thrash to windward.

As they drew near the mark, both were traveling like express trains. *Columbia* reached the stake boat first, got in her light canvas in fine style, flattened sheets in smartly, and made a fine turn just 17 seconds ahead of *Shamrock,* having beaten her opponent 1 minute and 18 seconds on the run.

Shamrock did not take the turn as neatly, and was slow getting her main boom aboard, so that she sagged off to leeward. When she finally got settled down for the beat back she was well under *Columbia's* lee and was not pointing as high.

All through that magnificent fifteen-mile beat home the *Shamrock* tried her best to get away from *Columbia,* but whether she was sailed fine or full her big white opponent kept eating out to windward under lower sails only. Toward the end the quarterdeck gang on *Shamrock* tried setting a club topsail in place of the jib-headed one, in a last desperate effort to catch *Columbia,* but it only made her lay over farther and did not help her any.

Columbia crossed the line an easy winner with over six minutes to spare, and the series of 1899 was at an end.

The times:

NAME	START	FINISH	ELAPSED TIME	CORR'T'D TIME
	H. M. S.	H. M. S.	H. M. S.	H. M. S.
Columbia	11 01 35	2 40 00	3 38 25	3 38 09
Shamrock	11 00 34	2 45 17	3 44 43	3 44 43

Columbia won by 6 minutes 34 seconds. She undoubtedly could have made it more if she had been pushed.

If ever man and a crew were "vindicated" by the result of a race it was Charley Barr and the crew of the *Columbia,* forward and aft. At all times during the racing *Columbia* was better handled than *Shamrock,* despite the array of professional talent that was sailing the latter. Barr showed excellent judgment, was cool in a pinch, and sailed his boat like the master hand that he was acknowledged to be later. The newspaper critics were forced to eat their words and give him the praise that he deserved.

Columbia's superiority was conclusively shown, though it is probable that *Shamrock* might have done better with Mr. Fife on board, or if she had been tuned to a higher pitch.

After the series the New York Yacht Club elected Sir Thomas Lipton to honorary membership, his name being proposed by Commodore J. P. Morgan, and another challenge from the same source was talked of for 1901. On November 2 the *Shamrock* left this country for England in tow of the steam yacht *Erin.*

Chapter XIII

THE SECOND LIPTON CHALLENGE. THE "SHAMROCK II —
COLUMBIA" RACE OF 1901

AFTER WAITING long enough to give another challenger an
opportunity to come forward, if any so desired, Sir Thomas had
the Royal Ulster Yacht Club send a challenge in his behalf
October 2, 1900, asking for a series of races in August of the
following year and naming a ninety-foot cutter as the boat. The
New York Yacht Club did not insist on any other measurements
than the waterline length, and the minor details of the match
were easily arranged to the satisfaction of both sides, Sir
Thomas being then in high favor in the club.

For *Shamrock II*, Lipton went to George Watson for the
design. Watson was probably the foremost designer in England
at that time, if that adjective can be applied to any one man
in a profession. His *Britannia* was one of the most wonderful
racing yachts ever turned out, and he had also designed the
little *Madge,* and the *America's* Cup challengers *Thistle* and
the two *Valkyries.* He had thus had ample experience in our
waters.

Before building the new boat, he conducted an exhaustive
series of tank experiments with small models to try out various
forms. It is believed that this is the first time this had been
done with sailing models, though it was quite common with
those of steam vessels. The angles of heel and courses when on
the wind complicated the problem for sailing models. However, Watson put much faith in these tests.

No expense was to be spared in this second *Shamrock,* **and**
again lightness of construction with the least possible **displace-**

140

ment, or "body," was sought. The boat was plated with a new alloy called immadium, light but strong, and though the yacht was broken up after two years this material appears to have lasted satisfactorily.

In shape, *Shamrock II,* was an extremely flat boat with long ends (she was almost ten feet longer over all than her predecessor), full water lines, and a deep, narrow fin drawing twenty feet of water. When she was measured her dimensions were found to be: length over all 137 feet, waterline 89 feet 3 inches, beam 24 feet, and draft 20 feet, while Watson tacked on some 600 feet to the first *Shamrock's* already large sail area and gave the new boat 14,027 square feet. She was, up to that time, the most extreme type of racing machine, though she was to be outdone two years later.

As soon as the challenge was received and accepted, another syndicate was in order, there being hardly a thought as to whether *Columbia* would be good enough to take *Shamrock II's* measure. This new syndicate was composed of August Belmont, Oliver H. Payne, F. G. Bourne, James Stillman, and Henry Walters—all men of ample means who could afford to see that no money was spared on the new boat. Herreshoff again got the order, and with the last successful defender as a guide, he started in on a boat that was confidently expected to be even faster than *Columbia.*

Constitution, as this new craft was named, showed many differences in construction from previous defenders, if not in shape or type. A new form of "web" frames was used in her, which, while more expensive, gave a lighter construction, with, it was said, equal strength. These frames were placed about six feet apart instead of the ordinary distance of about a foot and a half. The plating was bronze. Though in many ways similar to *Columbia,* especially above the water, Herreshoff went back to the successful *Defender* for much of her underwater form, her midship section being quite similar to the 1895 yacht.

She was launched May 6, and was put in charge of W. Butler Duncan, Jr. Mr. Duncan, it will be remembered, was in charge of *Defender* during her trials against *Columbia,* and he also sailed on the *Columbia* with Mr. Iselin during the last Cup series.

For captain, Uriah Rhodes was chosen. This was a poor choice, with such a man as Barr in the field, for Rhodes had not had the experience on big racing machines, nor was he as good a helmsman as the other man. But there was still some feeling against Barr, both on account of his not being a native born American, and, possibly, on account of his success, though it is not known that this influenced the *Constitution* syndicate in its selection.

Constitution's length over all was 132 feet, waterline 89 feet 6 inches, beam 25 feet 2 inches, and draft 19 feet 7 inches. Her sail area was given as 14,290 square feet.

In order to give the new boat the advantage of trials against a boat of known caliber, Mr. E. D. Morgan bought Mr. Iselin's share in *Columbia* and fitted her out. While he managed the yacht himself he gave the command to Charley Barr, who picked a Scandinavian crew which he trained into a perfect machine.

Work on the *Constitution* was no sooner under way at the Herreshoff shop than word came that Boston would also be in the field for the honor of defending. It had been eight years since Boston had been represented by a Cup yacht and this word came with something of a shock to the complacency of the two New York Yacht Club syndicates and was received with poor grace.

The owner of the Boston boat was Thomas W. Lawson, a rich stock broker and speculator, possessed of ample means to build the boat alone and do her justice. He was not a practical yachtsman, however, and, besides, he was not a member of the New York Yacht Club.

Now, the New York Yacht Club had held a monopoly on Cup defense so long that it had construed the various Deeds of Gifts to imply that the defending boat *must* belong to a member of the Club and sail under the Club burgee. Every boat that had so far represented this country in these matches had done so; and while there was nothing specific on this point in any of the three Deeds, the fact that the last Deed specifically made over the Cup to the New York Yacht Club, to be held by it until won by a foreign club, made the Club feel that it was responsible for the defense and it was not right to make it assume this responsibility unless it had complete control of the yacht chosen to defend. It could only have this control if the yacht were owned in the club. This may have been round-about reasoning, but still it must be remembered that the Cup was in the possession of the New York Yacht Club, and possession implies a good deal in yacht racing. The Club's attitude in this matter did not find favor in the eyes of the majority of the American public, yet it was in keeping with racing custom.

Mr. Lawson was informed of the interpretation the New York Yacht Club placed on the trust by which it held the Cup, and that if he wanted to race this boat in the trial races to pick a defender, he would have to either join the New York Yacht Club, or put his boat temporarily in the possession of some member of that Club.

Mr. Lawson was a very aggressive and outspoken man, and he declined to comply with these suggestions. He told the committee who saw him in regard to this matter, when they intimated that he might have a boat on his hands and nothing to race against, that that was his concern and not theirs.

Thus the yachting season opened with three big sloops in the field, considerable hard feeling, and every prospect of a lively time.

Constitution and *Columbia* met early in the season, and in the first races the former did fairly well, proving very fast in light winds, as she carried over 1000 square feet more sail than *Columbia.* However, with this great spread it was soon found that her spars were not strong enough to stand the strain, and she had endless trouble with them. They were of steel, braced, and trussed, and they buckled badly. In one of her earlier races she carried away her mast and had to go back to the shop for a new one. So marked was this weakness of her spars that it is said everyone aboard her was wrought up to a high state of nervousness over them, and that all hands would turn a back-hand-spring to get out of the way whenever there was a snap aloft, or the boom fetched up hard on the mainsheet in coming about or jibing.

Along about the middle of the season *Columbia* began to win. Especially in a breeze of over ten or twelve knots' strength did she show her superiority. Besides, she was better sailed and was much easier to handle than *Constitution* and was in much better shape all around.

While this matter of choice was bothering the *America's* Cup Committee in mid-season, the Boston sloop, which had been named *Independence,* arrived off Newport, after a rough voyage around Cape Cod at the end of a towing hawser. She was a big, flat, "brute" of a boat, some 140 feet long on deck, built like an enlarged "scow" with very flat body, long ends, a deep fin-like keel, and a balanced rudder. However, after it was found that this "tin pan" of a rudder would not hold her off in a breeze, and that she would "take charge" herself when off the wind, it was discarded and a regular type of rudder, set into a socket at the bottom of the keel, was substituted. Even with this it was hard to hold her, and old "Hank" Haff, who was in command of her, had his hands more than full in keeping her on her course and clear of the other boats.

Independence had a whopping big sail spread and was virtually a racing "scow," enlarged to unwieldly proportions. Under favorable conditions and on certain points of sailing she was undoubtedly very fast, but, on the whole, she was a failure. She was designed by B. B. Crowninshield, a well-known Boston naval architect, and was built by Lawley. She was a good deal in the nature of an experiment—the extremely flat boat not having at that time been tried in such a large size.

Lawson still refused to let his name go up for membership in the New York Yacht Club, or to place his boat in charge of some member of that organization, so the yacht was not allowed to enter any of the Club races. This called forth much popular criticism, until it was seen that *Independence* was not the fastest boat.

At this stage of the proceedings the Newport Yacht Racing Association, a new organization composed of some prominent Newport yachtsmen, came upon the stage and arranged a series of races off Brenton Reef between the three boats. While this did not relieve the New York Yacht Club of criticism, it gave the *Independence* the opportunity she was looking for.

In all, the Lawson boat sailed in six races, four against the *Columbia* and the *Constitution,* and two against the *Columbia* alone. In all of these races she finished last, thereby taking away all of Lawson's thunder.

In the first two races it was noticed that she was very sluggish, moving much slower in the light air than the other boats, and this, together with the fact that water was seen constantly running down her side in the second race, led to the surmise that she was leaking. This turned out to be the case. Her flat nose had received a hammering coming around the Cape that started the plates, and until she could be docked it was necessary to mount an extra pump below to keep her clear. In the fourth race she lost her topmast, and though she finished, it was in the last position. These races, of course, eliminated her as a further factor and cleared the air somewhat.

Still there was the vexing problem of a selection between the other two boats to bother the committee, for *Constitution* had been showing such in-and-out work that it was by no means certain that she was the best all-round boat.

After her early success *Constitution* lost more races than she won, and never seemed to get in quite the proper trim. This, of course, started the cry that Herreshoff had reached his limit in *Columbia,* and that *Constitution* was a failure. The fact was, that *Columbia* was better handled in all her races than the new boat. Barr "put it over" Rhodes and *Constitution's* afterguard right straight along. He nearly always got the best of the start, putting *Constitution* just where he wanted her, until it almost seemed as if he had them all scared aboard of her. He frequently bluffed *Constitution* out of her rights and, incidentally, he came in for a good deal of criticism for the high-handed way in which he carried things when at close quarters.

As a matter of fact, Butler Duncan and Rhodes had a great responsibility on their shoulders, for if they insisted on their rights and damaged or sank both boats, they might have left the Cup without a defender.

It is doubtful, though, if Barr would have gone so far as to let the boats actually get together. *Columbia* was a quick handling boat, and Barr usually had her well in hand for fast maneuvering. He knew the caution with which *Constitution* was being handled, and he was smart enough to make the most of it and get away with situations where his boat was in the wrong. As long as his "bluffs" were not called he could continue "to make a monkey" out of Rhodes. It is only fair to say that the skipper of *Constitution* was probably held back somewhat by those over him.

During the season *Constitution* and *Columbia* met in twenty-two races. Eighteen of these were finished, and each boat won nine. In two that were not finished *Columbia* had a commanding lead when they were called off. Besides this generally unsatisfactory record of *Constitution's,* she did not do as well in the latter part of the season as at first. This was said to be due largely to her poor sails, which when new were in good condition, but after being stretched and recut several times, did not hold their shape. The new suits she received from the Herreshoff shop seemed no better. Her sails came in for a lot of criticism, justly or unjustly, and everyone was asking why some other American sailmaker was not given a chance. But the contract called for sails from Herreshoff, and from the Herreshoff loft they came.

The later races, and especially the nine held between August 10th and 25th, so clearly demonstrated that *Columbia* was the most consistent performer, in all around weather conditions, that she was chosen by the *America's* Cup Committee on September 5th, to meet *Shamrock II.*

This was a great disappointment to the *Constitution* syndicate, to Herreshoff, and to many yachtsmen, and the feeling was quite general that *Shamrock II* had an excellent chance to win the Cup in meeting a boat two years old, the new Lipton boat being admittedly faster than the first *Shamrock.* Herreshoff was never satisfied that *Constitution* was the slower boat, and felt that with a little longer time to get her into form, or with a man like Barr at her wheel, the result would have been different.

On the other side of the Atlantic, meanwhile, *Shamrock II* was having her own troubles. She, too, did some in-and-out sailing while her skipper and crew were working her into shape, and she also lost her mast in one race. This happened while King Edward VII was aboard her; but that good sportsman, so the story runs, merely lighted a fresh cigar as the mast crumpled up and inquired if anyone was hurt. This accident caused Sir Thomas to ask for a postponment of the races for a month, which was granted by the New York Yacht Club.

This carrying away of masts was getting to be altogether too

common in Cup racers and showed that the limit of sail carrying capacity on one "stick" had about been reached. It was
pretty nearly time to call a halt when a 135-foot yacht could
not go out in a breeze of over ten or twelve-knots' strength
without danger of losing her entire rig overboard.

Before leaving for this country *Shamrock II* was strength-
ened internally by braces, struts, and extra stringers, to with-
stand the voyage. She had a small jury rig of head sails and
loose-footed mainsail, but it was only for emergency use, as she
was towed across by the steam yacht *Erin.* She arrived here in
time to get thoroughly tuned up and to instill in the minds of
many of those who saw her sail, or who got a look at her shape
in the drydock, a fear of what she might do to the *Columbia.*
Reports credited her with making fourteen knots on several oc-
casions when tuning up, and stories were told of her leaving
fast tugboats behind as if they were anchored.

She certainly had all the earmarks of speed and was conceded
to be the fastest boat that had ever come over after the Cup.
She was a much bigger boat than *Columbia,* and spread 800
square feet of sail more than the American boat, yet by some
clever rigging of the peak halyard block that saved something
in the measurement of sail area, she only had to allow *Columbia*
43 seconds on a thirty-mile course.

With the prospects good for the closest match yet seen for the
historic trophy, much would probably depend on handling, and
Shamrock II was in the capable hands of Captains Wringe
and Sycamore. Wringe had been here with the first *Shamrock,*
and Sycamore, it will be remembered, was helmsman of *Valkyrie III* so they were both familiar with the courses of Sandy
Hook.

The first race was scheduled for September 26th. The start
was made in a light breeze that became fluky and lighter as
the hours wore on; and when it was found that the race could
not be finished in the five and a half hour's time limit, it was

called off. At that time *Columbia* was about a mile ahead, though it was no real test of the boats.

On September 28th they tried it again, with a moderate breeze of eight to ten-knots' strength, a smooth sea, and the course fifteen miles to windward and return. Those on the big excursion fleet were treated to a fine exhibition of jockeying before the start. Barr had met his match in this respect in Sycamore and could not get away with any "bluffs." The two boats hung together waiting for the gun, and when the puff of smoke from the Committee boat said that it was eleven o'clock, both were close to the line. They went over lapped, *Shamrock* first and *Columbia* only two seconds behind her.

The beat to the outer mark in conditions that just suited *Shamrock* was full of excitement, as the boats had it nip-and-tuck the whole way. On this point of sailing the *Shamrock* did her best work of the day, gaining 39 seconds on *Columbia* and turning 41 seconds ahead. With *Shamrock's* immense sail spread it looked as if Sir Thomas was at last to get a race, and everyone expected to see his boat run away from the *Columbia* on the homeward leg.

To the surprise of all, however, the finer lined *Columbia* not only made up what she had lost on the beat, but actually passed the *Shamrock* and crossed the finish, amid a fearful din of whistles, 35 seconds ahead of the challenger.

The times:

NAME	START	FINISH	ELAPSED TIME	CORR'T'D TIME
	H. M. S.	H. M. S.	H. M. S.	H. M. S.
Columbia	11 00 16	3 31 23	4 31 07	4 30 24
Shamrock	11 00 14	3 31 58	4 31 44	4 31 44

The *Columbia* won by 1 minute and 20 seconds, corrected time.

Another attempt at a race was made October 1st, but again there was not sufficient wind, and the race was finally abandoned, this time with *Shamrock* some half mile ahead.

Two days later the yachts met again off the Hook, finding
a rattling breeze of some twelve-knots' strength. The course
this time was triangular, ten miles to a leg. The starting signal
caught *Columbia* some distance from the line, and she was 1
minute and 34 seconds behind the Irish boat in crossing. The
first two legs were reaches, and *Columbia* immediately started
in to show what she could do on this point of sailing.

Despite the fact that a reach in a moderate breeze was considered *Shamrock's* long suit, the two-year-old American yacht,
traveling at a twelve-knot clip, gained 22 seconds on the first
leg, and 30 seconds on the second. As they rounded the last
mark for the beat home *Shamrock II* was still 42 seconds in the
lead, and then, as the wind freshened to about fifteen-knots'
strength and the sea became flecked with white, *Columbia*
proceeded to give an exhibition of what she could do on the
wind in a breeze. Before the leg was half sailed she had waded
by *Shamrock,* and with her lee rail buried, her crew flat along
the weather rail, and Barr standing at the wheel as if only on a
practice spin, she crossed the line one minute and 18 seconds
ahead of Lipton's hope, having gained two minutes on the beat.
The times:

NAME	FINISH	ELAPSED TIME	CORR'T'D TIME
	H. M. S.	H. M. S.	H. M. S.
Columbia	2 15 05	3 13 18	3 12 35
Shamrock	2 16 23	3 16 10	3 16 10

The *Columbia* won by 3 minutes and 35 seconds, corrected time.

This was something of a damper to the spirits of Sir Thomas
Lipton and the crew of *Shamrock,* but they were at the line
the next day as full of fight as ever, and not yet ready to admit
that they were beaten. The breeze was again kind, blowing at
about ten knots, though it lightened somewhat before the finish. The wind was off shore and the course was a leeward and
windward one of thirty miles.

As the start was down the wind neither boat was anxious to be first over to be blanketed by the other, so they hung back and the allowance of two minutes in which to cross had expired before either started, the time of both being thus taken as at 11:02 A.M. *Shamrock* crossed thirteen seconds behind *Columbia.*

It was again *Shamrock's* weather, and if she had been as cleverly handled as *Columbia,* the chances are good that she would have won. The challenger's skippers did not seem to make the most of their opportunities, while Barr handled *Columbia* with excellent judgment and great skill. He showed to special advantage in the windward work. In the run down wind *Shamrock* gained 49 seconds, though as she was 13 seconds behind in starting her actual gain was one minute two seconds. On the beat home, in a softening breeze, *Columbia* gained 47 seconds.

As they neared the finish line after the long fifteen-mile beat to windward the two boats were right together, and it was a toss-up as to which would cross first. As they slipped over the two boats were lapped, and *Shamrock* wrested the honor from *Columbia* by *two* seconds. Two seconds apart after thirty miles of sailing is something of a finish, and the fact that after *Shamrock* allowed the 43 seconds of time to *Columbia* she lost by 41 seconds did not detract from the excitement of the last moments of the race.

It was the closest finish in the history of the Cup, and the first time when there was no open water between the boats at the end of thirty miles of sailing. The times:

NAME	FINISH	ELAPSED TIME	CORR'T'D TIME
	H. M. S.	H. M. S.	H. M. S.
Columbia	3 35 40	4 33 40	4 32 57
Shamrock	3 35 38	4 33 38	4 33 38

The *Columbia* won by 41 seconds, corrected time.

This ended it. *Shamrock II* had fulfilled the prediction that she was the fastest boat ever sent after the Cup, but she wasn't quite fast enough for the clean-lined boat that had taken the first *Shamrock's* measure two years before. Truly *Columbia* and Charley Barr were a hard combination to beat!

To show how evenly the two boats were matched, in the three races they sailed ninety miles (considerably more than that if the windward work was counted for what it actually was) yet *Columbia* only beat *Shamrock II* by a total of 3 minutes and 27 seconds, actual time, or 5 minutes and 36 seconds, corrected time.

Shamrock II was not taken back to England, but was laid up at the Erie Basin, in New York, and was broken up in November, 1903, as another fruitless sacrifice to a coveted bit of silver.

Chapter XIV

AFTER THE Cup Race of 1901 it began to be apparent to every-one who had followed yacht racing closely that the limit to which everything could be sacrificed for speed in racing yachts had about been reached. The tendency in Cup defenders was naturally reflected in smaller yachts, and, on the whole, a very unsatisfactory type of racing boat was being developed. Dissatisfaction with this tendency was already becoming apparent, though it took another Cup race, and a still more extreme defender, to bring it to a head and to lead to the adoption of a measurement rule that put a stop to the flat, scow-like racing shells.

Lipton waited a decent interval to allow anyone else who might be covetous of the *America's* Cup to make a try for it; but no one came forward. The cost of a race was getting to be prohibitive with the chances of success very slim and the return in sport altogether incommensurate with the outlay, the boats being useless except for this one event. *America's* Cup racing was not particularly popular, just then.

The following summer word came that Sir Thomas Lipton was making plans for another assault on the New York Yacht Club, and in due time a third challenge arrived from the Royal Ulster Yacht Club, asking for a race in August, 1903, and naming another ninety-foot cutter as the boat. Accompanying this challenge of October 7th, 1902, Sir Thomas sent a personal letter to the New York Yacht Club regarding his persistence in trying to "lift" the Cup, in which he said: "In thus desiring an opportunity of making a third attempt to obtain possession of the *America's* Cup I hope I may not be deemed importunate or unduly covetous of the precious trophy so long and so securely held in trust by the New York Yacht Club." These were fine words, and showed a true spirit of sportsmanship in the face of two defeats.

No trouble was had in arriving at an understanding as to the terms of the match, the conditions asked for and granted being practically the same as in the previous races. The series was to consist of the best three out of five races with the usual five and one half hour time limit.

For the new boat Sir Thomas turned back to William Fife, the designer of the first *Shamrock*. The boat was built under lock and key, and until she was launched nothing was known of the kind of craft Fife would turn out.

When she slid overboard early in the season it was seen that *Shamrock III* was a beautifully modeled boat in spite of some extreme features, such as excessively long ends, low freeboard, etc. She was of the semi-fin type, though not as extreme in this respect as *Shamrock II,* and throughout Fife had kept as close as he could, with due regard to modern practice, to some of the older principles of the regular cutter type. *Shamrock III* was much nearer the proper balance between moderate form and dimensions and economical driving power, than was the American boat, as we shall see when we study the latter's dimensions. She was not as big or as powerful a boat as *Shamrock II,* yet she was sweeter and abler in every way.

In *Shamrock III* Fife had swung back toward the narrow cutter. She was the narrowest boat since the *Valkyrie II* of 1893, being only some eight inches wider than the latter boat, though she was seventeen feet longer over all. She was built of nickel steel, a very strong alloy, coated with white enamel, giving a very smooth surface. Her dimensions were: Length over all 134 feet 4 inches, waterline 89 feet 10 inches, beam 23 feet, and draft 19 feet, while her sail area was 14,154 square feet.

She was also the first English challenger of cutter rig to adopt the American type of steering gear, being steered by a wheel instead of by a long tiller.

While we are looking at *Shamrock* we might also turn to the new American defender, and see what kind of a boat Herreshoff had turned out to meet the latest English creation. A new millionaire's syndicate had been formed in the New York Yacht Club as soon as Lipton's challenge was received and took upon itself the task of financing a ninety-foot, up-to-the-minute racing machine.

This syndicate was composed of Cornelius Vanderbilt, William Rockefeller, Elbert H. Gary, Clement A. Griscom, James J. Hill, W. B. Leeds, Norman B. Ream, Henry Walters, and P. A. B. Widener. The syndicate gave Herreshoff practically unlimited financial backing, and the result was a boat that was extreme in every way. With the waterline length practically the only fixed restriction, Herreshoff took all kinds of liberties with the other factors, and "went the limit" as regards ends and sail area. It is said that her first cost was $175,000, exclusive of her equipment or of the expenses of running her throughout the season.

It will be remembered that in *Independence,* two years before, Crowninshield had experimented with the extremely flat, almost scow-like type of boat in a ninety-footer, and while the boat was practically a failure as a factor in the season's racing, she showed herself extremely fast on certain points of sailing and under conditions just suited to her. Herreshoff undoubtedly watched the flat boat's performance with considerable interest and noticed her good points, and in *Reliance,* as the new defender was christened, the influence of *Independence* was apparent, if we can judge by certain points of similarity.

The new boat was an extremely flat craft, with shallow body, long and flat ends, and a very deep fin or keel. In other words, though she might not properly be called a scow, she was a "skimming dish" of the most pronounced type, with a fin keel attached. To show how extreme she was her forward overhang was twenty-eight feet long, and the after one twenty-six feet; and these long ends, with a flat floor, little deadrise, and moderately rounded bilges, gave very straight fore-and-aft lines, and a full waterline.

To see what she gained by this it need only be said that on a measured waterline of less than ninety feet when on an even keel, when she was heeled so that her lee rail was just awash, she increased this waterline length, or bearing surface, to 130 feet. Her quarter was very wide on deck, and she resembled aft "a saucer afloat." With it all, however, Herreshoff had "fined" the lines wonderfully, and there was nothing "brute-like" or heavy about the boat.

On this immense, flat hull Herreshoff piled a mass of canvas such as was never before (or since) seen on a single-sticker. Jumping some 3,000 feet from *Columbia*, the *Reliance* spread 16,160 square feet of sail. This was over 2,000 square feet more than Fife had given *Shamrock III*, and when the two boats came together the *Reliance* towered well over her English rival. It was "some sail" to ask one mast to carry, but a steel spar was built for it with a wooden topmast telescoping inside, that managed to keep the canvas in shape when it didn't blow too hard, though the topmast broke in one of the races during the summer. The spars and rig of *Reliance* were a wonderful piece of engineering work.

The new boat w᷵᷵ built of Tobin bronze, and her general dimensions were: length over all 143 feet 8 inches (as long as a 600-ton sailing ship), waterline 89 feet 8 inches, beam 25 feet 8 inches, and draft about 20 feet, an immense chunk of lead being hung at the bottom of her fin.

Shamrock III was launched at Dumbarton on March 17th, and was immediately fitted out for a series of races with the first

Shamrock. The new boat was in charge of Captain Wringe, who had been on both the other *Shamrocks.*

On April 17th, or just a month after she was launched, the new boat was dismasted in a race with *Shamrock I* in Weymouth Bay on the south coast of England. She was carrying a club topsail at the time when a puff hit her, and the whole rig crumpled up and went over the side. Several of the crew were injured, and one man was knocked overboard and drowned.

This cast quite a damper over the trials. Sir Thomas was badly cut up over the loss of the man and said, "I can stand the loss of the rig, but that poor fellow! This is the first life that has been lost in my service—and the poor chap leaves a wife and child. I'd give the yacht sooner than lose a man!" It took nearly four weeks to get a new mast and the boat in shape again.

The seven trials between *Shamrock I* and *Shamrock III* before the accident showed conclusively that the new boat was greatly superior to the 1899 challenger. In windward work the new *Shamrock* outsailed the *Shamrock I* in the early trials from twenty to thirty seconds per mile. Off the wind her gain was not as marked, but was still very apparent, and she was conceded to be the fastest of the three Lipton boats.

While the two *Shamrocks* were busy with each other in England things were happening fast in this country. The *Reliance* had been launched April 12th, and even in her sail-stretching spins showed evidence of great speed, particularly in smooth water and light airs. In order to give her a thorough trying out Mr. E. D. Morgan put *Columbia* in commission and gave the command to Captain "Lem" Miller, who was mate with Barr in the races of 1901 and so knew the boat. The *Constitution* syndicate fitted out its boat under Mr. Belmont's management. Captain Rhodes was again given charge of her.

On board *Reliance* was C. Oliver Iselin, who had once more been persuaded to take up the task of managing a cup defender.

This time no mistake was made in the choice of a skipper, and Charley Barr was found in charge of her, with a big crew of Scandinavians.

The three boats raced throughout the summer, and *Reliance* proved herself the fastest beyond a doubt. The general result of these races showed *Reliance* to be about ten minutes faster than *Columbia* in light weather, and about three minutes faster in a strong breeze and sea, over a thirty-mile course. With her immense sail area *Reliance* heeled to her sailing lines in about a seven-knot breeze which, of course, made her very fast in light airs; yet in breezes up to twelve-knots' strength she was still powerful enough not to bury her lee rail except when caught broad off with sheets amidships.

In these races *Constitution* appeared to better advantage than she had two years before, yet she never showed consistent form or fully justified the faith of many yachtsmen who believed that she should have been chosen as the defender in 1901. *Columbia* was not as well handled as when Barr had her, and *Constitution* was undoubtedly in better shape than during her first season.

The handling of a large racing yacht plays so great a part in her success or failure that it is often hard to say just how much of her showing is due to the man at the helm; and more and more the successful skipper of a large racing machine has to be a man who is something more than a mere helmsman and sail trimmer. He must have also the faculty of getting a boat into trim, and properly tuning the whole fabric of sails, spars, and hull into perfect harmony, and rounding it into winning form.

Three official trial races were arranged off Newport, beginning July 27th. On that date *Reliance, Columbia,* and *Constitution* met in a thirty-mile race and *Reliance* won, beating *Columbia* by 46 seconds and *Constitution* by 2 minutes and 29 seconds. This was the only official trial race held, as others were deemed unnecessary after *Reliance's* showing throughout the summer. After the boats finished the cup committee met on the steam yacht *Rambler* and formerly selected *Reliance* to meet *Shamrock III*.

As the first race for the Cup was scheduled for August 20th, it was planned to bring *Shamrock III* over early in the year so as to give her plently of time to get into proper shape on this side of the water. Instead of fitting out *Shamrock II*, which was already in this country, to race against her here, it was decided to bring over the first *Shamrock*, as she was already in commission and was sailing in consistent form. So a small flotilla belonging to Lipton left Gourock on May 28th and headed out across the Western Ocean. It consisted of the steam yacht *Erin*, towing *Shamrock III*, and the ocean tug *Cruiser* with *Shamrock I* in charge. The new challenger was rigged with a small cutter rig, short mast and bowsprit, two headsails, and a loose-footed trysail, while the older boat had the ketch rig under which she crossed in 1899. Each of the racing yachts had forty-one men aboard her, and with the crews of the *Erin* and the tug there was quite a party in Sir Thomas's pay.

The trip was made *via* the Azores, and the fleet arrived off Sandy Hook in good shape after a passage of 15 days and 23 hours. The racers immediately went to the Erie Basin to get their racing spars on end and to refit. This was the first time a challenger had ever had another yacht on this side of the water to race against in her tuning-up spins, and it was, of course, expected to be a great help to the new boat and to enable her crew to know when they had her at top form.

After arriving in this country the original agreement for the sailing of the races was amended by the addition of a number of clauses governing possible contingencies that might arise, one of which was especially significant as showing the limits to which racing machines had gone and how far they had departed from the older types of able, weatherly and withal, fast racing yachts of the past. This clause read: "If in the opinion of the

Regatta Committee the weather shall at the time appointed for the start of any race be, or threaten to be, of such severe character as not to afford a reasonable opportunity of fairly testing the speed of the two vessels, the race may be postponed in the discretion of the Regatta Committee, unless either contestant shall insist on its being started."

This was quite necessary, perhaps, in view of the enormous spread of canvas that was carried on one mast, but in its spirit it was enough to have called forth a protest from the shades of that great crew that had striven for the Cup in the past. What would old Commodore Stevens, James Gordon Bennett, of the old *Dauntless,* Commodore Douglas, Lieutenant Henn, or Sir Richard Sutton have thought of such a clause inserted in any agreement for an *America's* Cup Race?

Both boats were measured before the first race of August 20th by C. D. Mower, measurer of the New York Yacht Club. The racing length of *Reliance* was found to be 108.41, and that of *Shamrock III* 104.37. *Reliance* had to allow *Shamrock III* 1 minute and 57 seconds over a thirty-mile course.

On the morning of August 20th both boats were towed from their anchorage in the Horseshoe, back of Sandy Hook, to the starting line off the lightship. It was a calm morning with a light SSW air with just enough force to make the tall racers move. As the big excursion fleet was keeping discreetly in the background under the watchful eye of a navy and revenue cutter patrol, the starting gun was fired punctually at 11 A.M., and the boats were sent off on a fifteen-mile windward leg.

Wringe, of *Shamrock III,* with Captain Bevis of *Shamrock I* at his side as second captain, judged the time more closely than his opponent, and was in a better position to cross first, which he promptly did. Only he undid his good work by tacking right on the line and killing his boat's headway. Barr crossed 33 seconds behind, but he had his boat going fast and soon passed *Shamrock III.*

It was a long, slow beat to the outer mark in a falling wind, and it took *Reliance* 4 hours 35 minutes and 31 seconds to sail the fifteen miles. *Shamrock* was then far astern, and as she saw the race could not be finished in the time limit she gave up and did not even get to the mark. This race was no test of the comparative abilities of the boats except that it showed, what all Americans knew, that *Reliance* was fast in light airs and a good "drifter," with her immense club topsail sticking over 175 feet into the air to catch the zephyrs.

A day intervened and on August 22nd the boats were at the line once more to do battle for the Cup that had been won fifty-two years before, to a day, for it was on August 22nd that the old *America* "trimmed" the British fleet in the race around the Isle of Wight. A moderate southwest wind was coming across from the Jersey beach, and there was something of a sea on. The course was signalled to windward, fifteen miles and return, and the starting gun banged at 11:45 A.M.

Both boats crossed on the starboard tack with sheets flattened down hard, and Wringe again beat Barr to it, crossing four seconds in the lead but with *Reliance* glued on his weather quarter.

Reliance made considerable fuss under her bows with the head sea, but *Shamrock* slipped along easily and seemed to pull ahead a bit. Barr finally tacked to get away from *Shamrock's* back wind, and stood toward the Jersey beach, sailing his boat a good rap full to drive her, while *Shamrock,* when she came about, seemed to be pinched a little.

When they came together on opposite tacks about an hour after the start, *Shamrock* found she could not cross the American boat's bow, and had to tack under her lee. There was smoother water under the beach and as the outer mark was neared the wind lightened, both of these things helping *Reliance.*

When they came about for the mark the last time both boats

were on nearly even terms; but the wind hauled suddenly toward the west and put *Shamrock* to leeward. Both boats then had to make several more tacks to fetch the mark, and of course *Shamrock* got the worst of it, and rounded 3 minutes 15 seconds behind the defender.

After turning, *Shamrock's* crew handled her light sails in a slovenly manner, and eventually had to reset the ballooner on account of its having been sent up with a twist in it.

Reliance was now too far ahead to be caught on the run home, her "square acre" of canvas making her move at an 11-knot gait, and she slid across the line 8 minutes and 56 seconds ahead of Lipton's boat. When allowances were figured *Reliance* won by 7 minutes and 3 seconds. The times:

NAME	FINISH	ELAPSED TIME	CORR'T'D TIME
	H. M. S.	H. M. S.	H. M. S.
Reliance	3 17 38	3 32 17	3 32 17
Shamrock III.	3 26 34	3 41 17	3 39 20

A Sunday and a weekday intervened before the next race, on August 25th over a triangular course of ten miles to a leg. A light south wind greeted the racers outside Sandy Hook, and the first leg was in that direction. In the preliminary maneuvering Wringe seemed a little afraid of Barr and disinclined to come to close quarters. When he found *Reliance* on his weather, he hung back and let the American boat go over first, thirty-six seconds after the gun. He hung back too long, however, and did not cross until nineteen seconds after the two-minute handicap, actually losing the nineteen seconds.

The wind freshened on the first leg and both boats sailed evenly. When they rounded the first mark *Reliance* was only 2 minutes and 37 seconds ahead, 1 minute and 43 seconds of which she had at the start, so that *Shamrock* only lost 54 seconds on the 10-mile beat.

The second leg was a broad reach and toward the end of it

both boats tried to carry spinnakers. The crew of the *Reliance* got theirs drawing better and she pulled away slightly; but the wind backed again and the sails had to come in. *Reliance* gained on the leg, but only 1 minute and 20 seconds, largely due to the better handling of her sails.

On the last leg both boats had to trim in somewhat, as it was a fairly close reach. *Reliance* tried to carry a ballooner only to find she could not make it draw. As they neared the finish *Reliance* ran into a soft spot and *Shamrock,* still carrying a good breeze, closed up so fast that it seemed to the spectators as if she would save her time. On she came, hand over fist, only to drop into the same soft spot that had caught *Reliance,* and she lost out on corrected time by just 1 minute and 19 seconds.

The times:

Name	Finish	Elapsed Time	Corr't'd Time
	H. M. S.	H. M. S.	H. M. S.
Reliance	2 15 30	3 14 54	3 14 54
Shamrock III	2 20 10	3 18 10	3 16 13

From August 25th to September 3rd, a period of nine days, many attempts were made to sail a race, but without a single one being finished. There was either not enough wind, too much, or else that arch enemy of yachtsmen, fog. On August 27th a start was made in a light southeast air but the time limit expired after *Reliance* had beaten *Shamrock* 12 minutes 31 seconds to the outer mark.

On August 29th there was the rare condition of too much wind. It was blowing a moderately heavy breeze, though hardly a gale of wind, but it was accompanied by a heavy mist or fog that prevented any of the marks from being seen, so the race was postponed. It is worthy of note that this was the first race for the Cup that had to be postponed by reason of too much wind. But it would have been foolhardy to have sailed under the conditions with two racing machines, one of which carried on her single mast as much sail as was spread by the Cup defenders *Puritan* and *Mayflower* combined.

After this postponement it was agreed to sail every day instead of every other day, until a race was finished. Still the elements were obdurate. On August 31st a race was started but not finished. On September 1st and 2nd there was a flat calm and the boats were not even started.

On September 3rd, as the yachts were towed wearily out to the starting line the day seemed to hold little of cheering prospect. There was almost no wind and the sky was gray and misty. The committee waited a long time, whistling for a wind. About 12:30 P.M. the breeze was coming in from the south and the preparatory signal was fired at 12:45, with the course signalled as a 15-mile beat to windward and return.

In the jockeying before the start Wringe again displayed his aversion to coming to close quarters with Barr, and the starting gun at one o'clock found both boats some distance from the line. Barr got over first with only four seconds of his two minute handicap left, while Wringe was again behind, and lost seven seconds.

It was a long, slow beat to the outer mark and *Reliance* kept eating out to windward in masterful style, dropping *Shamrock* on every tack. Barr sailed her beautifully in the light air and again proved the assertion that it is the man who gets the most out of his boat in light breezes that wins. Any sailor can make a boat go in a breeze, but it is the master hand who makes her move in light weather. At the weather mark *Shamrock III* was 11 minutes and 7 seconds astern. After rounding in smart style *Shamrock's* crew got the jump on *Reliance* and beat her setting light canvas, getting up the big spinnaker and ballooner in less than two minutes—remarkably fast work.

After they turned, the wind hauled two points to the eastward, and presently it rolled in a big fog bank, shutting out from view first one boat and then the other. Fog whistles on the excursion steamers were going mournfully, while down near the committee boat the hoarse siren on the lightship boomed out its blasts to let the racers know where the finish line was.

On the yachts came, through the dripping fog, neither aware of the position of the other, and nothing was known of the two racers by anyone until the slatting of a huge sail was heard from the watching Committee boat, and *Reliance* loomed out of the mist with her crew muzzling the big spinnaker. She had hit the line nearly on end, and crossed at 5:30:02 P.M. As she slipped over, her crew broke out an immense American yacht ensign at her truck and another at each spreader in token that it was all over. Then a line was passed to a waiting tug and she started back to the city.

After a long wait for the *Shamrock* some anxiety began to be felt for her, when the fog lifted enough to show the Irish boat well to the northeast of the lightship. She had got off her course in the fog. and had missed the lightship and its fog signal entirely. When she discovered her mistake she did not even bother to come back and cross the line.

The series of 1903 was over. Lipton had tried as no man had tried before to win the Cup, but had failed. Indeed he did not come as close to winning as he had in 1901, with the *Shamrock II,* and in the three races and all the unfinished trials of 1903 his boat was never ahead at any single mark of the course, after crossing the starting line.

His failure to win was a keen disappointment, but he took it in good part. Many Americans were also sorry to see him lose, as they felt that it might be a good thing for international racing if the Cup went back to England for a time. We had held it so long, and had defended it so successfully, that it rather frightened prospective challengers away, and it was felt that it would be a long time before another race for it would be held in this country.

Chapter XV

NEW MEASUREMENT RULES—LIPTON'S FOURTH CHALLENGE
—WAR INTERVENES

AFTER 1903 a decade passed during which no foreign yachtsman (save Lipton) came forward with even a prospective challenge—the longest such period since the first challenge of 1870.
There were rumors that some English, or Swedish, or German yachtsman was contemplating an assault on the *America's*
Cup, but none were heard from. Off and on during this period
Sir Thomas was in communication with the New York Yacht
Club, but nothing actually came of the letter writing until
1913.

Several things were responsible for this lack of interest in the
America's Cup. It had been apparent for some time that the
trend of these Cup contests as outlined in the last chapter was
greatly narrowing their scope, and restricting competition to
those who could afford to spend a good sized fortune on a very
slim chance of success. *Reliance* marked the extreme limit in
the development of the racing machine and, in general racing,
there had been already a swing toward a saner and more healthy
type of yacht.

In 1903 the New York Yacht Club adopted a rating rule that
sounded the death knell of the flat, light-displacement, scow-
like boats. This rule took into account displacement as well as
length and sail area, and by putting a premium on the first
named encouraged a sharper, fuller-bodied hull instead of the
flat freaks that had grown up under the old rule. At a conference of most of the leading yacht clubs and racing associations
of the East, held in 1905, this rule was pretty generally adopted.

Although called the "Universal Rule," it was only used in this country, England and the other European yachting countries having adopted a rule to bring about the same desired results, known as the International Rule. Under these two rules a fine type of racing craft was produced—able, seaworthy, safe and yet fast, which had value as cruisers when their racing days were over.

Although it was now holding all its regular races under the Universal Rule, the New York Yacht Club declined to commit itself to a suggestion from Sir Thomas that it accept a challenge to race for the Cup with challenger and defender built to this rule. The club, instead, seemed determined to negotiate only under the strict letter of the Deed of Gift.

Lipton, as well as most other yachtsmen abroad and at home, believed that we should get away from boats of the *Reliance* type; and with this point unsettled no unconditional challenge was received, though Sir Thomas actually sent a conditional challenge in 1907.

There seemed to be some sentiment in the holding club that Lipton had been given enough chances for the Cup, and the members guiding the club's Cup policy were loath to make any concessions to him. To put it in another way, they would have welcomed more heartily a challenge from another quarter.

Yet in 1899 they had welcomed the Irish baronet when he was unknown in the yacht racing world. He challenged after the unpleasant Dunraven incident, at a time when the New York Yacht Club needed a challenge badly, and he raced in a sportsmanlike manner. In the intervening years, by consistent racing in home waters, he had become the foremost big-boat racing yachtsman in Great Britain, and as such was entitled to the consideration due a sportsman.

Late in 1912, no other challenger being in sight, Lipton opened negotiations again, and intimated his readiness to challenge if any assurance could be had of racing with a boat of a certain size, and under the new rules. The Club still refusing to commit itself, he finally sent a definite challenge, naming a boat of 75 feet waterline length, and stipulating that the New York Yacht Club meet him with a boat of not over that length. This the Club refused to do, claiming for the sake of precedent, if nothing else, that it could not and would not waive its right to meet him with any sized boat it saw fit that was eligible under the Deed. Sir Thomas then withdrew his qualifications and sent, in April, 1913, through the Royal Ulster Yacht Club, an unconditional challenge. The New York Yacht Club accepted this challenge, and in drawing up the conditions of the series by "mutual consent" agreed to race under the new measurement rules, with a 75-foot waterline boat. Having maintained its position as to its "rights," the Club met Sir Thomas Lipton fairly on the points for which he had stood out.

The conditions called for three races out of five, alternating windward and leeward and triangular, of thirty miles, outside of Sandy Hook, with a time limit of six hours. The dates selected started September 10th.

In selecting a designer for his fourth attempt, Sir Thomas Lipton had gone to C. E. Nicholson, one of the most successful designers of racing yachts in England, although he had had no experience in an *America's* Cup race.

In designing *Shamrock IV*, Nicholson, to all appearances, paid but scant attention to the American rule of measurement and turned out a boat with long, flat ends, which took considerable quarter-beam penalty, with a straight or even slightly reverse sheer, a straight transom that looked as if the stern had been sawed off short, and a lot of tumble home to the topsides. Above water she looked like an extreme scow, and Nicholson himself called her "the ugly duckling." He evidently designed what he figured was the fastest type of hull for the conditions he expected, and was willing to pay any penalty incurred under the measurement rule. She was of laminated wood construction over steel frames.

Shamrock IV was a big powerful boat for her size, being 75 feet on the water, 110.3 feet over all, with a "whopping" big sail area of 10,459 square feet of canvas, or nearly 1,700 square feet more than was carried by *Resolute*, the yacht finally chosen to defend. This, of course, made her rate high, 94.4 feet, or some 10 feet more than the American boats, and forced her to give a lot of time to the defender. She also took a slight draft penalty, and in addition carried a narrow centerboard which housed in her keel. She was, without exception, the homeliest yacht that ever challenged for the Cup.

On this side of the water three boats were built to defend the Cup, each from the board of a different designer. One of these was by Herreshoff, for a New York Yacht Club syndicate formed by Henry Walters, and composed, besides himself, of Commodore J. P. Morgan, Cornelius Vanderbilt, F. G. Bourne, George F. Baker, Jr., and Arthur Curtiss James. This yacht was named *Resolute*.

The second boat was built for Alexander S. Cochran from designs by William Gardner, a New York naval architect with long experience. Among the better known craft from his board may be mentioned the schooner *Atlantic*, which won the trans-Atlantic race of 1905 for the German Emperor's Cup, establishing a record for the course from Sandy Hook to Land's End, and the cutters *Irondequoit, Liris* and *Medora*. This Cup yacht was built of bronze at George Lawley & Son's, Boston, and was named *Vanitie*.

The third candidate was designed by a Boston naval architect, George Owen, for a syndicate of New York Yacht Club members headed by George M. Pynchon and E. Walter Clark. This boat, named *Defiance*, was her designer's first attempt at a 75-foot racing yacht, though he had turned out many very successful smaller racing craft.

While these three yachts were approximately the same waterline, 75 feet, they differed greatly in form and looks, and there was much speculation before the season of 1914 opened as to which would prove the fastest. The fact that three boats were being built, with the best one to be chosen to defend, rather gave us the edge on the challenger at the start, as all of his eggs were in one basket. They also assured a most interesting summer's racing in our waters prior to the actual match for the Cup.

Several series of races for them were arranged during the summer of 1914, starting in June. The three boats first came together off Sandy Hook. *Resolute* was sailed then, as she was in most of her races throughout her career as a Cup yacht, by Charles Francis Adams, of Boston, one of the most successful amateur skippers in America, assisted by Robert W. Emmons, who acted as manager and who built up an efficient organization which was largely responsible for the excellent condition in which the yacht was always kept. He and Charlie Adams got together an efficient and well-drilled crew. *Vanitie* was in charge of a professional skipper, "Bill" Dennis, in all of her early races. His previous experience had been largely in schooners. *Defiance* was sailed by her owners, but chiefly by George M. Pynchon, with a professional skipper on board in charge of the crew.

In the first series of seven races *Resolute* won five and *Vanitie* two, although in one race credited to *Resolute, Vanitie* had two sailors washed overboard while she was leading and had to quit the race to pick them up. *Defiance* only appeared in one of these races, which she did not finish. She appeared to be over-canvassed and had great difficulty in getting into racing shape.

To show how even the two first-named yachts were in these seven races, during which about 180 miles were sailed, *Vanitie's* total elapsed time was 17 minutes 22 seconds *better* than *Reso-*

lute's, but as she was rated higher than *Resolute* she had to allow 19 minutes 17 seconds, so that *Resolute's* corrected time was the better by one minute 55 seconds. Which is pretty close sailing.

There was much dissatisfaction in this series over the way Dennis sailed *Vanitie,* and he was replaced before the yachts met again by another professional, Harry Haff, son of old "Hank." While there was some improvement, things still did not go smoothly and *Vanitie* evidently was not showing her best form. In the next nine races *Resolute* won six and *Vanitie* three. *Defiance* started in five of these races but never crossed the finish line a winner, subsequently being withdrawn from the trials as a failure. The trouble seemed to be mostly with her rig, which she had difficulty in carrying.

On the New York Yacht Club cruise *Resolute* and *Vanitie* met again in four races, the former winning all of them on corrected time.

During this cruise World War I broke out in Europe, and at Sir Thomas Lipton's request the *America's* Cup match was postponed indefinitely. *Shamrock IV,* on her way across and actually at Bermuda when hostilities opened, completed her voyage to New York safely and was laid up in this country.

Summarizing the twenty races sailed, *Resolute* had won fifteen and *Vanitie* five, but in two of those which *Vanitie* won *Resolute* did not start. But the latter yacht had to go repeatedly to her builder's yard for repairs, and it looked as if Herreshoff had rather overdone it as regards lightness of construction and rig, while *Vanitie* was always ready and never parted a rope yarn, earning a name for herself as a good boat in a breeze.

Chapter XVI

THE "RESOLUTE"–"SHAMROCK IV" MATCH OF 1920

THE WAR was over in November, 1918, but it was not until 1920 that conditions in Great Britain or the United States justified the sailing of the postponed series of races for the *America's* Cup. Negotiations were opened by Sir Thomas Lipton in 1919, looking towards a race in 1920. July 15th was finally agreed upon as the date for the first race, with racing every other weekday until one yacht won three races.

A course off Newport was suggested by the New York Yacht Club instead of the old course off Sandy Hook. It was pointed out that winds were better there than off the Hook, and that there would be less interference with the racing yachts by the big fleet of sight-seeing boats. But Sir Thomas Lipton desired to sail off Sandy Hook, as in his previous races, and that course was decided upon. The length of the courses was to be thirty miles, alternating between windward and leeward and an equilateral triangle, with a six-hour time limit. *Shamrock IV* was named the challenging yacht, and the New York Yacht Club was to name the defending yacht one week before the first race.

The two American Cup yachts were under sail in May. "Charlie" Adams and "Bob" Emmons were again in charge of *Resolute,* but this time *Vanitie* was in the hands of George Nichols, assisted by another of our best amateurs, C. Sherman Hoyt. Under Nichols' guidance the bronze sloop did very much better, and the racing was nip-and-tuck between the two yachts, making the choice a difficult one.

The two boats met for the first time that year on May 22nd

off New Haven. In this very first go *Resolute* lost her mast in a squall, the hollow wooden spar letting go some ten or twelve feet above the deck. She was immediately towed to the Herreshoff yard at Bristol for repairs, and the yachts did not meet again until June 3rd, when *Resolute* won, though she broke the jaws of her gaff.

After this a new steel mast was stepped on *Resolute,* and the two boats were again at the line on June 7th. *Vanitie,* splendidly sailed, won, saving her time by 34 seconds.

Altogether the two Cup yachts met in eleven races, counting the first in which *Resolute* was dismasted. Of these the Herreshoff sloop won seven and *Vanitie* four. On one occasion, however, *Vanitie,* while leading, picked up a lobster pot buoy on her keel, and this slowed her up enough to kill her chances in that particular race.

As a result of these races the Cup Committee picked *Resolute* to defend. In spite of *Vanitie's* improved showing, and the fact that many observers considered her the faster boat when she was well sailed, as she had been this last season, the choice was a logical one. In the three seasons they had met, the Herreshoff sloop had had overwhelmingly the best of it, and her skipper and crew had been together so long that they got the most out of the yacht. She was a "surer bet" than *Vanitie,* no matter what one thought of the capabilities of the Gardner boat.

While all this racing to pick the defending yacht had been going on, *Shamrock IV's* crew had not been idle. With Captain Albert Turner in charge, the green yacht was also under sail early in the season. Sir Thomas Lipton's 23-meter cutter *Shamrock* was brought over that spring and used as a trial horse to help in the challenger's tuning up. The two yachts were taken down to Sandy Hook and had early spins whenever the weather suited.

In the Cup races *Shamrock IV* was to be sailed by William P. Burton, one of the best-known amateur helmsmen in England. He arrived in the United States early in the season and did much of the work of tuning up the challenger, assisted by Charles Nicholson, her designer. This marked the first time on record that the challenger was to be sailed by an amateur, and as it even then seemed probable that *Resolute* would be chosen to defend, it meant that Burton and Adams, the outstanding amateur skippers of each country, would be pitted against each other. As yacht racing in America had grown from a sport largely in the hands of professional sailors to a strictly amateur sport, it was most fitting that the two Cup yachts should be handled by amateur skippers.

When the two yachts were towed out to the starting line off Ambrose Light-vessel, a little before noon on July 15th, every eye was focussed on them to see how they moved in the light breeze that was coming in from SSW. The wind was hardly strong enough to keep the sails filled, and they moved sluggishly in the smooth sea, but it was black off in the southwest with indications of thunder squalls later in the day.

The course was to be windward and leeward, with the start at noon. Both skippers kept their boats to windward of the line, being afraid of getting caught too far to leeward in the light air, and neither attempted to bother the other. After taking *Shamrock* around the committee boat two minutes before the start and tacking to starboard to cross, Burton found he was too soon, and after luffing he had to come about so as not to be over before the gun. Adams, farther back, had *Resolute* going fast, and he crossed close to the lightship before *Shamrock* was straightened out and going again. So Burton was 58 seconds behind the defender, but as the actual time of crossing was still taken, up to two minutes after the starting signal, it cost him the advantage of position rather than loss of time. However, it was a poor getaway for the series.

Seeing that he was in a bad position, Burton tacked and tried to get clear, but Adams put *Resolute* about also. Then, as they stretched away to the westward on a long leg, came the first real chance to see what they could do. *Shamrock* was footing very fast and drew slowly ahead and out from *Resolute's* lee, but she was either being sailed wide or was sagging off to leeward, whereas *Resolute* seemed to look up at least half a point higher and to fetch where she looked. The wind was fluky and whenever the two boats were apart there was no certainty that they were holding the same breeze.

The wind got so light that both boats took in baby jib topsails and set No. 2 jib topsails. *Resolute* got the advantage of a shift of wind at this time and still further increased her lead. Then came a thunder squall with a deluge of rain, but not much wind. With it, a shift of wind to the southwest headed the boats, and at 12:54 they came about and made a long leg on the starboard tack down the Jersey coast. *Shamrock* was then about half a mile behind. At 1:40 she had closed this up to not over a quarter mile and was sailing fast and overhauling *Resolute* in a failing breeze when Burton made his second mistake. Notwithstanding the fact that he was gaining, was nearly laying the mark, and was holding the same wind as *Resolute*, he tacked inshore, evidently hoping for a stronger breeze, though none was in sight, and held that tack for nearly six minutes while *Resolute* was keeping on about her business. When he came about again he had not only lost nearly half a mile, but he had to bear away to clear Shrewsbury Rocks buoy, which he had stood inside of. It was a most costly tack.

Both boats were standing up nearly straight in the light breeze, and *Shamrock* was being troubled somewhat by the southerly swell. Her flat nose did not take kindly to it, and she would roll out a big wave every time she pitched over a swell.

Burton tried to split tacks when some three miles from the outer mark, in the hope of picking up a more favorable slant, but Adams tacked when the green yacht did so as to keep be-

tween her and the mark. Finally, seeing that he could lay the
mark in the breeze, which was backing to the southeast, he let
Shamrock take a short hitch off shore. As soon as she felt the
increased breeze *Shamrock* commenced to travel, and in the
next ten minutes she showed the best speed of the day, as she
was down to her rail and going very fast. In a few minutes she
slammed about to lay the mark, some half a mile behind the
American boat. As she did so *Resolute's* mainsail seemed to
wrinkle and sag at the throat. The gaff dropped down and
then fell away from the mast, and in a few seconds what had
been a perfect setting mainsail was a bag of canvas draped over
the quarterlifts. *Resolute* was only about one quarter of a mile
from the mark and could lay it easily, so she kept on and jibed
around it with her sail only half up.

Once around, the mainsail was lowered and the staysail
taken in, and she headed back up the coast under jib alone.
Her wire throat halyards had parted at the hoisting winch below decks, and the goose-neck of the gaff had jumped the mast,
making it impossible to reset the sail. What had caused it was
probably the soaking the mainsail had received in the showers,
which made it shrink, and the extra strain proved too much
for the halyard. The wind was of only eight or nine knots'
strength at the time.

Shamrock, coming fast, rounded the mark four minutes and
45 seconds after *Resolute*. She stood over near the disabled
boat and without setting any light sails kept on towards the
finish, on a broad reach, the wind having settled in the southeast. Before she reached the finish another thunder squall was
making up ahead of her and Burton took in his club topsail,
finishing at 4:26:26, or 4:24:58 elapsed time. *Resolute* did not
finish.

The race furnished no real test except to show that both
were fast going to windward in light breezes. *Resolute* seemed
to eat out to windward better, but *Shamrock* footed faster, and

when down to her lines seemed to close up on the defender. The sea bothered her more than it did the *Resolute,* which went through it with no fuss at all. The difference in elapsed time to the outer mark was only three minutes and 47 seconds, and Burton threw away more than this in his one bad tack inshore.

There was some criticism of *Resolute's* crew for not making an effort to finish. The remainder of the race was "downhill" and, after *Resolute's* mainsail had been rolled up, many expected to see her set a spinnaker which, with her headsails, might have still given her a chance, as *Shamrock* was a long distance astern. She would at least have gone down fighting. And in no other race for the *America's* Cup had the defender failed to finish.

An attempt to sail the second race on July 17th, in a light, fluky, shifting wind, was called off at the end of the six-hour time limit.

The outstanding feature of the second race, sailed July 20th, was *Shamrock's* demonstration of her ability to travel in light breezes. It is true that the race was fluky in that the wind favored one boat more than the other; but *Shamrock* had worked into the lead by clever sailing after some bad luck with her light sails at the start, and thereafter got most of the breaks, as the leading boat usually does.

Burton sailed his boat cleverly and with good judgment. The green boat gained on every leg of the course, and while there was no windward work, the shifting wind making the second leg a close reach instead of a beat, she showed herself very fast reaching and running.

There was the usual light breeze to greet the yachts at the lightship, barely four knots' strength at the start at 12:15. The first leg was a broad reach with ballooners, and neither skipper was too anxious to be first over, each being more intent on keeping his wind clear. A minute and a half before the gun

Shamrock tacked to starboard and stood for the line, well clear of *Resolute*. She sent up a balloon jib in stops, and as she crossed it was broken out. But it fouled about 25 feet above the bowsprit and did not fill, while *Resolute*, with her ballooner drawing like a house afire, crossed 38 seconds behind her.

It seemed to take *Shamrock's* crew forever to get the ballooner straightened out, and in trying to do so they tore it badly and it had to be taken in. Burton then set a spinnaker to starboard, but the wind was too far ahead to let it draw, and it did him practically no good. Something had to be done, and done quickly, as *Resolute* was going by to leeward fast, her ballooner drawing beautifully. So a sailor was sent aloft and put a strap around the mast about two-thirds of the way to the lower mast head, into which was hooked a block. Then a small, light sail was set flying from the bowsprit end to this block—a sail that defied yachting sharps to name. It was a very light sail, and with it and the jib topsail filling in the failing breeze they pulled the *Shamrock* along after the *Resolute,* which was now some 500 yards ahead.

In order to get the best out of these two headsails, which did not begin to fill the fore triangle, Burton looked up higher to windward and everyone expected to see Adams edge up there also to keep between *Shamrock* and the mark. This he did not do. As *Shamrock* was holding high on the course Adams may have thought it better judgment to keep on about his business. Soon *Shamrock,* with her two small light sails filling nicely, was closing up on *Resolute* and going out to windward. At 12:50 the wind backed a little and *Resolute's* big ballooner backed and fluttered. But it was sheeted in and Adams hung on to it. *Shamrock* merely got her sheets in a trifle and from then on she walked by *Resolute* fast, opening up a lead of about half a mile and seeming to hold a little air while the American boat was practically becalmed.

Both boats had overstood the mark considerably before they jibed over and headed for the buoy. Every time the green sloop changed tacks she had to lower this reaching sail to get it over the forestay, and set it again on the other side, but she kept her lead and rounded the mark at 2:26:20, just four minutes and 32 seconds ahead of *Resolute,* showing a gain on the leg of three minutes and 54 seconds.

It was a close reach to the next mark, and at first the breeze was very light. Adams kept *Resolute* pointing higher and working up to windward, evidently looking for a freshening breeze to come from the north'ard. Though both boats rolled the wind out of their sails, *Shamrock* continued to increase her lead, until she was something over a mile ahead. Then, at 4:05, a puff came in from the southwest, and, of course, reached the leading boat first. *Shamrock* eased her mainsail across and began to move, close hauled, in the freshening breeze. Five minutes later *Resolute* caught it, but by that time *Shamrock* had still further increased her lead and *Resolute* was farther to leeward.

Down they both came for the second mark, moving better than they had yet done, and *Shamrock* rounded at 4:26:40. *Resolute* rounded nine minutes 10 seconds after the challenger, and began a hopeless stern chase. As the wind hauled to the westward about two miles from the finish *Shamrock* was jibed over, the spinnaker taken in, staysail and jib topsail set, and she headed for the line on a reach, moving very fast. As she crossed amid a din of whistles Burton swung her off close to the lightship and in the best breeze of the day jogged around back of the line, anxiously counting the minutes as the defender came on to see if he had saved his seven minutes and 39 seconds time allowance.

It was apparent after five minutes had passed that *Resolute* could not make it, but she crossed ten minutes and five seconds behind the challenger, losing the race by two minutes and 26 seconds corrected time.

The times:

NAME	FINISH	ELAPSED TIME	CORR'T'D TIME
	H. M. S.	H. M. S.	H. M. S.
Shamrock IV	5 38 06	5 22 18	5 22 18
Resolute	5 48 11	5 31 45	5 24 44

The count now stood two races for the challenger to none for the defender, and it looked as if the Cup had a good chance of going back to the country of its origin. *Shamrock* had only to win once in three possible races to turn the trick.

With the fate of the Cup depending on the third race the crew of each yacht came to the line on July 21st, prepared to put up the fight of their lives—and they did. It was the closest race, boat for boat, that had ever been sailed for the Cup, the two sloops making it a dead heat on elapsed time for the thirty miles, each yacht taking exactly the same time to cover the course. At no time were they separated by more than a quarter of a mile of water. It was also the first race of the series sailed in a true breeze, and although it was light at the start and for some time thereafter, it furnished a good test of the two yachts.

The course was windward and leeward again, 15 miles to a leg, and as the previous races had shown *Resolute* better to windward in light airs, it seemed to be her chance to win. At noon, the starting hour, the breeze was very faint, and the start was postponed. As the wind freshened the preparatory signal was given at 12:45 for a 1:00 start, the course being S by W. The wind was still too light for quick work at the start, but with so much at stake each skipper was on the alert for the best position and watched the other like a hawk. *Shamrock* crossed first, 19 seconds ahead of *Resolute*. The breeze was freshening, and one minute after crossing *Shamrock* came about on the port tack to make a leg in towards the Jersey beach. *Resolute* followed almost immediately.

Shamrock footed faster than *Resolute,* but as in the previous races, *Resolute* seemed to look higher and to eat out to windward. After a long leg inshore *Shamrock* finally came about and *Resolute* crossed her bows, when Adams immediately tacked on Burton's weather, a position that he never relinquished throughout the windward leg, though *Shamrock* tried hard to split tacks with the American boat. Altogether *Shamrock* took 19 hitches in this long beat to windward, and as she was slower in stays than *Resolute* she lost about five seconds each time she came about. By this time the wind was freshening to a good sailing breeze, and when they reached the outer mark *Resolute* rounded one minute 47 seconds ahead of the green cutter.

Both yachts set spinnakers for the run home. As the breeze freshened on the homeward leg the green yacht closed up on the flying *Resolute.* Halfway home she was only some 300 yards astern. Three miles from the finish she was only two lengths astern. Here she began to blanket the defender, smothering her under a towering mass of canvas. Foot by foot the challenger crept up until she had poked her flat nose out in front, and then drew entirely clear. The line was only a mile off, however, and *Shamrock* could not save her time, barring an accident. Slowly lengthening out the open water between them the *Shamrock* swept on, her crew huddled aft, and tore over the line with everything drawing, getting the whistle from the committee boat just 19 seconds ahead of *Resolute.* It was just the margin by which she led at the start, and it meant that both boats had sailed the course in exactly the same time to a second, so that *Resolute* was the winner by just the time of her allowance, seven minutes and one second. *Shamrock* had gained on the 15-mile run just the time she had lost on the beat to windward, two minutes and six seconds.

The times:

NAME	FINISH	ELAPSED TIME	CORR'T'D TIME
	H. M. S.	H. M. S.	H. M. S.
Resolute	5 03 47	4 03 06	3 56 05
Shamrock IV	5 03 28	4 03 06	4 03 06

A day intervened after the third race, and *Shamrock* came to the line fresh from the dry dock where she had had her bottom cleaned and polished in the hope of winning the series on this triangular race, knowing that it was her best chance.

When the two yachts reached the lightship a thick fog had rolled in on the SSW breeze, which hid the line and made maneuvering impossible, so there was another postponement. But by 12:15 the fog had burned away, and though the breeze was still light, some four knots, it gave promise of holding.

The preparatory signal was given at 12:45. Both boats were back of the line at this signal. It was apparent that neither skipper was going to give up the advantage of the weather berth in this crucial race without a struggle, and some of the prettiest jockeying of the series was seen in the next 15 minutes, although as the wind was light it was not very spirited. Just before the whistle *Shamrock* tacked to starboard, and *Resolute* jibed quickly between her and the line. Being nearer the line, she had the advantage of being first over, though *Shamrock* was to windward of her. Adams went close to the stern of the committee boat and then held off a little to get going, while Burton squeezed in around the stern of the tug, also, and shot his boat into the weather berth as he crossed 23 seconds after *Resolute.*

Shamrock was being pinched too much to get going, and *Resolute* drew out ahead, but to leeward. They held this starboard tack for only a few minutes and though *Shamrock* seemed to be holding *Resolute,* and was so close that the latter could not come about and cross her bow, Burton split tacks and headed off towards the Jersey Beach. Whatever his reason for coming about (it may have been that he was afraid of dropping into *Resolute's* wake if he held *Shamrock* off) it was a costly move, for he ran into a soft spot as he tacked and was some time in getting way on his boat again, while *Resolute* held her breeze and stood on two minutes more, then came about a good bit to windward of her rival.

This windward leg was sailed in just three hitches. The wind, except for swinging a point to the southward for a few minutes, held true and was freshening all the time. It was blowing about ten knots when they reached the mark, with whitecaps flecking the tops of the seas, and both boats were down to their lines and traveling better than at any other time in the series. On the last part of the leg the challenger gained perceptibly, but *Resolute* rounded the first mark with a lead of two minutes and ten seconds, the British boat having lost one minute and 47 seconds on the ten-mile beat. She had held *Resolute* better than in any previous windward leg she had sailed.

Again the smarter sail handling of the American boat was in evidence, and 30 seconds after rounding she had broken out and sheeted home a No. 1 jib topsail for the close reach to the second mark, while it took *Shamrock's* crew two minutes and 12 seconds to do the work. The wind had freshened to 12 knots or over, and *Shamrock* began a stirring chase to the second mark. As she did not seem to gain she took in her jib topsail and set a larger one that her crew called the "Yankee," cut for the racing on this side. With this she moved faster in a constantly freshening wind and overhauled *Resolute,* but not rapidly enough to justify any belief that she could save her time. Though she covered the ten miles in 49 minutes, 52 seconds, or at the rate of better than 12 knots, she had only gained 43 seconds on *Resolute* when she jibed around the mark one minute and 27 seconds behind the flying Yankee.

Both boats carried the same sail on the first part of the next leg, though it was a somewhat broader reach. Then began a hectic leg that kept one busy following the shifts of sail on each boat. There was a squall making up ahead, and while it looked bad overhead it did not appear to be very heavy. *Shamrock* got in her jib topsail, and then sent down her big club topsail, it being on the windward side, so that it could be got in easily. *Resolute* first changed to a No. 2 jib topsail and when she saw *Shamrock's* topsail come down she took this jib topsail in. At 3:50 the squall hit and both boats luffed sharply. There was little wind in it, although a sharp shower hid the boats for a time. The rain killed the wind, what was left going to the NW, and while *Resolute* was headed to the westward, *Shamrock* on the other tack drew up to her and actually passed her to windward. But Adams went back to the other tack again and with his club topsail and a baby jib topsail filling nicely, he pulled away again. Burton, knowing it would be a job to set the club topsail again, tried all kinds of headsails, but to no purpose. The wind finally backed to the old quarter, but was much lighter, and *Resolute,* some two miles from the finish, sent up a ballooner and went off to the westward, jibed, and stood for the line. She crossed with ballooner drawing nicely just three minutes and 41 seconds before the green yacht.

Resolute had actually gained two minutes and 14 seconds on the leg.

The times:

NAME	FINISH	ELAPSED TIME	CORR'T'D TIME
	H. M. S.	H. M. S.	H. M. S.
Resolute	4 39 25	3 37 52	3 31 12
Shamrock IV	4 43 06	3 41 10	3 41 10

The fifth race was to have been sailed the next day. The crews of both yachts, and especially of the challenger, had been asking for a good breeze. They found it when they got to the lightship on the morning of the day the deciding race was scheduled—and something more. There was a puffy sou'wester of from 23 to 25-knots' strength, and both boats were under shortened canvas, *Resolute* having only mainsail and jib, *Shamrock* having a single reef with the small working topsail set above it. The sea was lumpy, but as the wind came off the Jersey Beach it was not very rough and conditions were not such as to prevent a race with *real boats*. Yet, after weighing conditions of wind and sea, the Regatta Committee, with the assent of the skippers of both boats, postponed the race for the day, much to the disgust of every true sailor and of the big fleet of excursion boats.

This postponement caused much caustic comment on *America's* Cup yachts, when it appeared that both were so lightly built and rigged that they would not race in what to a 75-foot waterline boat should have been just a good sailing breeze. At the time the race was abandoned a little 30-foot waterline schooner yacht was beating to windward not far from the lightship under full sail. It was not blowing then over 23 knots, and yet either one of the Cup boats would have been taking chances of losing her rig had they been started.

After this fiasco, more unsatisfactory conditions for sailing the last and deciding race could hardly be found than those of July 27th. A light northwest wind inshore that did not have strength to reach the lightship made a postponement necessary until 2:15, at which hour the lightest of airs was coming in from about SSW and the racers were sent off on a long beat to windward for the first leg.

In the breeze of only some four knots' strength, the maneuvering for the start was slow, but was well planned. Both boats were late in reaching the line and did not cross until after the two-minute handicap signal, so that both were timed as crossing at 2:17. Burton, however, put *Shamrock* over first on the starboard tack at the westerly end of the line, with *Resolute* to leeward of him and 40 seconds behind—a clear gain of 40 seconds for *Shamrock*. After two minutes on this tack both boats went about for the Jersey beach. *Shamrock* not only held her lead but increased it, though, as usual, *Resolute* was holding higher. The challenger was looking up better than heretofore, however. Fifteen minutes after the start *Resolute* took a short tack to clear a tow, but was soon back after the green sloop again.

The windward leg, which lasted over three hours, was a repetition of most of the others, except that *Shamrock* held her advantage for a longer time. When she came about inshore the first time, after nearly an hour's sailing, she forced *Resolute* about when they came together, and on the long offshore tack seemed to gain still more. The wind lightened to some three knots, and was very streaky, but about four o'clock *Resolute* got a slant which did not seem to reach *Shamrock*, and she drew out ahead. At 4:08 Adams tried to cross Burton, who was on the starboard tack. Seeing that he could not make it he went back on the old tack again, and 15 minutes later tried it again. This time he got across and tacked on *Shamrock's* bow. With this commanding position he never lost the lead thereafter.

At the mark *Resolute* had a lead of some one-third mile and rounded four minutes and seven seconds ahead of *Shamrock*. In the light breeze neither skipper elected to set spinnakers, but preferred to reach down wind with ballooners. *Resolute* jibed and immediately started to work out to the eastward, but *Shamrock*, knowing she could not save her time if she kept with the defender, eased her sheets, set spinnaker, and worked in toward the shore on the other tack, taking a gambler's chance to find wind. Adams would not let Burton get very far away, however, and jibed and headed over with *Shamrock*.

As *Resolute* neared the finish line *Shamrock* changed her spinnaker in favor of a ballooner again, but could not gain by

it, and as the sun was sinking behind the Highlands *Resolute*
slid over the finish line with ballooner drawing well at 7:52:15,
amid the whistles of those steamers still on hand. She had won
three races in a row after the challenger had taken two, and
she kept the Cup on this side after one of the closest calls
the famous piece of silverware had ever had since it came to
the United States in 1851. She had been cleverly handled in the
last three races, and, undoubtedly, the faster boat under the
conditions had won.

The times:

NAME	FINISH	ELAPSED TIME	CORR'T'D TIME
	H. M. S.	H. M. S.	H. M. S.
Resolute	7 52 15	5 35 15	5 28 35
Shamrock IV	8 05 20	5 48 20	5 48 20

Chapter XVII

FOR NEARLY 10 years after the defeat of *Shamrock IV* there was
no challenge for the *America's* Cup. Sir Thomas occasionally
talked of trying again, but he was getting on toward 80 and,
while other British yachtsmen held back from challenging out
of respect for his "prior claim," his intentions were not taken
too seriously. Then, in May, 1929, came another challenge
from the Royal Ulster Yacht Club in behalf of Lipton and
Shamrock V.

The conditions arranged contained some new features. The
challenge had specified a cutter of 77 feet waterline but the
New York Yacht Club's *America's* Cup committee, headed by
W. Butler Duncan, countered with the suggestion that Sir
Thomas build a yacht to the top rating of either Class J (76 feet)
or Class K (65 feet) under the Universal Rule of Measurement;
that we meet him with one of like rating, and that they race
boat-for-boat, without time allowance. This was virtually what
Lipton had asked for in 1914, and he readily agreed, selecting
Class J.

Though Sir Thomas seemed reluctant to get so far away
from the admiring throngs of New York, he agreed to give up
the old Sandy Hook course and sail in open water off Newport,
R. I. Always an area of fluky, undependable breezes, the old
course off New York had become so over-run with commercial
traffic, and the water so foul with flotsam and jetsam from the
port, that racing there was impractical. Steadier breezes also
normally prevail off the Rhode Island coast. Sept. 13 would

open the series, the first boat to take four races winning the
Cup.

Resolute and *Vanitie* had been racing for years as schooners,
but for the 1929 season had been reconverted by their owners,
E. Walter Clarke and Gerard B. Lambert, to sloops, carrying
jib-headed rigs. The latter, becoming popular on small craft
in the early 1920s, were still untried in yachts of this size. Many
still felt the old gaff rig might be better, and to head off costly
experimentation, the conditions specified that both yachts
carry jib-headed mainsails. A number of other experiments in
the rigs of *Resolute* and *Vanitie* that summer were watched
with special interest.

Meanwhile there was great activity as to potential defenders,
and it turned out to be the first time since 1893, when *Vigilant*
had won the trials from *Colonia, Jubilee,* and *Pilgrim,* that
four boats were built. The "old guard" of the New York Yacht
Club formed two syndicates. One, headed by Winthrop W.
Aldrich as manager and Harold S. Vanderbilt as skipper,
selected W. Starling Burgess, son of Edward and a worthy
successor to his genius, as the designer of its sloop, *Enterprise.*
The other, with Junius S. Morgan as its manager and George
Nichols, who had sailed *Vanitie* in the 1920 trials, as skipper,
went to Clinton H. Crane, veteran designer of successful racing
yachts, large and small, for plans of its *Weetamoe.*

Boston yachtsmen formed a group of which John S. Lawrence
was manager and for which Frank C. Paine (of the Paine family
of *Puritan, Mayflower* and *Volunteer* fame) designed *Yankee.*
Charles Francis Adams, who had defended the Cup in 1920
with *Resolute,* was *Yankee's* skipper, with Lawrence occasionally relieving him when Adams's duties as Secretary of the Navy
called him to Washington. A fourth syndicate, formed in New
York by Landon K. Thorne, Paul L. Hammond, George M.
Pynchon and others, went to L. Francis Herreshoff for the
design of their candidate, *Whirlwind.* L. Francis was **a son of**

Nat who, though now over 80 and past his active designing days, was still a keen observer of the sport and of the activities of the old Herreshoff plant, now under other ownership.

Enterprise and *Weetamoe* were built in the Herreshoff shops at Bristol, R. I.; *Yankee* and *Whirlwind* at Lawley's in Boston. *Whirlwind* had a double-planked wooden hull; the other three were bronze-plated over steel frames and somewhat lighter.

These four yachts, along with *Resolute* and *Vanitie* which did yeoman service as trial horses, had a keen summer of racing right through the final trials. Two of them, *Yankee* and *Weetamoe,* were also to figure prominently in later defense campaigns.

This was the first time in Cup history that all the contenders were designed to rate equally and to race "on the flat," eliminating the time allowances which in the past had confused landlubber followers of the sport, who couldn't see why a boat, finishing ahead of her rival, sometimes turned out to be the loser.

The principal dimensions of the four new defense sloops, and of *Shamrock V,* were as follows:

YACHT	Water-line length (feet)	Overall length (feet)	Beam (feet)	Draft (feet)	Displace-ment (long tons)	Sail Area (square feet)
Enterprise	80	120.9	22.1	14.6	128	7583
Weetamoe	83	125.6	20.3	15	143	7560
Yankee	84	125.5	22.4	15	148	7550
Whirlwind	86	130	21.8	15.5	158	7550
Shamrock V	81.1	119.1	19.8	14.8	134	7540

Comparing the four boats, as they took form in the builders' shops, were rigged, and started sailing, was a fascinating study in naval architecture. *Enterprise* was the smallest but her generous beam and powerful sections kept her from being "dainty," a word that cropped up when the experts got a look at the challenger. *Weetamoe* was all easy lines and soft curves, a hull that promised to move easily through the water, blow low or high. *Yankee* was a big, powerful craft that gave early promise of the heavy weather star she proved to be. *Whirlwind*, with her sharp-sterned hull and deep keel, was the biggest of the lot, and looked, on the stocks, faster than she ever was proved to be. All were true keel boats, but all except *Whirlwind* had small centerboards in their keels—in fact *Enterprise* had two. They were there not so much for the slight extra lateral plane they provided as to balance the boats and make them steer easily under different combinations of sail and weather.

The rigs showed less variety than the hulls. The rule held the sail areas within narrow limits—7550 to 7583 square feet. Mainsails were all triangular, but forward of the mast, except that they were all "knockabouts," with no bowsprits, the rigs were not unlike those of older boats. All had triple headrigs—forestaysail, jib and jib topsail—with the fore and jibstays coming in to the mast at about the same heights they would have on gaff-rigged sloops. They had several sizes of jib topsails, for varying strengths of wind. Genoa jibs were being used on smaller craft, like Six-Meter sloops, by 1930, and the Cup boats experimented with them, but used them only in the lightest breezes. In winds over seven knots, they made the headstays sag off, and set badly, and most of them were of too-light material.

The spinnakers were of the old pattern; with the clew sheeting over the foredeck between mast and stemhead. Double-luffed spinnakers were a brand new idea in a highly experimental stage, and deemed too unwieldy for a yacht 130 feet on deck, though *Enterprise* used one with some success late in the season.

Technological developments in sailmaking and rigging were to change this before the J Class was finished. The 1930 Cup boats, under their triple headrigs for windward work, carried just about the amount of canvas their rating certificates showed —just over 7500 feet. By 1937 *Ranger,* with her parachute spinnaker drawing, was spreading about three times that area.

Even with the small headsails of 1930, Ratsey and Lapthorn cut up something like 10 acres of canvas to make sails for the four Cup boats that year. Independent of but associated with the old sailmaking firm of the same name in England, which made the *Shamrocks'* sails, this sail loft at City Island had nearly a monopoly of sails for the J boats in the '30s, though Prescott Wilson turned out a number of excellent sails for them.

Below decks, the Js of 1930 were not yachts at all—they were aptly described as machine shops. There were no accommodations for afterguards or forecastle hands. The former lived aboard other yachts, while the crews were quartered aboard "houseboats" fitted with comfortable living accommodations. These varied from the hulk of the old Cup candidate *Corona* (ex-*Colonia*), used by *Enterprise,* to that of the coasting schooner *Minas Princess,* for *Whirlwind's* crowd. Between decks, the space was devoted to sail stowage and machinery for the handling of sails and gear, including a battery of halyard and sheet winches, some of which came down from older Cup defenders and other big yachts. Much of the pulling and hauling was done in 1930 by men who rarely saw the race, but took their orders from a mate standing in a hatchway. Navigators' chart desks, minimal pantries where a racing lunch could be served, three "heads," and a couple of bunks where an exhausted or injured man might stretch out, were all the living quarters these huge sloops had.

Pushed by Vanderbilt's energy and forehandedness, *Enterprise* was the first launched, on April 14, just two days after *Shamrock V* had slid down the ways of the Camper and Nicholson yard at Gosport, England. By April 20 *Enterprise* was under sail. *Whirlwind, Weetamoe* and *Yankee* were launched in early May and *Weetamoe* stuck on the ways for a day—an omen of bad luck, according to old sailors' superstition.

Enterprise beat *Resolute* and *Vanitie* in informal races in May on Long Island Sound. The first formal competition was held in mid-June on the Sound by the New York and Sea-wanhaka Corinthian Yacht Clubs. *Enterprise* and *Weetamoe* each won one of the New York series, and *Weetamoe* and *Enterprise* finished one-two both days off Seawanhaka.

From there they moved to Newport where the Eastern Yacht Club of Marblehead, home club of the *Yankee* group, held a three-day series. *Enterprise* won all three, although in one *Weetamoe* finished first, only to be withdrawn because of a starting-line foul. Of the races so far, *Enterprise,* which had the advantage of nearly a month's tuning up before the others were in commission, had won four and *Weetamoe* three. The others had won none.

The official observation races began July 7, over the new *America's* Cup courses which started and finished at a buoy nine miles southeast of Brenton's Reef lightship, off Newport. The four candidates were raced in pairs to simulate actual *America's* Cup match races, the pairings being changed each day. Thirteen such races were completed, in a variety of weather conditions, over the standard 30-mile Cup courses, alternately windward-leeward and triangular.

When the series was over, *Weetamoe* had won five races and been beaten only once, by *Yankee* in a fresh breeze. *Enterprise* had won four but had never been able to beat *Weetamoe*. *Yankee,* winning three, had proved a fast boat in strong breezes, and off the wind, but no match for *Weetamoe* or *Enterprise* up wind or in light going. *Whirlwind* had won her first —and as it turned out her only—race, from *Yankee,* thanks to a favoring fluke in the wind. *Weetamoe,* at this stage, was a strong favorite to defend the Cup.

But Vanderbilt was a hard man to discourage. He and Burgess kept thinking up changes in *Enterprise's* rig, sails and gear that they felt would improve her. Nothing was too minor or too troublesome to try. Vanderbilt's book "Enterprise," published after the races, gives a fascinating account of these improvements, which were too many to enumerate here but which, in the aggregate, made the difference between being winner or runner-up in the struggle for selection. As Vanderbilt later wrote, "A large racing yacht such as *Enterprise* is never finished; never perfect."

When the New York Yacht Club cruise started early in August, they were still shaking down some of *Enterprise's* new tricks. *Weetamoe* won the first run; *Enterprise* took the second when *Weetamoe* fouled out, and *Yankee* won the third. The fourth was a triangular race in a breeze on Buzzards Bay, and a contemporary newspaper account reports it as *"Enterprise's* first clean-cut triumph over *Weetamoe* since June." Looking back, it was the turning point of the campaign, with the Vanderbilt boat now a real threat to *Weetamoe's* chances. *Enterprise* won next day, and then gave *Weetamoe* a hard fight for the Astor and King's Cups. Of the seven races on the cruise, *Weetamoe* and *Enterprise* each won three and *Yankee* one. *Enterprise* was making increasing use of her genoa jib, which improvements in the rigging of her backstays now made it possible to carry on the wind with the luff standing quite straight.

In the meanwhile *Shamrock V* had made port at New London after an uneventful tow across the ocean, and Sir Thomas Lipton arrived in New York by steamer Aug. 17, accompanied by Col. Duncan Neill, his long-time yachting adviser and manager; Captain Ted Heard, a professional who had sailed in all the *Shamrocks* and was skipper of this one; and Charles E. Nicholson, designer, builder, and the real brains of *Shamrock V*. Sir Thomas, at 82, was rather a shock to people who had known him earlier. He was a weak and weary old man. He did his best to put on a good show, cracking his old jokes and expressing his habitual confidence in the final success of his 31-year quest of "the ould mug," but there were moments, aboard his steam yacht *Erin* during the Newport campaign, when he didn't seem quite sure where he was or what was going on. This, for sure, was his last try, and a good many people hoped it would be a winning one.

Shamrock V was refitted at New London, and was well looked over there and later at Newport by the experts. They found her a lovely sloop—in marked contrast to the powerful but ugly *Shamrock IV*—and one promising speed, especially in light going. She was on the small side, compared to the American J Class sloops; closest to *Enterprise* in dimensions, which boosted the latter's hopes of being selected the defender.

The final trials started over the Cup course on Aug. 20. Over the whole season to date, *Enterprise* and *Weetamoe* had won just about an equal number of races, but in their vital two-boat match races *Weetamoe* had always had the upper hand. But *Enterprise* was a faster boat now. *Yankee* was acknowledged the fastest of all in a strong breeze, but only if the trials were all held in heavy weather was she conceded a chance. *Whirlwind* could be ignored. Like *Enterprise,* she had had changes made, but hers did her no good. Whether the cause of her failure lay with the boat, her rig, or the way she was handled, was the subject of some discussion that summer. That fall, she was broken up for scrap.

Enterprise and *Weetamoe* sailed 15 miles to leeward and back, in a breeze rising from six to 12 miles an hour, in the opening trial. *Enterprise* led by a length at the lee mark, and stretched the lead out to about a minute on the beat back, to win her first match from *Weetamoe*. *Whirlwind,* racing *Yankee,* blew out her mainsail.

Next day, in a whistling 25-mile northeast wind and rough

sea, *Enterprise* did it again. Vanderbilt put her over the line
in a perfect start and pulled out a lead of 24 seconds on *Weetamoe* on the first 10-mile reach. Then he hammered his way
10 miles up wind, driving *Enterprise* unmercifully into the
seas while *Weetamoe* repeatedly eased up in the heaviest puffs.
Enterprise led by four minutes at the weather mark and took
it easy on the final reach, on which George Nichols piled sail
on *Weetamoe* but could only cut a minute off *Enterprise's* lead.

That day *Yankee*, in beating *Whirlwind* by 6½ minutes, set
a new record for the 30-mile America's Cup course. Standing
up like a brick church on the gruelling ten-mile beat, the Paine-
designed sloop sailed the 30 miles in 2 hr., 47 min., 59 sec.,
which was 3 minutes 49 sec. faster than *Columbia*, a bigger
boat with twice as much sail, did it in the previous record race
of 1901. Had *Yankee's* people realized at the time that a record
was at stake, they might have cracked on a jib topsail, reaching
for home, and made it even faster. As it was, she averaged 10¾
knots for the course, and sailed the first 10-mile leg at 13¼
knots. *Enterprise* beat the old record too, but not by as much.

That breeze was the start of a three-day northeast storm
which kept the boats in port. A calm followed that, and the
next race wasn't held until Aug. 27, when *Enterprise* raced
Yankee in light airs, and was far ahead of her when the drifting
match was called off.

That night the selection committee named *Enterprise* to
defend the cup. The *Weetamoe* and *Yankee* people felt that
they should have had another chance, but Butler Duncan and
his committee had seen enough to convince them that *Enterprise* and Vanderbilt was their surest combination to beat
Shamrock V.

"Mike" Vanderbilt had won the selection the hard way.
From playing second fiddle to *Weetamoe* up to early August,
he and his afterguard and crew had fought *Enterprise* to the
top of the heap by ceaseless efforts to make her faster and by

fine sailing. Boat and men were honed to a keen edge for the coming job of defending the Cup—a job that was to prove easier than the selection campaign.

Vanderbilt, who was to defend the *America's* Cup three times, must be ranked among the all-time top sailors. He had beaten two of the country's best, Charles Francis Adams and George Nichols, in the trials. He was an excellent helmsman, tactician, strategist and judge of boats and weather. He had, practically from boyhood, always sailed big yachts. Probably plenty of men could have beaten him in small-boat racing classes, but he had what a big-yacht skipper needs; the ability to pick good men to sail with him, to delegate responsibility to them and benefit by trusting their advice and actions, and he was master organizer of racing crews.

Vanderbilt was a man of studious, inquiring, scientific mind, always ready to try any promising experiment. He and Starling Burgess made a perfect team. Burgess was a somewhat erratic genius, but he had all his famous father's gift for progressive yacht design, plus a background of aircraft engineering and aerodynamics which showed up in much of *Enterprise's* gear. Burgess was often amazed at Vanderbilt's quick, complete grasp of obscure engineering theories, and under Vanderbilt's guidance he produced near-miracles. *Enterprise's* 4000-pound duralumin mast and her "Park Avenue" boom, whose broad top and transverse slides allowed the foot of her mainsail to take an efficient aerodynamic curve, were two conspicuous examples. Dozens of lesser features of the rig reduced weight and windage aloft and improved efficiency—all to the credit of the Burgess-Vanderbilt team.

Of the rest of *Enterprise's* afterguard, C. Sherman Hoyt was one of the world's great helmsmen and sail trimmers, who had won international fame in all kinds of racing yachts. Winthrop Aldrich, veteran racing skipper, handled the important post of navigator with ability, and Charles F. Havemeyer was another able yachtsman whose calm efficiency in many important duties took much worry off Vanderbilt's mind.

Nor can we overlook the professional sailing master, Captain George Monsell of Greenport, L. I., who had served under Vanderbilt since the latter's early racing days in the schooner *Vagrant.* Cap'n George was a master hand at putting a crew together, training it to perfection, watching every man's performance of duty, and above all, building up morale and keeping it at top competitive pitch throughout a long, hard series. Monsell and his mate, Harry Klefve, trained *Enterprise's* mixed crew of 20-odd Scandinavian and Yankee yacht hands into one of the best organizations of its kind ever put together.

The two weeks between *Enterprise's* selection and the start of the Cup series was a period of intensive preparation. Yachts and rigs were put in top shape between practice sails. The afterguards of the two contenders amicably looked over each others' yachts, and designers Burgess and Nicholson exchanged views on their work. Riggers and sailmakers swarmed over the boats. *Enterprise* now had an inventory of 50 sails—quite adequate for a yacht that cannot set more than four sails at once.

"Old Mr. Nat" Herreshoff was taken for a sail on *Enterprise* and pronounced her "one of the finest yachts he had ever seen" —lavish praise from this taciturn veteran who had seen them all.

Shamrock wasn't the "mechanical ship" *Enterprise* was—she had far fewer winches and most of the work was done by the sweat and muscle of her British tars. They liked it that way. She didn't have 50 sails, but she had plenty, and, as one of her afterguard pointed out, they wouldn't have as much trouble deciding every morning which sails to take aboard and which to leave on the tender.

The U. S. Coast Guard set up a plan for patrolling the course to prevent interference from the spectator fleet, and from coastwise traffic which might have to be diverted during a race. The Coast Guard pulled in half a dozen big cutters and as many destroyers, plus many smaller craft, off "rum patrol" duty (nobody, probably, enjoyed the week of the Cup races more than the rum-runners). They planned two lines of ships flanking the race at a good distance, with all spectators outside the lines. It was well they did, for the spectator fleet included several big passenger steamers of the "luxury cruise" type, many smaller excursion steamers, big steam and diesel yachts, and hundreds of smaller yachts and fishing craft. Uncontrolled, they would have crowded in on the racing yachts so badly as to prevent a fair race.

The first race was described by a reporter who had followed the selection campaign, as "the dullest race sailed all year." A thin fog and a calm greeted the racing sloops, and the fleet of more excursion vessels and yachts than had ever followed a race off Sandy Hook at the race buoy nine miles offshore. But after an hour or so a light northerly breeze struck in and a course of 15 miles to leeward and return was signalled by the race committee—Edmund Lang, Colgate Hoyt and Philip R. Mallory.

The antiquated two-minute "free" starting interval was no longer in use, and the yachts were timed as starting at the instant the starting signal was made.

With little preliminary maneuvering, Vanderbilt put *Enterprise* over the starting line ahead and to windward of *Shamrock V* and going faster. She continued to go faster. Under spinnakers, they steered offshore. *Enterprise* held a bit higher and sailed farther but considerably faster than the green sloop—the "tacking to leeward" technique. Half-way down the leeward leg *Enterprise* jibed over and presently *Shamrock,* by now nearly a quarter-mile astern of the defender, followed suit.

With the wind hauling more easterly, they took over two hours to make the buoy, having to haul quite sharply on the wind when they sighted it wide off their port bows in the haze. Seeing *Enterprise,* which sighted the buoy first, haul up for it,

Shamrock "cut the corner" a bit. Even so, *Enterprise* rounded one minute, 56 seconds ahead of her.

By now the formerly north wind was out of the northeast, and instead of the intended beat home, both yachts could lay the course for the finish line, though *Enterprise* did have to take one very short hitch at the finish. She continued to pull away from *Shamrock,* and finished a winner by 2 min. 52 sec. Elapsed times were: *Enterprise,* 4 hr., 3 min., 48 sec.; *Shamrock,* 4:06:40. So far, the defender looked like the faster boat, but a race with no windward work in it doesn't prove very much.

The next day—Sunday and hence a lay-day—*Shamrock V* took out a ton of ballast. They sailed the next day over a triangle— a 10-mile beat and two reaches—in a 7-10-mile sou'wester and a sloppy sea and when that race was over the defenders could breathe easy. Barring miracles, the Cup was safe. *Enterprise,* going very fast, started on *Shamrock's* lee bow and sailed away from her. Ted Heard, at the Lipton sloop's helm, tried a series of short tacks, and lost on each tack as *Enterprise* covered her. It appeared to observers that *Shamrock* was being "starved" at times; i.e., her helmsman was sailing her too close to the wind, pointing high but not footing. She rounded the weather mark 5 min. 58 sec. after *Enterprise.*

Reaching down the next leg under balloon jibs, *Enterprise* added another three minutes to her lead, bowling along with her head up and her mainsail, ballooner and staysail drawing nicely. *Shamrock* was slogging into the sea, her bow appearing heavy and failing to lift as it should, and observers criticised the trim of her sails, which appeared to be sheeted in much too flat.

Some time after *Enterprise* rounded the second mark the wind veered more aft, and she broke out a spinnaker. It drew beautifully, but *Shamrock V* didn't bother to set hers. Oddly enough, in spite of that, she lost less than she had on the other

Resolute (white) and *Shamrock IV* starting at Ambrose Lightship in 1920.

Shamrock IV (left) leading *Enterprise* in a 1930 race, one of the few times she was ahead.

Crew relaxes for a moment on *Yankee*.

two legs—apparently because the swell was now from aft and she wasn't diving into it. They finished the race with *Enterprise* 9 minutes 34 seconds ahead. Elapsed times were: *Enterprise*, 4:04:44; *Shamrock V*, 4:10:18.

Enterprise was clearly the faster boat all around. Keen observers of the races, however, felt that *Shamrock V* was a better boat than she had looked, and that if Charles Nicholson were at her helm and in command, she'd make a better showing. But nothing of the kind happened. There were even a few people mean enough to say it was too bad the selection committee hadn't picked *Whirlwind* as the defender—it would have made a more interesting race.

Coming in from that race, it was a miracle that there were no serious accidents. The fog that had been hanging on the racing sloops' mastheads settled down, burgoo-thick, and there were many near-collisions as the several hundred spectator and official craft groped their way back to Newport. The fog kept the yachts in port next day, and *Shamrock V* put back her ton of ballast.

Captain Heard retrieved his reputation a bit next day when, started to windward in a fine 12-mile sou'wester, he outmaneuvered Vanderbilt, who was making one of his well-timed reaching starts. Heard, maneuvering close to the starting line, "laid for" *Enterprise*, made her choose between going over the line before the signal or bearing away under *Shamrock's* stern and, when Vanderbilt elected the latter, planted *Shamrock* neatly on *Enterprise's* wind.

But she didn't stay there. Vanderbilt waited until the British crew were busy hardening in their sheets, snapped *Enterprise* around, and was off with his wind clear before the challenger could cover him. *Enterprise* now ate out to windward. *Shamrock* sagged down onto her quarter and had to tack again to keep out of *Enterprise's* backwind. From there on the defender edged out to windward, while going fully as fast as

Shamrock, until *Enterprise* had what amounted to a two-minute lead.

At this point *Shamrock's* mainsail came fluttering down. She took a tow from her tender and went home, leaving *Enterprise* to sail the course alone. It is racing tradition that if one boat breaks down the other finishes the race. *Shamrock's* wire main halyard had parted at the spot where it made the sharp bend over the sheave at the masthead—a point which sooner or later develops metal fatigue from constant sharp bending under strain. To avoid just such a failure, *Enterprise's* halyard had been renewed several times during the season. *Shamrock V* had used hers once too often.

Next day the final race was sailed in the freshest wind of the series, at 14 knots out of the west northwest, over a triangle. Both yachts hit the line at just about the same moment, but *Enterprise's* afterguard had been keen enough to notice that a two-point shift in the wind, a few minutes before the start, had made the buoy end of the line clearly the windward end. She crossed at that end while *Shamrock* went over close to the committee boat, a little to windward of *Enterprise's* wake but half a dozen lengths astern of her. The defender sailed into the puffs of a freshening breeze first and walked up wind almost a minute a mile faster than her rival, to round the weather mark 9 min. 10 sec. ahead.

With the series in the bag, *Enterprise* took it easy reaching and running on the other two legs, carrying smaller headsails than she would have in a close race and allowing *Shamrock* to cut the lead down to 5 min. 44 sec. at the finish. For all that, *Enterprise's* elapsed time of 3 hr., 10 min., 13 sec. was the fastest that had ever been made over a 30-mile course in an actual race for the Cup, the previous mark having been *Columbia's* 3:13:18 in a race against *Shamrock II* in 1901. *Shamrock* finished this last race in 3:15:57.

Poor old Sir Thomas, viewing the collapse of his hopes from

the deck of the *Erin*—he had never sailed on *Shamrock V*—said, "I willna challenge again. I canna win." When he got back to England, Sir Thomas received a social honor that would have meant a lot to him in earlier years—membership in the Royal Yacht Squadron, which had once blackballed him because he was "in trade." In October, 1931, he died.

The experts who hold post-mortems over yacht races reached the conclusion that *Shamrock V's* wooden hull was probably potentially as fast as *Enterprise's* and that with a better rig and different handling she might have won the Cup, or at least put up a good fight.

Harold Vanderbilt's own theories as to why *Enterprise* beat *Shamrock,* given in his book "Enterprise," are:

"*Sailing to windward:* The luffs of *Enterprise's* headsails, owing to shorter headstays and greater tension thereon, sagged off to leeward much less than *Shamrock V's. Enterprise's* lighter mast and rigging made her stiffer and easier in a sea. *Enterprise* had more efficiently shaped headsails. *Enterprise's* sliding-foot boom allowed the foot of the mainsail to take a correct aerodynamic curve.

"*Sailing free: Enterprise* used sail combinations better suited to conditions. *Enterprise* had more diversified headsails to meet varying conditions. *Enterprise's* afterguard had a greater appreciation of the value of tacking to leeward. *Enterprise's* sliding foot main boom."

Chapter XVIII

SOPWITH CHALLENGES — "RAINBOW'S" UPHILL FIGHT FOR
SELECTION — THE CLOSEST MATCH IN CUP HISTORY

IN THE THREE YEARS following the defeat of the last *Shamrock*
there were rumors of probable challenges for the *America's*
Cup. Several British yachtsmen were mentioned as wanting a
shot at it, and it was no surprise when, early in the fall of
1933, a challenge came from the Royal Yacht Squadron in
behalf of T. O. M. Sopwith.

Mr. Sopwith was well known, by reputation at least, to
yachtsmen in this country, and he shaped up as a worthy opponent. As early as 1912, while barnstorming as a stunt flier
in this country, he had had his baptism of salt water off our
shores by falling into it off Coney Island when one of the stunts
went wrong. He had also driven racing motorboats in this
country. He became a top figure in the infant aviation industry
and the Sopwith firm supplied a major share of British military
aircraft during World War I, and later.

He had taken up sailing, and had won the 1927-30 Twelve-
Meter championships of England. After Lipton's death he
bought and raced *Shamrock V*. So he was well prepared for the
job in hand, and his aviation connections gave him all the
knowledge of that branch of engineering which had helped
Burgess and Vanderbilt make *Enterprise* a winner.

Sopwith would be the first British yacht owner to command
his own boat in an *America's* Cup challenge series. Hitherto
the challengers had been sailed either by professional skippers
or, like Burton in *Shamrock IV,* amateurs representing non-
sailing owners.

With the first rumors that a challenge was on the way, speculation bloomed as to defense. *Enterprise* was out of it, for reasons that go back to an international conference held the winter after the 1930 races, which had adopted new rules to make better boats of the Js. One was a minimum mast weight of 5500 lb., to make the spars more dependable and rigid, and at the same time less expensive, than *Enterprise's* 4000-pound aluminum spar. Another was that the boats should have accommodations for the crew to live aboard, answering the "hollow shell" criticism of the 1930 J boats.

Burgess and Vanderbilt had sharpened up their pencils and figured that the additional seven or eight tons—some of it above deck—would cook *Enterprise's* goose. She just wasn't a big enough boat to take the weight and still have the stability to carry her sail. *Enterprise* never sailed again, though much of her gear and some of her sails helped defend the cup aboard her 1934 and 1937 successors.

Starling Burgess had, on speculation, designed a J boat after the new rules were made in 1931. With a challenge assured for 1934, a syndicate was formed, with "Mike" Vanderbilt as manager-skipper, and Herreshoff's went to work on this new hull. The name selected was *Rainbow*—an omen of fair sailing and better times ahead, Vanderbilt explained hopefully.

Two of the 1930 candidates were still available. Frederick H. Prince owned *Weetamoe*, and she would be altered to meet the new rules. Her lead would be lowered, for added stability, and her new mast would be a duplicate of *Rainbow's*—a possible spare for the new boat in case of accident.

Yankee had been laid up at Herreshoff's for three years. The Boston syndicate that owned her, now headed by Chandler Hovey, had her towed around to Lawley's, and her bow was rebuilt to an improved design by Frank Paine. Her forward sections were made V rather than their old U shape, which gave her a sharper entrance and proved to make her a faster all-around boat than she had been in 1930. A big boat to start with, the extra weight was no problem for *Yankee.*

Ratsey's and Prescott Wilson's lofts got busy cutting new headsails. The old mainsails were all right and there were plenty of them, but everything forward of the mast had to be new and bigger, in line with the improvements in rigs and rigging since 1930. Jib topsails were out. Double headrigs, much taller than the jibs and staysails of 1930, were cut. Genoa jibs, of heavier material and better shape than those of 1930, were standard equipment and used regularly in light and moderate weather. The double-clewed or quadrilateral jib, first used in *Endeavour,* was developed during 1934. Double-luff spinnakers, far larger than the old spinnakers though not quite as voluminous as parachutes were to become, were now standard gear on the J Class sloops.

The terms of the challenge, made public in February, 1934, called for a four-out-of-seven series, off Newport, starting Sept. 15, with conditions much like those of 1930. An innovation was that the challenging club was, for the first time, given the option of naming another boat at any time up to 60 days before Sept. 15. The Royal Yacht Squadron had in mind substituting W. L. Stephenson's *Velsheda* if Sopwith's new *Endeavour* should prove a failure. In the spirit of the new class rules, the professional crews were to live aboard the sloops during the season.

Rainbow's dimensions, when announced, showed her to be, though larger than *Enterprise,* still the smallest of the three defense candidates. She was just enough bigger than *Enterprise* to accommodate the added weights, being 82 feet waterline, 127.3 feet over all, 21 feet beam, 14.6 feet draft, displacing 141.1 tons and carrying 7572 feet of sail.

When *Rainbow* was launched at Herreshoff's, May 15, *Endeavour* was already sailing. At first the British experts shook their heads and said the challenger wasn't as fast as the older

Velsheda, but they had to change their tune before long.

By late May, *Rainbow* was beating Gerard Lambert's old *Vanitie* in trial spins. Sherman Hoyt and Starling Burgess were again in Vanderbilt's afterguard, along with John Parkinson, who had sailed in *Vanitie* in 1920 and *Weetamoe* in 1930, and Professor Zenas Bliss of Brown University, navigator. Charles Francis Adams was again at *Yankee's* helm, while Richard de B. Boardman, another top Boston skipper, sailed *Weetamoe* for Frederick Prince. In Boardman's afterguard was a lad in his early twenties, learning about *America's* Cup racing, in which he was to be heard from again—Olin J. Stephens.

The preliminary race series for the Cup boats started June 16, with the boats racing in pairs. *Vanitie* did her earnest, elderly best to give one of the newer boats a race each day while the other two went at each other. It was a helpful series for tuning-up purposes. *Rainbow* beat *Weetamoe* four times and lost a race each to *Yankee* and *Weetamoe*. *Yankee* had beaten *Rainbow* once and split a pair with *Vanitie*. *Weetamoe* had beaten *Rainbow* and *Vanitie* once each, and lost four to the new Vanderbilt boat.

The observation races, which followed a period of tuning up and overhaul, were rather unsatisfactory, with not a single good sailing breeze. *Yankee,* however, emerged from this series as the outstanding boat, having beaten *Rainbow* and *Weetamoe* four times each.

In two months racing, *Rainbow* had now beaten *Yankee* only twice—once on a disqualification and once by a fluke in a drifting-match that went over the 5½-hour time limit. *Yankee* was now a better boat to windward and in lighter breezes than she had been in 1930. *Weetamoe,* while not as sad a case as *Whirlwind* in 1930, had been unable to beat anyone important. Her changes apparently had done her little good.

Rainbow, definitely second choice so far, like *Enterprise* in 1930, had become a beehive of activity and a laboratory of experimentation. The Vanderbilt-Burgess team was at it again. Though regularly beaten by *Yankee,* the time margins had been small. If they could just make *Rainbow* a couple of minutes faster over a 30-mile course, they still had a fighting chance. They experimented with her ballast. They had bigger headsails made to give her more driving power. They gave her a flexible boom, which could be mechanically bent into an aerodynamic curve and which they considered even better than the old Park Avenue boom. They left nothing untried in this second up-hill fight for selection.

Meanwhile, the challenger arrived and was being hauled and rigged at Herreshoff's. She attracted much favorable comment, even from "Old Mr. Nat" Herreshoff himself. Without doubt, she was one of the handsomest and slipperiest-looking J boats anyone had ever seen. Her light rigging, reflecting the aircraft influence, held up the tallest mast in the J fleet.

Once tuned up, *Endeavour* had clearly proved faster than *Velsheda* and the other big British cutters. There was one big "if" in her prospects. Shortly before she left England, most of her professional crew had struck for higher wages. Bitterly disgusted with what he regarded as a hold-up, Sopwith let them stay struck, and filled up his crew from among a lot of husky, enthusiastic young amateur sailors who were anxious to take part in the match. Several of these made the ocean passage, along with nine loyal professionals, and Captain George Williams reported favorably on them. They had the spirit, and they were experienced sailors in smaller yachts. It remained to be seen how their muscles and hands would stand up under the back-breaking, hand-tearing work of handling the gear of so big a yacht, with its heavy sails, tremendous forces, and wire sheets.

Like *Enterprise* in 1930, *Rainbow* showed improvement on the New York Yacht Club cruise. *Yankee* and *Weetamoe* split the first places on the first four runs of the cruise, but *Rainbow,* after taking in extra ballast, beat them both in the Astor and King's Cup races which wound up the cruise. However, analyzing the season's results to date on the standard point basis—a point for finishing and a point for every yacht beaten—*Yankee* had 22 points to *Rainbow's* 16. *Weetamoe's* point score was 14 —two less than the old reliable *Vanitie*. So the final trial series started with *Yankee* the favorite.

Rainbow took the first trial race from *Weetamoe,* but was paired with *Yankee* next day and beaten by 15 minutes in light weather—*Yankee's* former bane. The two boats ran the 15 miles to leeward on even terms, but Adams made the better turn at the buoy and worked into the leader's usual better luck beating home. Then *Yankee* and *Rainbow* each beat *Weetamoe* again, and the Cup committee eliminated *Weetamoe* from further consideration.

In the next race *Rainbow* beat *Yankee* by over three minutes, in light airs. The next one, in a fresher breeze, saw *Yankee* well out ahead of *Rainbow* when the jumper strut on *Yankee's* mast broke and she had to drop out. It was more than a strut that broke in that race. It came out later that if *Yankee* had won that day, the Cup committee would have named her the defender. But the breakdown, added to some earlier gear failures and a few tactical errors, shook their confidence, and the series went on. *Rainbow* added greatly to her stature in the committee's eyes next day by beating *Yankee* 2 min. 21 sec. in a fresh breeze.

The next race was a thriller. *Yankee* split her genoa jib and as a result was a minute and a half behind *Rainbow* at the weather mark, but she ran home faster, both boats carrying parachutes before a good breeze. They crossed the finish line overlapped, with *Rainbow* a winner by just one second. Had they had another 50 yards to go, *Yankee* would have won. Yet that evening they were notified that *Rainbow* was selected.

It was a bitter pill for *Yankee's* afterguard, for they regarded that one-second defeat as a moral victory, considering the earlier mishap, and were sure that they had the faster boat.

But, as in 1930, the selection committee had seen enough to convince them that Vanderbilt and his boat and organization was the safer bet to defend the Cup. With the boats so evenly matched, this seesaw series might have gone on indefinitely, had they not settled it on that one-second finish. And the defender had to be prepared for the match. There was plenty to be done.

Rainbow borrowed a particularly good mainsail from *Weetamoe,* making ten mainsails in her sail locker, which at $8,000 or so per mainsail represented a tidy investment in canvas. Most of them had been *Enterprise's.*

The worried look that Harold Vanderbilt had been wearing all season remained on his face. *"Endeavour* is a fast boat—a very fast boat," he remarked frequently. Everyone who saw her sailing or hauled out—including "Old Mr. Nat" Herreshoff who took a good look at her when she came up on his railway for a bottom job—shared that opinion. But there was one remark that you heard around Newport, and Bristol and the New York Yacht Club—"Mike beat one faster boat, *Yankee.* Maybe he can do it again against *Endeavour."* Prophetic!

Endeavour was sailing daily, and held several long starting practice drills with *Vanitie,* which Gerry Lambert had offered as a trial horse. Yachtsmen who saw them at it off Brenton's Reef came in saying Lambert was making all the best of the starts, which was encouraging. The British boat was having blister trouble with the paint on her bottom—she was all steel, as against *Rainbow's* steel topsides and smooth, bare bronze bottom—but that didn't reassure anyone much.

Sopwith's afterguard consisted of Mrs. Sopwith, Charles E. Nicholson, Frank Murdoch, an aviation engineer who had designed much of *Endeavour's* rig, and Gerald Penny. His mixed crew of 12 pros and 14 amateurs were shaping up well. The more you saw and heard of the big blue sloop, the better she looked. *Endeavour* was a trifle larger boat than *Rainbow* in every dimension except sail area, which was practically identical, as it had to be under the Universal Rule.

Their dimensions were:

YACHT	Water-line length (feet)	Overall length (feet)	'Beam (feet)	Draft (feet)	Displace-ment (long tons)	Sail Area (square feet)
Rainbow	82	126.7	21	14.6	141.1	7572
Endeavour	83.3	129.7	22	14.9	143.1	7561

The day before the first race Vanderbilt and Sopwith posed together for movie cameramen at the Ida Lewis Yacht Club. "We don't really wish each other good luck, you know," the British skipper remarked, "but we *can* wish each other 'no bad luck'." Final instructions were issued aboard Commodore Junius Morgan's flagship, *Corsair,* by the race committee, Edmund Lang, E. Vail Stebbins and Clinton MacKenzie. The war was on!

The first attempt to hold a race—though it fizzled when the 5½-hour time limit ran out with the leading boat still half a mile short of the finish, bred a false confidence in the Americans who saw it. And plenty of them did. It was estimated that 10,000 spectators were aboard the fleet, ranging from big passenger liners to lobstermen's open launches, which ranged along outside the Coast Guard patrol lines. That fleet made the seascape look like a distant view of a big city against the skyline.

In a light easterly breeze, the course was 15 miles to windward and return. After the warning gun Sopwith decided to shift from working headsails to a genoa, one of which *Rainbow* was carrying, and that delay resulted in the challenger starting almost a minute late. Vanderbilt covered her, tack for tack, in a breeze that never blew over eight knots, and at the weather mark *Rainbow* led by 2 minutes, 46 seconds. Running back, *Rainbow's* light parachute pulled better than *Endeavour's* heavier one and she gained steadily. But the wind slowly died, and when the committee boat's whistle signalled "Race Off," the defender, now three-quarters of a mile ahead of *Endeavour,* was still half a mile from the finish.

The defenders would have liked to have had that victory in their pockets to start the series off, but they were encouraged by the fact that the British boat, while showing plenty of speed at times, had been slower in handling sail, and not as smart tactically as *Rainbow.* The race, however, had given Sopwith and his crew valuable experience in the use of the genoa jib, which was practically unknown on yachts of this size in England —in fact. the one *Endeavour* carried had been borrowed from *Vanitie.*

Two days later they sailed the first completed race, and that was another story. In a 16-mile breeze and rough sea, one of *Endeavour's* men was hurt while aloft in a boatswain's chair freeing the main halyard, which had fouled on the spreaders in the heavy pitching on the tow out to the buoy. The race committee saw the accident and signalled a 15-minute postponement. It was a sporting gesture, if a bit out of line with a strict interpretation of *America's* Cup racing rules and customs, and it made it possible for the challenger to get a perfectly timed start.

Her sails weren't quite sheeted home, however, and by the time her mainsail, staysail and "quad" jib were trimmed properly *Rainbow,* carrying the same sail combination, was up on her weather quarter and going fast. It was a nip-and-tuck battle up wind, with both boats plunging into the head sea. First one, then the other, appeared to have the advantage, but *Endeavour* came up with a rush near the buoy. She rounded it 18 seconds after *Rainbow* and the latter luffed sharply to prevent the challenger passing her then and there.

Rainbow's crew, as usual, made a faster job of setting her parachute spinnaker, but once the sloops were squared away with spinnakers drawing *Endeavour* outsailed the defender in no uncertain manner. She passed well to windward of *Rainbow* and, 20 minutes after rounding, was clear ahead of her and going away. Vanderbilt tried tacking down wind, and other maneuvers, but the blue challenger swept across the finish line 2 minutes, 9 seconds in the lead. The elapsed times were: *Endeavour,* 3 hr., 43 min., 44 sec.; *Rainbow* 3:45:53.

The second completed race was a fast one over a triangle in a raw, damp, 14-mile northwest wind and a long swell. They got away to an even start, and for half an hour, as they sped along under genoa jibs, it was hard to say which was going the faster, but, inch by inch, the blue hull drew ahead of the white one, to lead by a length of open water at the first turn. On the second leg, a beat with both boats carrying quad jibs and sailing fast, Sopwith covered *Rainbow's* every tack and edged out to weather of her so that at the weather turn *Endeavour's* lead amounted to a minute and a half. Slow sail handling in shifting back to genoa jibs, and a lightening of the breeze which *Rainbow* seemed to like better than *Endeavour,* cost the latter some 40 seconds of her lead on the last leg, but the result was never in doubt. The elapsed times were: *Endeavour,* 3:09:01; *Rainbow,* 3:09:52.

Both yachts had bettered the former *America's* Cup race 30-mile course record set by *Enterprise* just four years earlier—*Endeavour* by one minute 12 seconds, *Rainbow* by 21 seconds. *Endeavour* was now half-way to victory—only two more wins needed—and those responsible for keeping the *America's* Cup in America were pretty glum. As Vanderbilt put it, "Perhaps it would be a good thing for the sport to have the Cup cross the Atlantic . . . still I hated to go down in history as the first skipper to lose it."

The third race was started in a six-mile breeze from northeast by east and, to quote the defending skipper again, "This was in many ways the most startling race I have ever sailed—a constantly changing panorama of breaks and mistakes."

The two yachts went over the starting line side by side, and the *Rainbow* crew's quicker spinnaker setting gave her a fleeting lead. But once her kite was drawing the big blue Britisher walked off and left *Rainbow* as if the latter were aground. Vanderbilt held high, to port of the course, for a faster sailing angle and a possible break if the wind, as seemed likely, shifted through east into the south. It shifted enough so they both substituted balloon jibs for spinnakers, but *Rainbow* trailed *Endeavour* around the lee mark by 6 minutes, 39 seconds.

When *Endeavour* rounded, the wind was enough into the east so she could steer within two points of the course to the finish, on the starboard tack. By the time *Rainbow* rounded and set her genoa, it had shifted more and she could lay the finish line. *Endeavour* was a little on *Rainbow's* lee bow, but so far ahead that it seemed nothing but a flat calm and the time limit could save *Rainbow* another licking. Vanderbilt turned the wheel over to Sherman Hoyt and went below to drown his sorrows in coffee and sandwiches. Fifteen minutes later he was back on deck, looking at a new yacht race.

Endeavour may already have been losing a little ground to *Rainbow,* which in that light air was carrying a much better-setting genoa jib than the one the challenger had borrowed from *Vanitie*—the only one she had. It wouldn't have mattered, though, except that *Endeavour* ran into one of those local calm spots common in light, fluky weather. Sopwith looked back and saw *Rainbow* coming up on his weather quarter, and decided to tack across her bow and cover her—not realizing, apparently, that both boats would be able to lay the finish line on the tack they were on.

Endeavour came about very slowly, crossed *Rainbow's* bow and tacked again. Two tacks in this drifting air almost completely killed the big boat's headway. With *Rainbow's* crew lying along her lee rail to heel her enough to keep her sails asleep, and with Sherman Hoyt putting all his skill as a helmsman into steering her, *Rainbow* ghosted through the almost motionless *Endeavour's* lee and out ahead. The British boat, gathering way very slowly, sagged down to leeward and presently she had to make another short tack to keep out of the defender's backwind. And that was the boat race! *Rainbow* held on, worked through the flat spot into a steadier breeze, and crossed the finish line a winner by 3 minutes, 26 seconds. The elapsed times were: *Rainbow*, 4:35:34; *Endeavour*, 4:39:00.

At Sopwith's request, the committee declared the next day a lay day, partly to give both crews a needed rest, partly to allow time for a new genoa jib, being made for *Endeavour* by Ratsey at City Island, to be delivered.

Rainbow now had one race won—or rather, one handed to her by her rival's mistake, for *Endeavour's* four unnecessary tacks must have cost her 15 minutes—but there was no assurance that she could win another. That evening Vanderbilt hollered for help. Frank C. Paine, designer and sail-trimming officer of *Yankee*, had made that yacht do wonders under her parachute spinnaker. *Rainbow* had been using a 'chute supposed to be a duplicate of *Yankee's* but Vanderbilt was now convinced that either it was not as effective a sail or *Rainbow's* people weren't getting the most out of it. That night a phone call went through to Paine in Boston, an urgent invitation from Vanderbilt, via Jack Parkinson, to join *Rainbow's* afterguard. Paine had been sadly disappointed when the committee had selected *Rainbow* over his beloved *Yankee*, but he was no sorehead. Next morning he drove down to Newport, with *Yankee's* best spinnaker in the back of his car. As another measure of desperation, Vanderbilt had two more tons of ballast stowed in *Rainbow's* bilges—just about all she could take without putting her over her rating limit.

Rainbow evened the series next day in a way that suggested both her extra ballast and her new sail-trimmer were doing her good, but it was a race that stirred up international ructions with the first protest that had developed in an *America's* Cup race since the days of Lord Dunraven, back in 1895.

The race, over a triangle, started in an 11-knot breeze. At the end of some very close-quarters maneuvering behind the line, *Rainbow* started on *Endeavour's* weather bow, in an ideal position to backwind the challenger. This advantage she was able to hold for 10 miles up wind, covering the British boat's every tack closely and giving her no chance to get clear. Coming up to the mark, however, Sopwith was so close up on *Rainbow's* weather quarter that the latter couldn't tack around the buoy without fouling *Endeavour*. This enabled Sopwith to "ride her off the mark" and he carried the defender several lengths past the buoy, then tacked and rounded it 23 seconds ahead. The British crew, however, was slow setting their genoa, and within a few minutes *Rainbow* was passing *Endeavour* to windward.

Under the racing rules then in force, if an overtaken boat is being passed to windward, she may luff up into the wind to prevent the windward boat getting by her, provided she could, by holding her luff, strike the weather boat forward of the mast, but *not* if the point of contact would be abaft the mast. Sopwith threw *Endeavour* into a sharp luff, but Vanderbilt didn't change course by so much as wheel-spoke. Rather than cut the white sloop in two, Sopwith bore off. Nobody will ever be sure whether *Endeavour* could have hit her rival forward of the mast or not. Sopwith thought he could; Vanderbilt thought he couldn't. It was purely a question of judgment, incapable of final proof except by actual contact, which in 140-ton yachts in a fresh breeze is unhealthy.

Incidentally, it is largely through Vanderbilt's efforts that this rule has since been altered so that the determination of the

Rainbow leading *Endeavour* in 1934.

Rosenfeld photo

Ranger leading Endeavour II in 1937. Note the quadrilateral jibs.

critical point is now a matter of observable fact rather than personal judgment.

Rainbow swept past, rounded the second mark a minute ahead of *Endeavour,* and added 15 seconds to her lead reaching home. She was reaching better, and Vanderbilt credits this and subsequent improvements in *Rainbow's* down-wind performance to the sail-trimming of Frank Paine, whom Vanderbilt, in his second book, "On the Wind's Highway," calls "Saviour of the *America's* Cup, 1934."

Sopwith finished the race with a red protest flag flying in his rigging, and that evening handed the race committee two written protests, one based on the luffing incident, the other on another occurence in the close maneuvering before the start. The next day, a Sunday with no race, he was notified that the race committee declined to hear the protest, because his red flag had not been displayed immediately after the alleged foul.

This quite understandably enraged Sopwith and the British contingent. The rules state that a protest flag should be displayed as soon as possible after an alleged foul has been commited, but this technicality is commonly honored more in the breach than in the observance. Sopwith had felt that showing the flag at the finish would be enough, and the New York Yacht Club's observer aboard *Endeavour,* C. F. Havemeyer, concurred. The committee was widely criticized at the time for being stuffy about the matter, and for using a technicality to save the American boat from disqualification. They didn't grin, but they bore it in silence.

Along about Christmas time, when the flames of this hassle had died down to sullenly glowing embers, the committee made a statement that explained its action. In the close-quarters maneuvering before the start, they, from their bridge, had clearly seen a violation of the port-starboard tack rule by *Endeavour.* Had the matter come to a hearing, the committee, on its own evidence, would have had to disqualify *Endeavour* for that first foul, long before the luffing incident occurred, and a boat that has already fouled out cannot disqualify another. The committee felt that the course it took would, of the two alternatives, cause less international unpleasantness, and grimly "took the rap" for its decision. No one who knew Chairman Ed Lang or his two associates on the race committee, Vail Stebbins and Clinton MacKenzie, would ever question either their intentions or their impartial application of the rules.

So the series stood even, two races to two, and with no love lost on either side they went out for the fifth race, 15 miles to leeward and back in a fresh northeaster. Vanderbilt describes this race as "the only decisive defeat we administered during the series." Again the two boats went over the line side by side, and again *Rainbow* pulled out ahead while *Endeavour's* crew were fumbling with their spinnaker. But this time *Rainbow* kept on gaining, a fact which Vanderbilt credits to Frank Paine's selection and trimming of spinnakers.

Halfway down wind *Rainbow's* spinnaker ripped badly at the foot and, while setting a new one, they decided to jibe. In jibing, the boom hit the lee backstay and the boatswain, Ben Bruntwith, who was just releasing the backstay jig, was knocked overboard. Ben, most of the time underwater, hung onto the end of the backstay whip like death to a dead mule; several of his shipmates grabbed the other end of the whip and hauled on it, pulling Ben out of the water like a jigged mackerel, and in 30 seconds he was back on deck. Had he let go the backstay, the time lost in rescuing him would have cost *Rainbow* the race. As it was, eight minutes from the time the spinnaker started to rip *Rainbow* had jibed, retrieved her boatswain, set a new spinnaker, and was still ahead of *Endeavour*. She led at the lee mark by 4 minutes, 38 seconds. The challenger could gain back only 37 seconds of this in the 15-mile beat home, and for the first time *Rainbow* led in the series, three races to two. The elapsed times: *Rainbow*, 3:54:05; *Endeavour*, 3:58:06.

The final race, in a way, characterized the whole series—a faster boat being beaten by a better-sailed boat, with a futile display of protest flags thrown in for bad measure. The breeze was moderate northeast and for almost the first time in ten days of gray, dour, overcast weather the sun came out. Before the start the two skippers circled each other like a couple of fighting dogs in a pit—you could almost hear them snarling. Protest flags were up on both boats before the starting signal, but just what incident in the close-quarters maneuvering brought them up never came out for, in the cool of the evening after they got back into port, both skippers withdrew their protests.

Sopwith had the better of it, and went over the line 48 seconds ahead of *Rainbow* on a reach for the first mark. *Rainbow* gained at first, and *Endeavour* luffed her head to wind (*Rainbow* responded promptly this time) to keep from being passed. As they filled away again the blue boat picked up her heels and started to go, and at the end of the 10-mile reach she rounded the buoy with a lead of a minute and eight seconds.

Sopwith was roundly criticised for a breach of sound match-racing tactics in that, shortly after rounding, he failed to cover *Rainbow* when she took a tack to the eastward. But he probably risked it because experience had shown that *Rainbow* with her faster-working crew could short-tack the British boat to death by superior sail-handling. *Rainbow* was carrying a staysail and quad jib, *Endeavour* a genoa which would take her crew much longer to sheet down after each tack.

A mile or two to the eastward, *Rainbow* tacked again, and both held a long board to the northward. And as so often happens when the leading boat in a match leaves the other uncovered, the trailing *Rainbow* got a break. The wind hauled gradually more to the eastward, letting them up, which shortened the distance for *Rainbow* and made *Endeavour* sail around the long rim of the arc as they headed up toward the mark. When she finally did tack, *Endeavour* crossed a quarter-mile under *Rainbow's* stern, and at the weather mark the defender led by 2 min. 47 sec.

If they'd had 15 miles to run to the finish, the challenger still might have won, for once squared away with their big parachute drawing she outfooted *Rainbow* all the way. In the 10 miles of the last leg she regained most of her lost ground, but she still finished 55 seconds astern. The elapsed times were *Rainbow,* 3:40:05; *Endeavour,* 3:41:00.

Thus ended the closest shave the New York Yacht Club has yet had, in over 100 years tenure of the *America's* Cup, to losing that trophy. Charles E. Nicholson had designed the fastest Class J sloop ever seen up to that time, and Mike Vanderbilt and his afterguard and crew, by magnificent competitive sailing and with the aid of a little bit of luck, had beaten her.

One contributing factor to the slowness of the challenger's sail handling became evident when, the night after the last race, the amateurs of her crew came ashore. To a man, the palms of their hands were a mass of raw meat and blisters. That they ever hauled on a rope at all, those last few days, was a feat of courage. At that, they had handled the gear as fast as *Shamrock V's* professionals had done four years before.

As for *Rainbow's* horny-handed forecastle gang, they didn't come ashore until late next morning. As Captain Monsell—a teetotaller himself—told it, that night when they were notified that the protests were withdrawn and it was all over, every man jack of them produced a bottle from somewhere—everything from Scotch to aquavit. They poured it all into the cook's big kettle and went to work on it. When they did straggle up the dock next morning they were a sick-looking lot of heroes, but they were still grinning from ear to ear, and every one of them was singing the praises of the skipper who had steered them to victory.

There was no great effort to save weight in *Galatea's* palatial accommodations. Compare with next picture.

Ranger's spartan accommodations.

Chapter XIX

"RANGER," LAST AND FASTEST OF THE CLASS J SLOOPS

ANGRY AS SOPWITH had been after the race committee declined to hear his protest in the fourth race of 1934, he had cooled off considerably by the time he sailed for home a week or two after the series, and he left with a promise to come back and try again. He raced *Endeavour* in 1935 in the then-active class of big British cutters, and one of his rivals that year was *Yankee*, which Gerard B. Lambert had bought and taken abroad for what proved a fairly successful season's racing.

For the 1936 season, Charles E. Nicholson designed a new *Endeavour II*, a big, powerful J boat which proved faster to windward than even the first *Endeavour*, and fully as fast off the wind. The new boat carried away two steel masts that season, indicating that even the new 5500-lb. minimum was too light for a J of her size and power, so a new mast rule was agreed upon, with weights and diameters somewhat higher, varying with the dimensions of the boat. For an 87-foot water-line sloop like *Endeavour II*, the minimum weight came to about 6300 pounds.

The expected challenge came in mid-summer of 1936, while *Rainbow*, now wholly owned by Vanderbilt; *Yankee*, Gerard Lambert, and *Weetamoe*, Chandler Hovey, were racing on the Eastern and and New York Yacht Clubs cruises, and dividing honors fairly evenly.

It was obvious that there would have to be a new defender. *Endeavour* had been a faster boat than *Rainbow* in 1934, and while the latter, judging by her showing against *Yankee* and *Weetamoe* in 1936, was now, thanks to ballast and rig changes, a trifle faster than she had been in '34, the new *Endeavour II* was faster than her older sister.

She was also a bigger boat—Nicholson had gone to the limit in size under the J Class rules—and the New York Yacht Club couldn't afford to risk meeting her with an old or a smaller boat. The dimensions of the 1937 rivals, when they were measured for the Cup races, were:

YACHT	Water-line length (feet)	Overall length (feet)	Beam (feet)	Draft (feet)	Displace-ment (long tons)	Sail Area (square feet)
Endeavour II	87	135.8	21.5	15	162.6	7543
Ranger	87	135.2	21	15	166	7546

The new *America's* Cup Committee appointed by Commodore W. A. W. Stewart turned to Harold S. Vanderbilt as the logical man to head up a new defender. For the design, Vanderbilt worked out a collaboration of the veteran Starling Burgess and 29-year-old Olin J. Stephens, rising young star in the racing yacht design field—a combination of talent that produced the finest Class J yacht the sport has ever seen.

At this point the Stevens family, of *America* fame, turns up again in the *America's* Cup picture, for it was in the new model-testing tank at Stevens Institute of Technology in Hoboken, N. J.—named for and founded by that same Stevens family—that the defender's model was selected. Burgess and Olin Stephens designed four different sets of lines, models of which were built and tested in the tank. Tank tests of hulls—principally steamship hulls—were nothing new, but under Professor Kenneth S. M. Davidson's inspired direction the Stevens tank had developed new techniques which gave reliable results on the performance of sailing-yacht hulls at all combinations of heeling angles, wind strength and wind angles. The four models were tested against each other and against models of *Enterprise, Rainbow* and the first *Endeavour,* whose lines

Nicholson had made available. The tests clearly pointed to the superiority of one of the four models—which became *Ranger.* One surprising discovery from these tests was that the new 87-foot waterline model proved faster than any of the smaller boats not only in fresh to strong winds, as expected, but also in lighter breezes, which was contrary to accepted theory.

Efforts to form a syndicate in the New York Yacht Club to finance the new boat found the members backward about coming forward with the funds—there seemed to be a widespread "let Mike do it" sentiment on this subject. Mike did. Along about October, Vanderbilt made up his mind to go it alone. For a name he went back to the early American Navy's successful vessels, like *Enterprise,* and called the new one *Ranger,* after John Paul Jones' ship which had made things so tough for the British during the Revolution. No more "Rainbows in the Sky," after 1934's uphill struggle! Vanderbilt was the first individual owner of an *America's* Cup defender since General Paine with *Volunteer* in 1887. All actual defenders in between had been syndicate-owned boats, although there had been some privately-owned candidates in the trials.

There was a new afterguard, too. Zenas Bliss, Jr., *Rainbow's* navigator, was the only veteran—youth was the keynote. The other members would be Olin Stephens, his brother, Roderick, Jr., 27, and Arthur Knapp, Jr., 31. Mrs. Vanderbilt officially shipped as observer and member of the board of strategy—the first woman to sail on a defender in the Cup races. Mrs. Sopwith, of course, had sailed in *Endeavour.*

Construction was contracted for with the Bath Iron Works, in Maine. The new boat was to be of steel, saving several tons off the weight of an equivalent bronze hull, and Bath was famous for its steel construction. *Ranger* was the first Cup defender built elsewhere than in the old Herreshoff plant since 1890.

Rainbow was towed to Bath, where all her gear that could

be used on the new boat—including some Herreshoff winches
and hardware that dated back to *Reliance* of 1903—was stripped
off. With the exception of a new duralumin mast and standing
rigging of solid bar steel instead of conventional wire, *Ranger*
was to be "a well-tried old rig in a new hull." All this represented economies and, coupled with the fact that Bath Iron
Works built the hull practically at cost and Burgess and the
firm of Sparkman and Stephens pared the usual designing fees
considerably, tempered the financial wind to *Ranger's* owner
somewhat. No cost figures were ever given out, but credible
estimates at the time placed the first cost of the new boat at
between $150,000 and $200,000 and the over-all cost of the
racing season at under half a million. In 1930, one of the four
syndicates had spent over $900,000 before their boat was finally
eliminated in the trials.

   Ranger was launched at Bath on May 11—a beautifully
smooth job of steel plating—and three days later Vanderbilt's
diesel yacht *Vara* towed her down the Kennebec River with
flags flying, whistles giving her a send-off, and her new dural
mast and bar rigging standing bravely aloft. Next morning she
was a mess!

   Towing down the coast in a quartering swell, with her
forestaysail set to steady her, all went well until midnight when
her crew heard a clanging noise aloft and found that one of the
upper rigging spans, between the second and third spreaders,
had carried away—why or how no one ever found out. With
70 feet of it thus unsupported, the 165-foot spar started to sway
a little. Every roll made the remaining rigging slack up and
spring taut. Turnbuckles and lock-nuts began to back off with
this motion. One by one the bar shrouds worked loose. *Vara*
tried to tow her into Gloucester before the whole business
went over the side, but dawn showed the upper 130 feet of the
spar unsupported and whipping madly to port and starboard
as she rolled, the rigging hanging loose and clanging like a

boiler factory. Metal fatigue had its inevitable result. The mast snapped just above the lower spreaders and went over the side. *Ranger's* crew, who had stood by for hours with the tools in their hands, swarmed on deck and freed what rigging still held the wreckage to the ship, to save the hull from damage, and the whole costly rig sank in 60 fathom of water. It was a sad hulk *Vara* towed into Marblehead that morning.

The first scheduled race was only two weeks off. Bath Iron Works and its suppliers went to work to duplicate the mast and rig. *Ranger* was towed to Bristol where Vanderbilt and the Stephens boys, with all the aid Herreshoff's could give them, started cobbling up a temporary rig out of *Rainbow's* 1934 dural mast and a collection of rigging scraped up from among *Enterprise's, Weetamoe's* and *Vanitie's* spare gear. Nine days after she reached Bristol, *Ranger* was ready to sail, though her crew were by no means confident of her patchwork rig. They had a few days to tune up before the preliminary trials started.

Ranger had two rivals to beat for the selection. *Yankee* belonged to Gerard Lambert, and for this season he and Frank Paine had changed her rig, moving the mast six feet forward and giving her a single jib in place of her old jib and staysail. The racing results were to show it was anything but an improvement, and after the trials her old rig was restored.

Chandler Hovey, who had been racing *Weetamoe,* had bought *Rainbow's* stripped hull from Vanderbilt, replaced the gear taken off her for *Ranger* with corresponding equipment from *Weetamoe,* and had his heart set on winning the right to meet the challenger.

While *Ranger* was being re-rigged at Bristol, the challenger had arrived—both of them in fact. Sopwith still owned the older *Endeavour* and she was under charter to his friends Frederick Sigrist and Phillip Hall. Both sloops were brought over and would conduct their own trials, with the older boat a possible substitute for the new one in case of accident or unforeseen superiority. While the match conditions of 1937 followed closely those of 1934, at Sopwith's suggestion an earlier date had been set. The Cup match would start July 31. Sopwith had an all-professional crew this time, and in his afterguard were Mrs. Sopwith, Sir Ralph Gore, Frank Murdoch and Flight Lieut. Scarlett, RAF, navigator.

With the Cup races less than two months away, the preliminary trials for the American defense candidates started June 2. *Ranger's* afterguard, from their few shake-down sails, already felt that they had a new kind of J boat under them. So she proved to be, and after their up-hill climb to selection in *Enterprise* in 1930 and the even longer and harder struggle for *Rainbow's* selection and final victory in 1934, *Ranger* was to give her crew a real joy-ride this season.

Of six races in the preliminary series, *Ranger*, patchwork rig and all, won all four of those she was in. *Yankee* beat *Rainbow* twice but finished behind her in the last race, in which all three sailed.

Thanks to strenuous efforts by all concerned, *Ranger* got her new rig before the observation trial series started on June 19, and all hands breathed easier. The jury rig she had been carrying was not strong enough to lug sail in heavy breezes, and they had been prepared to drop out of any race if it breezed on too hard. The gear had been of ample strength for the older boats it was made for, but not for these 87-foot-waterline Js. Not only were the hulls more powerful, standing up to their sail in heavier breezes, but the actual sail area they had to carry was a lot bigger.

The old mainsails were fine—*Ranger* used *Enterprise's* No. 1 and No. 6 mainsails for the Cup series—but forward of the mast everything was bigger. Where the quadrilateral jibs of 1934 had had little more area than their triangular working counterparts, those *Ranger* used in 1937 were from 100% up to 250% of the measured area of her fore triangle. Quads almost completely replaced genoas on the big boats, in anything but drifting weather. Parachute spinnakers, too, had been vastly increased in size. A 1937 addition, too, was the equivalent of the modern balloon forestaysail—actually it was the genoa jib from Vanderbilt's Class M sloop *Prestige,* set on *Ranger's* forestay inside a spinnaker or ballooner when reaching.

Her new mast and rig made *Ranger* even faster. In the first of the observation trials, July 19, she set a new 30-mile course record for *America's* Cup boats. She went around the triangle in 2 hr., 43 min. 43 sec.—averaging 11.1 knots—in a breeze not nearly as fresh as the one in which *Yankee* made her record of 2 hr., 47 min., 59 sec. in 1930.

In this series *Ranger* beat *Yankee* twice and *Rainbow* once; *Yankee* beat *Rainbow* twice, and *Rainbow's* best showing was in an unfinished drifting match in which she was ahead of *Ranger* when the time limit ran out. The new boat's winning margins were large, and it began to look as if the final trials would serve no purpose except to tune up the defender.

So it proved. *Ranger* beat *Yankee* once by 15 minutes and was well ahead of *Rainbow* next day in a drifter when time ran out. There wasn't wind enough for a race the following day, which happened to be Vanderbilt's 53rd birthday, but the selection committee handed him a nice present anyhow by announcing that *Ranger* was selected as the defender. For once, there were no hurt feelings among the chosen boat's rivals—nobody had any doubts this time which boat was fastest.

Instead of further trials, the three sloops sailed four races for a cup put up by Commodore George Nichols. The finish order was the same in each—*Ranger, Rainbow, Yankee.* At this point, with the remainder of the season's racing in mind, Lambert and Paine restored *Yankee* to her 1936 rig.

This left *Ranger's* record at 12 races completed; 12 races won. Her crew wasn't superstitious, of course, but they'd be just as happy if the first race of the Cup match wasn't Number 13 for her. The Eastern Yacht Club cruise, a few days later, took care of that. *Ranger* sailed on two days of it. She won her thirteenth race safely enough, beating *Yankee, Rainbow* and the old *Endeavour.* But next day, in a confusion of fluky calms and swift currents in Vineyard Sound, she took her first defeat. *Endeavour,* with Sherman Hoyt as guest skipper, played the catspaws and currents just right and won, followed by *Yankee, Ranger* and *Rainbow.* If it's true that a boat ought to be beaten at least once before she's ready for a supreme effort, *Ranger* was now ready to take on *Endeavour II.*

Meanwhile the two *Endeavours* had been active, in a way that baffled American observers. They were out almost every day, but instead of actual races they went through an interminable series of comparative sailing and handling tests together, trying out various sail combinations, maneuvering, but never actually competing. Sopwith was satisfied that his new boat was the faster, and had no intention of exercising his option to name the old one. In his opinion the sort of experimentation and drill he was holding was the best way to get ready. Perhaps he was right—it wouldn't have mattered, anyhow, against *Ranger.*

When the two Cup rivals towed out to the race buoy, nine miles southeast of Brenton Reef lightship, on the morning of July 31, they found that a vast spectator fleet of some 800 craft, from passenger steamers to catboats, had gotten there ahead of them. It took the Coast Guard 45 minutes to clear the area around the buoy enough so the race could be started—the only time during the series that the patrol had serious trouble with the rubberneck navy.

By then there was a light southerly breeze. The postponement flag came down, and they went off on the starboard tack, *Endeavor II* on *Ranger's* lee bow and close enough to give the defender some backwind. Sopwith was carrying a genoa jib, while *Ranger* had a huge double-clewed jib which looked like

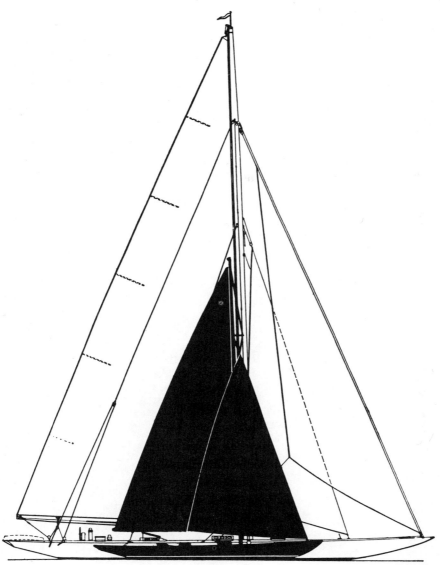

A 12-meter (black) looks small compared to a J boat.

Vim, one of the four 12-meter candidates for the defense of the cup in 1958.

a patchwork quilt made out of an old genoa, but was actually
a new sail, of a synthetic material and unusual construction,
that pulled like a tugboat. After a few minutes Vanderbilt
tacked to clear his wind, drove off to get her moving, and then
began to work up to windward. *Endeavour II* covered the tack
promptly, but once *Ranger* had her wind clear there was no
holding her, and in half an hour she was well out ahead of the
blue boat and going away.

Sopwith tried all the tricks, changing sails and short-tacking,
but while his professional crew handled their sails much faster
than the unfortunate amateurs of 1934 they couldn't hold
Ranger. She covered their tacks, continued to gain, and
rounded the buoy, after a 15-mile beat, with a lead of 6 minutes,
14 seconds. On the downwind leg—a broad reach rather than
a run, as the breeze had shifted a couple of points—*Ranger*
continued to gain. Sopwith tried the loser's gamble of reaching
off wide of the course, but it only cost him more time, and he
finished 17 minutes, 5 seconds astern of *Ranger.* Elapsed times
were: *Ranger,* 4:41:15; *Endeavour II,* 4:58:20.

It was the worst boat-for-boat licking a challenger had taken
since *Volunteer* beat *Thistle* by 19 minutes, 23 seconds back in
1887. There had been nothing to criticize, this time, in Sopwith's sailing of the race, nor in his crew's performance—
Ranger just sailed that much faster. Vanderbilt, in his own
account of this race, lists some errors his own crew made, but
they certainly didn't show in the final results. Perhaps Mr. V.
had been spoiled by the usually flawless work of his crews.

"You have a phenomenally fast boat," Charlie Nicholson,
Endeavour's amazed and disappointed designer, told American
reporters next day.

Just to prove it was no fluke, *Ranger* beat the challenger
even worse in the next race; by 18 minutes, 32 seconds, to be
exact.

For a second time Sopwith had the better of the start in a

light breeze, tacking under *Ranger's* lee bow and backwinding her on the line. Again Vanderbilt tacked to clear his wind, but this time his quad jib's upper sheet jammed in its block. It took a minute to clear it, letting *Endeavour* get well out ahead. For almost an hour it looked like a boat race. Once *Ranger* found she couldn't cross the blue boat, as they converged, and tacked under her lee bow. But superior speed told, and eventually *Ranger* had worked up under *Endeavour's* lee bow and backwinded her so that the challenger had to tack to clear her wind. From then on *Ranger* was going away and at the end of the ten-mile beat she was more than 10 minutes ahead. She added more to that lead on two uneventful reaching legs, to finish with the above-mentioned margin. The elapsed times were: *Ranger,* 3:41:33; *Endeavour II,* 4:00:05.

After that race Sopwith asked for a lay-day to haul *Endeavour II* out and look at her bottom. After two such lickings, it was hard to believe there wasn't something, such as a stray lobster pot, on the challenger's bottom holding her back. But there wasn't. Both boats were hauled, and as a matter of fact *Ranger* probably gained by that deal, too, for her bottom paint needed a smoothing-up more than the British boat's did. *Endeavour II* did take out three tons of pig lead—her only removable ballast—and possibly that helped her to keep her margins of defeat in the two remaining races a little more reasonable.

The third race was sailed in a steady sou'wester of from 11 to 15 miles strength, 15 miles to windward and back. Before the start *Ranger* followed close on *Endeavour II's* stern—a favorite maneuver of Vanderbilt's—as they tacked and jibed in a series of tight circles close to the line. At exactly the right moment *Ranger* broke away, headed for the line, and made a perfectly-timed start with *Endeavor II* in her backwind. A few minutes later, however, as *Ranger* was making her second tack, her upper quad jib sheet jammed on the winch and she had to fall back on the old tack for several minutes while a riding

turn on the winch was cleared. This left the challenger uncovered, and a slight favorable shift in the wind might have
put her in a strong leading position.

But Lady Luck wasn't riding *Endeavour II*—the wind remained steady. *Ranger* finally worked into a clear lead, which
she held through a series of short tacks that Sopwith initiated
on the off chance that *Ranger* might foul up another tack as
she had earlier. But she didn't, and she rounded the weather
mark 4 minutes, 13 seconds ahead of the challenger. With the
wind dead aft, they sailed the leeward leg with spinnakers out
on opposite sides, each jibing once near the finish. They ran
the 15 miles quite evenly, *Endeavor II* losing only 14 seconds
more. The elapsed times were: *Ranger,* 3:54:30; *Endeavour,*
3:58:57.

As an indication of how much faster these 1937 sloops were
than older J boats: *Ranger* in this race set a new *America's*
Cup record for 15 miles to windward, 2 hr., 3 min., 45 sec.,
in spite of the time lost due to the jibsheet jam and the short-
tacking duel and the fact that it was an absolute dead beat in
wind much lighter than on the day in 1934 when *Rainbow*
had made the previous record—40 seconds slower than *Ranger's*
time.

Another steady 15-mile sou'wester blew for the final race,
around a 30-mile triangle. The pre-start maneuvering was
much like the previous day's but this time Sopwith was over-
anxious, crossed the line five seconds before the signal, and
lost over a minute jibing around and re-starting. This put
Ranger in a commanding position and she held it, through
another short-tacking duel which Sopwith initiated as a forlorn
hope, for the 10-mile beat, rounding the mark 4 minutes, 5
seconds, ahead of *Endeavour II.* The latter out-sailed *Ranger*
for the first time on the second leg, a reach, cutting half a
minute off the defender's lead, and she lost only two seconds

to *Ranger* on the final reach. The elapsed times for this final race were: *Ranger, 3:07:49; Endeavour II, 3:11:26.*

Traditionally, the skipper steers a winning boat across the finish line, but Olin Stephens was at *Ranger's* helm as she finished, as Burgess had been when *Enterprise* wound up the 1930 series. It was Vanderbilt's characteristic way of showing appreciation to two great designers who had provided two superior boats for the defense of the *America's* Cup.

Incidentally, *Ranger* broke two more Cup race records in this final race. Her 1:14:45 was 34 seconds under the old 10-mile beat mark; and she sailed the whole race in a minute, 12 seconds less than the previous 30-mile record. Both old records were made by the first *Endeavour* in the second Cup race of 1934, with a fresher breeze. These are actual cup race records—faster times had been made by J boats in trial races when wind conditions had been more conducive to speed than they ever happened to be in a race for the Cup.

This 1937 series had been a happy one. The challengers had become resigned to their fate long before it ended, as a result of *Ranger's* obvious superiority. There were no over-stretched nerves, no protests or unpleasant incidents. Everybody connected with the rival yachts were firm friends when it ended. This lent itself to some enjoyable racing after the Cup series, which was one thing Sopwith had had in mind when he proposed the mid-summer date for the Cup event.

The two *Endeavours* joined the three American J boats on the New York Yacht Club cruise; and in races for two special trophies given by the cities of Newport and Marblehead, the latter a five-race series on Massachusetts Bay. Except on one run of the cruise, when the old *Yankee* beat her thanks to a successful wind-hunting expedition by skipper Gerry Lambert, *Ranger* showed the way in all these races, but the other four had a lot of fun scrapping for second places. Of 13 races sailed by the J Class after the Cup series, *Ranger* won 12 and was second once. *Endeavour II* took seven second prizes, *Rainbow* four and *Yankee* one. The old *Endeavour* had to be content with her one victory earlier in the season on the Eastern cruise.

Sopwith enjoyed one day of victory when, on a lay-day at Marblehead, some genius talked the five J-boat skippers into sailing a series of races in Brutal Beasts. These are Marblehead's junior training class boats—12-foot, V-bottomed, cat-rigged skiffs about as different from Class J sloops as anything could be and still sail. Sopwith won both the races, for a score of 12½ points. Chandler Hovey finished second with 9 points; Fred Sigrist of *Endeavour* third with 8, Lambert fourth with 7 and Vanderbilt fifth with 4. A pleasant afternoon was enjoyed by all.

Ranger was easily the fastest Class J sloop ever built, and probably, taking all points of sailing, the fastest yacht that ever raced for the *America's* Cup, although it is possible that some of the huge "fin-keel scows," of which *Reliance* of 1903 was the arch-type, might have beaten her under conditions that suited them best—a reach in a strong breeze. It appeared to some observers of the 1937 series that Starling Burgess and Olin Stephens, with the Stevens Institute model tank to help guide their experiments, had jumped over 20 years of normal progress in racing yacht design when they produced *Ranger*. Charles Nicholson had turned out, in *Endeavour II,* a faster boat than any J up to her time, but, with no comparable testing tank to aid him, had not been able to equal the big jump of the American naval architects.

It would have been interesting to see, had the *America's* Cup series continued in Class J sloops, how long it would have taken to develop a boat that would beat *Ranger*. But *Ranger* never sailed again after 1937. None of the American Js survived World War II—all ended ingloriously, broken up for scrap metal. The *Endeavours*—minus their lead keels—did come through the war, but the big class in England was dead and they have never raced since.

Two factors rang the death knell of the Js—confiscatory taxes on the kind of incomes that once supported such yachts, and skyrocketing costs in yacht building and every other requisite that goes into sailing. It is estimated that to build a yacht of their size and campaign her for a season on the scale of the '30s would now cost somewhere well over three million dollars in this country.

Chapter XX

THE SERIES REVIVED IN 12-METER SLOOPS—"COLUMBIA"-"VIM"
TRIAL BATTLES—"COLUMBIA" DEFEATS "SCEPTRE" EASILY

THE 20 YEARS following the 1937 match constitute the longest
period of inactivity in *America's* Cup history. World War II
and the impossibility of campaigning boats to fit the Deed of
Gift seemed to have finished the competition for all time. To
many younger yachtsmen, it had already become a relic of days
that would never return. Suggestions were made, as divergent
as an ocean race around Bermuda and back and a team race in
International 14 dinghies, but none of them seemed consistent
with the traditions of the Cup.

The idea would not die, however, for a closed-course match
race in yachts of the largest general class currently active, which
meant either ocean racers up to the 73-foot top limit placed
on Bermuda Race entries, or the International Rule Twelve-
Meter Class. There were a few aging sloops of these types,
approximately 70 feet overall and 45 feet on the waterline, still
in commission in England and America. Discussions centered
on these two types, with the Twelves more favored by those
who had the most say.

As a preliminary to possible action, the New York Yacht Club,
under Commodore Henry Sears, went to the Supreme Court of
the State of New York for permission to make certain changes
in the Deed of Gift—a necessary step since there was now no
survivor of the Cup's original donors to re-deed the trophy, as
George L. Schuyler had twice done. In December, 1956, the
court authorized two changes in the Deed.

One was the reduction of minimum waterline length from

65 to 44 feet, which opened the Cup up to Twelve-Meters and
the big ocean racers. The other was striking out the clause
that required challengers to "proceed under sail, on their own
bottoms, to the port where the contest is to take place." The
latter change was not meant to let unseaworthy yachts compete
—a Twelve can perfectly well cross the Atlantic under shortened rig—but to save the challenger the loss of valuable racing
and tuning-up time that such a voyage entails. Practically, this
provision had been nullified long since, as the Lipton and
Sopwith challengers had been allowed, by mutual consent, to
be towed across by steam or power vessels. Yachts 70 feet
overall can be shipped over on a steamer's deck much more
quickly.

With these points cleared up, informal discussions took on
real meaning, and in June, 1957, the anticipated challenge
from the Royal Yacht Squadron was received. Commodore
J. Burr Bartram had already appointed an *America's* Cup
Committee headed by former Commodore W. A. W. Stewart,
who had officiated in three previous Cup matches, and the
Squadron's challenge was accepted, subject to negotiations on
details. Its basic terms called for a match in Twelve-Meter
Class sloops, off Newport, R. I., during the latter part of September, 1958, four races out of seven to decide.

The *America's* Cup Committee included former Commodores
Stewart, Harold S. Vanderbilt and Henry S. Morgan, Vice Com-
modore George A. Hinman, Luke B. Lockwood, and Charles F.
Havemeyer.

The International Measurement Rule, under which the
Twelve-Meter Class yachts were designed and built, was used in
all of the yachting world except the United States, where the
New York Yacht Club's Universal Rule of Measurement, established at the turn of the century, had been in use. Only those
Americans who were interested in international competition
had turned to the so-called "meter boat" classes provided for

by the International Rule, but gradually the Universal Rule lost favor at home too, and *Ranger* had been one of the last boats built to it.

A meter designation for a class does not refer to any one dimension. There is a mathematical formula, stated as an equation, in which various factors, such as waterline, girth measurements, sail area and other elements having bearing on a boat's speed potential, are balanced out so that the product of the equation must be 12 meters. A designer therefore has freedom to choose how he will balance these elements in the lines and sail plan of the boat. The boats are not identical, as in a one-design class but, as long as they fit the formula, they are raced against each other without handicap. Under other rules, such as the Cruising Club of America Rule, for example, they might rate quite differently because of the emphasis there on different factors.

Although the International Rule was not used much by Americans, a few Twelve-Meters had been campaigned in the 1920's and '30's, and the last one built anywhere had been *Vim,* designed by Sparkman and Stephens and built by Nevins for Harold S. Vanderbilt in 1939. She had been campaigned by him very successfully in England that summer, and several of the boats she had raced against in England were still in commission there, notably the 1936-built *Evaine,* fastest of the pre-war British Twelves, owned in 1958 by a recently very active yachtsman named Owen Aisher.

A nine-member Royal Yacht Squadron syndicate was formed to build the new challenger—H. A. Andreae, Bertram Currie, Hugh L. Goodson, Group Captain Joel Guinness, Major Harold W. Hall, Sir Peter W. Hoare, Major R. N. MacDonald-Buchanan, Viscount Runciman and C. G. A. Wainman. They commissioned four leading architects to draw up designs, and models from them were tank tested. On the basis of the results, which later proved to have been based on rudimentary tech-

niques compared to those used at the Stevens Institute Towing
Tank in Hoboken, N. J., a design by Scotsman David Boyd was
selected. Construction began at the yard of Alexander Robertson and Sons, Sandbank, Argyll, of which Boyd was managing
director. The boat was named *Sceptre,* certainly a name with
a fine British imperial ring to it. It was arranged for *Evaine* to
be a trial horse.

Sceptre, following her acceptance trials, was sailed to the
south coast of England and began a long series of workouts
with *Evaine.* The objectives were to select a crew from among
a large group of candidates and to shake down crew, ship and
rigging. For some time reports from England intimated that
neither the ship nor her crew work were up to expectations.
Evaine was beating her, and remembering that *Vim* had beaten
Evaine badly back in 1939, the prospects didn't look good.

Gradually *Sceptre* improved, however. A crew was finally
settled upon—a well-balanced combination of able, experienced
afterguard and husky, enthusiastic young hands. *Sceptre* began
to beat *Evaine* consistently before the time came to ship the
new boat to America late in July.

Sceptre's most obvious deviation from the conventional 12-
Meter sloop was a huge midships working cockpit from which
most of her winches and gear were handled, keeping weights
lower and chances of a man going overboard less than in the
usual flush-decked Twelve. Whether this was a help or a hin-
drance was never agreed upon even among those who sailed in
her, and it probably affected her performance little if any. It
did dislocate the required minimum living accommodations
in a manner that made calling them "Spartan," a rank under-
statement.

Her other peculiarity wasn't realized in America until
Sceptre was hauled out at the Newport Shipyard in mid-August.
She was known to be a heavy-displacement craft, but a look at
her underbody revealed that she carried most of that displace-

ment in enormously full, almost bulbous, forward sections. Her waterlines were blunt forward, there was no true leading edge to her stem or keel. On the other hand, her run, aft, was remarkably fine. In fact she was a modern version of the "cod's head and mackerel's tail" principle of design that the *America's* triumph in 1851 had discredited.

As one American naval architect remarked, looking at her, "Either we or the British are awfully wrong!" Though *Sceptre* worked out off Newport with the old American Twelve *Gleam,* it was anybody's guess which was wrong until the first few minutes of the first Cup race supplied the answer.

Vim, newest and fastest Twelve built prior to 1958, had been thoroughly rejuvenated in 1957, under the direction of her designer, Olin Stephens, and with no expense spared by her owner, Capt. John N. Matthews. Her basic design, lead keel, frames and duralumin mast were 1939 vintage; her rig, gear, sails, and much of her fastenings and planking were new. In most respects that mattered she was as up-to-date as the 1958 boats. A crew headed by her owner's 24-year-old son Donald and his brother Dick Matthews, navigator, had sailed her enough in the fall of '57 to work out some of the "bugs" of the new gear and learn some of the tricks of synthetic sails, of Dacron and nylon, which were used for the first time in 12-Meter and in *America's* Cup racing in the 1958 match.

She was back in the water early in April, 1958, and a crew was signed on—mostly amateurs and several of them top skippers of their own boats—that rapidly developed into the crack crew of the trial series. They sailed her three or four days every week until the end of the trials, and under the inspired helmsmanship and tactical command of Emil Mosbacher, Jr., who in effect became her racing skipper, they were to bring the old *Vim* within seconds of being the defender.

Next boat out was the new Stephens-designed sloop *Columbia,* built at Nevins yard at City Island, N.Y., for a syndicate which besides Henry Sears and Briggs S. Cunningham now included Gerard B. Lambert, James A. Farrell, Jr., William T. Moore, A. Howard Fuller and Vincent Astor. *Columbia* was launched June 3 and within a few days was sailing against an older Twelve, *Nereus,* which under the handling of Bill Moore, Cornelius Shields and other crack skippers gave the new boat some real workouts.

Briggs Cunningham, a successful 12-Meter sailor of the late 1930s and with a fine record in international Six-Meter competition, was *Columbia's* skipper. Harry Sears was navigator and syndicate manager. Among her amateur hands were Olin and Rod Stephens, who had sailed in *Ranger* in 1937, and her professional sailing master was Fred Lawton, who had served in that capacity in *Vim* in 1939. With these and a bunch of good younger men, *Columbia* carried plenty of talent, but it took all season to weld them into a smooth-working crew that was a match for *Vim's* crowd with their two-months head start.

The other two crews never did catch up. *Weatherly* was launched about 10 days after *Columbia,* and *Easterner* 10 days or so later, but neither had any competition, and very little sailing of any kind, before they met off Newport July 9.

Weatherly, designed by Philip L. Rhodes and built by Luders for the syndicate of shipping executives Henry Mercer, Cornelius Walsh and Arnold Frese, all new to the sport, had Arthur Knapp Jr. as skipper, ably assisted by Edgar L. Raymond, Jr. as mate and Frank R. MacLear as navigator. They and the group of able yachtsmen who sailed with them developed into a fine crew—in some ways a match even for *Vim's* veterans. But they never had time to get fully to know their ship and her optimum performance under various sails in all kinds of weather on all points of sailing.

Easterner, designed by C. Raymond Hunt, built by Graves of Marblehead, and owned principally by Chandler Hovey of Boston, who had been managing or sole owner of *Yankee,*

Weetamoe and *Rainbow* at different times in the J-boat, era, had even less time. She was manned out largely "family style" at first, and part of the time carried no professional. Charles Hovey and Chandler Jr. were her helmsmen but with Ray Hunt in "complete command," according to Hovey, senior. With less than two months of sailing, they also were unable to get the best out of their sloop, day in and day out, though she often showed flashes of real speed.

The first scheduled meeting of the American defense candidates was on July 9 off Newport, in a race under Eastern YC auspices in which, appropriately, the Charles Francis Adams Memorial Trophy was at stake. Unfortunately *Weatherly* wasn't yet ready to leave her builder's yard, out of which she had been sailing between numerous odd jobs of completion and improvement, and *Easterner* was held up by weather north of the Cape Cod Canal and didn't make Newport until after the race. *Columbia, Vim* and *Nereus* sailed a 21-mile triangle which a shifting breeze made into three reaches, *Columbia* won by 46 seconds over *Vim* with *Nereus* last.

A few days later came the Preliminary Trials. Due to fog and calms, races were completed on only four of the eight scheduled days. They proved that neither *Weatherly* nor *Easterner* was anywhere near ready for serious racing; that *Vim* was very much in the running with an excellent crew; and that while a fast boat, especially to windward, *Columbia* and her crew needed a lot of improvement. Two of these races were three-boat affairs, due to first *Weatherly,* then *Easterner,* staying in port for repairs, and *Columbia* won both of these with *Vim* second each time. In the match races completed, *Vim* beat *Columbia* and *Weatherly; Columbia* and *Weatherly* each lost to *Vim* once and won from *Easterner; Easterner* lost to *Columbia* and broke down in another race.

The New York Yacht Club's annual cruise, while it didn't officially figure in the selection committee's decisions, gave the

Twelves some good practice and showed how they shaped up in fleet (as differentiated from match) racing. It left no doubt that *Vim* was the top boat as of now, for she won five of the seven races and port-to-port runs, finishing third and fourth in the others. *Columbia* won the other two and took a second, three thirds and a fourth. *Easterner,* looking much better than in July, took four second places and *Weatherly* two.

An unofficial point score on the four contenders for the cruise shows *Vim* with 24 points, *Columbia* 18, *Easterner* 16, *Weatherly* 14.

By now *Vim* was firmly established as "the people's choice," except east of Cape Cod where *Easterner* was the local favorite. The reading public had a vivid, if erroneous, mental image of *Vim* as an ancient and underprivileged warhorse putting up a game fight against new rivals who held all kinds of advantages. Actually, as noted above, *Vim* had everything the other boats had plus the smartest and most experienced crew in the fleet. Nevertheless, she and they deserved all the credit and admiration they got through the season.

The feature of the second or Observation series of trials, August 16–23, was *Weatherly's* improved performance. With favorable weather, the four boats sailed a pair of match races each day for eight days, and when it was over the Rhodes sloop had the best record of any of them—six victories in eight starts, including the last five races in a row. She had beaten each of her rivals at least once. *Vim* and *Columbia* had each won five races. *Easterner* had lost eight, most of them, however, by narrow margins.

The *Weatherly* camp was naturally jubilant, although some of her wins weren't wholly convincing to an impartial observer. One, over *Columbia,* came by virtue of the latter's missing the finish line, in a heavy fog, while in the lead. A couple more were scored in races which, due to wind shifts after the start, were almost entirely reaching—always *Weatherly's* best point of sailing, competitively.

The final trials, beginning Sept. 1, started and finished at the special *America's* Cup buoy nine miles SSE of Brenton Reef lightship. The courses were the same as for the Cup match—24 miles, either twice around a six-mile windward-leeward course or once around a triangle eight miles to a leg. This gave sea-room for starting all races to windward. The J boats, with their longer courses, had had to start to leeward when the wind was offshore.

The selection committee, headed by veteran Commodore W. A. W. Stewart, had until Sept. 13 to name a defender. Judging by the season's showing to date, they had two evenly matched top contenders and two that hadn't done so well. But both the latter had shown flashes of speed, and either might prove a real candidate this time out. So for the first three days *Easterner* and *Weatherly* were alternately matched against *Vim* and *Columbia*. *Easterner*, though she put up some good scraps, was beaten each time. So was *Weatherly*, to the bitter disappointment of her partisans, who had been encouraged by the previous series. After the third day's racing the committee eliminated them both and set the stage for the final *Vim-Columbia* battle.

And a battle it was! *Vim's* crew were at their excellent best and Bus Mosbacher's clever, aggressive tactics, especially at the starts, often gave *Vim* an edge that *Columbia's* slightly faster potential speed to windward could not overcome. But *Columbia's* crew had come a long way since the early trials. They could match tacks and tactics with *Vim* now. In some races, too, they had the help of a master racing skipper, Cornelius Shields, Sr., who came out of retirement (enforced by a heart condition) to be *Columbia's* part-time helmsman in several races, then stepped ashore again.

In their first match, in a 12–16-mile sou'west breeze, *Columbia* beat *Vim* handily. Next day, in lighter going, *Vim* got the better of the start and by superior sail handling stayed out ahead to win by 10 seconds. The third race, in a 20-mile smoky sou'wester, was *Columbia's* all the way. Most observers—and *Vim's* crew—expected *Columbia* to be named that evening but the committee ordered another race next day—which *Vim* won by again outmaneuvering her rival at the start. *Columbia* made some 35 tacks on the eight-mile beat, trying to break clear, but in the 10–12-mile breeze she didn't have enough speed advantage to do so, as *Vim* covered her every tack until both crews were ready to drop at their winches. The score was even again.

Vim led the first time around the fifth race's windward-leeward course; then the breeze freshened and *Columbia* stepped out and won. The score was 3-2 but still the committee called another race. This one turned out to be what no less a critic than Harold S. Vanderbilt, of the selection committee, called one of the greatest races he had even seen. It was sailed, windward-leeward, in a 15–17-mile nor'wester whose frequent slight shifts favored first one boat, then the other, about equally.

Briggs Cunningham got *Columbia* the best of this start and the breeze was fresh enough for her. *Vim* initiated many short tacks but *Columbia* walked out to windward to lead by 1:06 at the turn. Running back *Columbia,* whose huge spinnaker didn't draw too well, made two jibes, *Vim* none, and just before the turn *Vim* ranged ahead, to lead by nine seconds.

On the second beat upwind first one, then the other appeared to have a boat-length or two advantage. A quarter-mile from the weather mark *Vim* had the edge; then *Columbia* swept past her to lead at the turn by nine seconds. This time *Columbia* set a smaller but better-drawing spinnaker that kept her ahead —just barely. She won by 12 seconds—half a second a mile for the course. In these last six races *Columbia's* average had been 32½ seconds.

In port later, the selection committee notified the two crews that *Columbia* would defend the Cup. When the *"Columbias"* came ashore in their launch they found the whole *Vim* crew lined up to give them three cheers—a gesture typifying the spirit of the whole 1958 trial series.

The few days between the final trials and the Cup races were busy ones at Newport. *Columbia*—third of that name to defend the *America's* Cup—was offered the pick of her erstwhile rivals' sail and gear lockers. She took a spinnaker each from *Vim* and *Weatherly*. Both sails having bright red upper corners, they became known as "Big Harry" and "Little Harry" in honor of navigator Sears's flaming topknot. *Columbia* had already borrowed from the eliminated *Weatherly* her "turtle," from which her spinnakers had been set so fast, and along with it a *Weatherly* crew member particularly adept in its use, Victor Romagna. Vic and the "turtle" speeded up *Columbia's* spinnaker setting in the last few trials. It was reminiscent of Frank Paine's joining *Rainbow*, bringing *Yankee's* spinnaker, in 1934.

Sceptre had been sailing off Newport for over a month, trying out sails and maneuvers against *Gleam*. Owen Aisher, acting as *Gleam's* skipper, reported having to run his engine to keep up with *Sceptre*, but this wasn't surprising. The 21-year-old boat was carrying much extra weight and lacked a modern rig.

With both crews composed predominantly of amateurs for the first time in *America's* Cup history, friendly inter-yacht relations developed immediately and continued throughout the series. In the 1930's the big professional crews had lived aboard either tenders or the Class J sloops themselves; the afterguards aboard their power yachts. With the Twelves, all hands lived ashore in huge old Newport "cottages," relics of that town's heyday as a social resort. Briggs Cunningham had rented "Beechbound," overlooking the anchorage and with its own landing pier, where the *Columbia* crew lived. "Horse Head," on nearby Conanicut Island, had been loaned to the British expeditionary force, to whom the U.S. Army had contributed the use of nearby Fort Wetherill's pier and storehouses.

Sceptre's skipper was Lt. Cdr. Graham Mann, RN, 34, who though new at Twelve-Meters was a crack racing helmsman in smaller craft, with an Olympic medal and many other trophies in his locker. Lt. Cdr. Joe Brooks, RN, was navigator. G. Colin Ratsey was relief helmsman, other crew members being David Boyd, Jr. (son of the designer), Tim Langford, Denis Jackson, Mike Tremlett, Hamish Connell, Charles de Selincourt, Ian Lennox and Capt. Stanley Bishop. The latter, only professional yachtsman aboard, had sailed in the Class J challengers, and his father had been over with Lipton.

Several of *Sceptre's* 12 owners came over. The Royal Yacht Squadron syndicate now included H. L. Goodson, H. A. Andreae, B. Curry, Group Capt. L. Guinness, Maj. H. W. Hall, Sir Peter Hoare, Maj. R. N. Macdonald-Buchanan, Lord Runciman, C. G. C. Wainman, Lord Camrose, Lt. Col. A. W. Acland, and Sir John Wardlaw-Milne. What with numerous other associates and aides, it was quite a group of British yachtsmen that invaded Rhode Island.

When the American candidates were racing there were always a few British "scouts" following them in *Sceptre's* own tender, *Ravahine,* or one of the power craft made available to the visitors. What they learned about the four possible defenders and the ways of their skippers and crews would have been invaluable to the challenger's skipper in a close match.

Columbia's final crew list included Briggs Cunningham, skipper; Henry Sears, navigator; Olin Stephens, relief helmsman; Roderick Stephens, Jr., Colin E. Ratsey, Cornelius Shields, Jr., Wallace E. Tobin, III, Halsey Herreshoff, Palmer Sparkman, Victor A. Romagna and three professionals, Capt. Fred Lawton, Robert C. Pettway and James Haslam. As the rules allowed only 11 aboard in a race, some of these men alternated on different days.

The two Colin Ratseys were uncle and nephew, fourth and

fifth generation members of that international sailmaking family
to have figured in *America's* Cup affairs. Uncle G. Colin headed
the British Ratsey and Lapthorn firm, nephew Colin E. was an
official of the American company of the same name. Halsey
Herreshoff was a member of the Bristol Cup defender building
family, a grandson of old Nat.

Precise hull dimensions of the yachts varied slightly from time
to time with changes in ballasting and the like, but as given out
by the designers, they were:

YACHT	L.O.A.	L.W.L.	BEAM	DRAFT	DISPLACE- MENT
Columbia	69'7"	45'9"	11'9"	8'11"	58,000 lb.
Sceptre	68'11"	46'6"	11'9"	9'1"	60,000 lb.

Measured sail area was another variable, but when they met
in the Cup series each carried approximately 1950 sq. ft., *Sceptre's* a bit the lower to compensate for her longer measured
waterline, as the International Rule required.

Unprecedented advance publicity in papers, magazines, radio
and television had whipped up wide interest in the match. Newport and nearby harbors were filling up with yachts and excursion vessels, shore accommodations were crammed, and the
US Coast Guard had a task force on hand to carry out a well-
organized patrol of the course. The patrol was needed! By a
conservative estimate, more than a thousand spectator craft
came out for the first race. They ranged in size from big excursion steamers and the USS *Mitscher* carrying President Eisen-
hower, down to a horde of little open outboard and sailing
boats. That there were few accidents and no interference with
the race is a testimonial to the work of the Coast Guard.

Both yachts had been hauled out and polished up in the last
days before the race, sitting companionably on adjacent railway
cradles. Some experts shook their heads over *Sceptre's* blunt,
massive forward lines; others said, "Maybe the British have got
something we've overlooked." Coming on the heels of the

hammer-and-tongs racing of the finals trials, the public expected a battle royal. They were due for a let-down!

The First Race

The weather looked dubious for the opening race Sept. 20. The previous day's hard northeaster had blown itself out, but skies were leaden. Under a light northerly air, the water was smooth except for a barely perceptible old swell and the bobble kicked up by the spectator fleet, when the Twelves, under tow, reached the Cup Race buoy. The race committee, headed by John S. Dickerson, Jr., sent the mark boat—a Navy tug—six miles north for a twice-around windward-leeward course, and the Coast Guard herded the vast spectator fleet clear of the starting area. They started at 12:30 in a breeze of not over four m.p.h.

Cunningham brought *Columbia* up to the starting line with good way on, drove off across *Sceptre's* bow with a boat length or more of open water to spare, and started with her wind clear and the challenger well astern, to weather of *Columbia's* wake and moving slowly. It was the one tense moment of the day. What would *Sceptre* do once she got going? For a while the spectators could hardly believe their eyes. *Sceptre* just didn't get going!

She was sailing slower than the defender, she wasn't pointing nearly as high, and even so her genoa jib kept lifting. In spite of the smooth water she pitched in a sort of hobby-horse motion. In five minutes *Columbia* had a seven-boat-length lead. *Sceptre* tacked, *Columbia* covered, and they stood inshore on a port tack for an hour or more, as the breeze, backing a bit west of north, made the beat a long-and-short-hitch one. The amazed spectators watched *Columbia* draw steadily away from her rival, outsailing and outpointing her, to round the mark tug after a slow beat of an hour and a half with a lead of 7 min., 38 sec.

At this point, one of them said later, the pent-up tensions

Sceptre's mammoth French spinnaker was a stirring sight.

Columbia left *Sceptre* far behind in all their races.

Designer Olin Stephens (in dark glasses, lower left) confers with skipper
Briggs Cunningham (white cap) in *Columbia's* cockpit. Comm. Harry Sears,
syndicate head, is in hatch.

in *Columbia's* crew began to relax. They knew she "had it made."

Sceptre, taking a couple of short tacks as she neared the mark, moved into a shift of breeze to the NE and it stayed with her when she turned the mark and set her famous huge white-and-green French-made Herbulot spinnaker. For a while she did nicely, bringing up the new air that *Columbia,* up ahead, never did get. She cut *Columbia's* lead in half before the breeze collapsed, and both of them drifted along with bare steerageway. *Sceptre* tried three different spinnakers and *Columbia* experimented briefly with a "drifter" jib, but when three hours—half the time limit—had expired they were nowhere near the end of the first round. It looked like "no race."

They were still a mile short of the mark when the breeze backed slowly, first to NW, then west, and picked up to six knots. Moving well in the new air, *Sceptre* rounded the starting buoy only 2:29 after *Columbia.* The second round was now two beam reaches, with no windward or spinnaker work. Under these conditions in the trial races, no American Twelve had gained or lost more than a minute or so against a rival. But *Sceptre,* in the next six miles, sagged back to a depressing 8:16 astern of the defender.

The wind lightened as they reached offshore for the finish. *Sceptre,* away back there, held more air longer than the leader, and cut the final margin down to 7:44. The elapsed times were *Columbia,* 5:13:56; *Sceptre,* 5:21:40; very slow time for 24 miles of which only six were a beat, and even those not dead to windward.

The spectator fleet gave both winner and loser, impartially, a mighty salute with horns, whistles, bells and a few cannon.

The race had proved one thing for sure—*Sceptre* was no match for *Columbia* in light going. But, "Wait 'till you see her go in a breeze," said the Englishmen confidently. Everyone on both sides was hoping for a 25-mile smoky sou'wester on

Monday. In picking *Sceptre* from their tank tests, the British
had deliberately chosen a model that tested out well in heavy
weather conditions, as they expected fresh winds to prevail off
Newport late in September.

The Time Limit Wins

Instead, there wasn't even wind enough to finish a race, although the 20 miles of sailing they got in before the 5½-
hour time limit ran out was interesting. *Columbia* had the
weather berth at the start in a very light northerly air and was
soon out ahead and to windward. Then the breeze died out and
came in faint from the SW. *Columbia* set a spinnaker and
steered north for the first mark. *Sceptre,* under a big genoa, held
a couple of points high, to the west of the direct course, picked
up a little private breeze out there, and sailed right around and
200 yards out ahead of the defender. It was a demonstration
of the folly of a leading boat, in a match race, failing to stay
between her rival and the next mark, no matter how far off
course the rival steers.

Sceptre broke out her second French spinnaker—a huge red,
white and blue affair—and the rest of that leg was a slow run
with both crews struggling to keep their sails drawing as the
boats rolled and slatted in the slight swell.

Sceptre rounded the mark tug with a lead of 1:45. The eight-
mile drift had taken 3 hours 25 minutes of a 5½-hour time limit.
The spectator fleet gave the British boat a roaring blast from
its horns as she rounded the mark in the lead. It turned out
to be the only mark she ever led at.

The breeze picked up to about seven m.p.h. out of the south,
making the second leg a fairly close reach, and *Columbia* ate
up the distance between them in a few minutes. Cunningham
drove the American sloop off, sailed through *Sceptre's* lee a few
boat lengths from her, and rounded the second mark with
a 45-second lead. In the one hour of steady, though light,

breeze of the day, *Columbia* had outsailed *Sceptre* by 2½ minutes.

There was less than an hour of time left. The wind went into the SW, making the last leg a dead beat, and turned light and shifty again. When the time limit expired at 1750 *Columbia* was a good three-quarters of a mile ahead of the challenger, but four miles from the finish.

After the race the British skipper exercised his privilege of asking for a lay-day, in the hopes that fresher breezes might turn up in the meanwhile.

The Second Completed Race

Wednesday, Sept. 24, was a fine summer sailing day, with sunny skies and a southwest breeze of about eight m.p.h. at the start and 12 at the finish. It wasn't as strong a breeze as *Sceptre* was supposed to be built for, but it was a normal, average breeze, and steady. The more it breezed up, the slower, compared to *Columbia*, the challenger sailed!

In maneuvering for starting position Graham Mann seemed at first to have the upper hand, but in the end Cunningham put *Columbia* over with her wind clear and going fast on *Sceptre's* weather quarter. Again the Yankee sloop outpointed the challenger and moved faster through the water. They sailed the weather leg in two long tacks in an hour and 20 minutes. There was nothing the British crew could do to catch up. *Columbia* led by 3:05 at the turn.

Both boats had spinnakers pulling within a few seconds of rounding, *Sceptre* again sporting the huge red, white and blue 'chute stitched up by Mme. Herbulot of Paris. Now we'd see! We did see! We saw the challenger drop farther and farther astern. After a while she tried her "gennaker," a sail tacked to the spinnaker pole but shaped much like a genoa jib. It didn't help, and she tried another big 'chute. *Columbia*, with a staysail set inside her spinnaker, just kept on going away. She jibed around the second mark with a lead of 8:55.

Columbia carried the same sail on the third leg and sailed the challenger hull-down. *Sceptre* sailed much of that leg under her "gennaker," setting a spinnaker only about the time *Columbia* boiled across the finish line. By then her lead was 11:42 which, with the sloops making over eight knots, meant a mile and a half. The elapsed times were *Columbia,* 3:17:43; *Sceptre,* 3:29:25.

The Third Race, In A Breeze

Sceptre got the breeze she was asking for in the third race. It was a sou'wester that blew 22 m.p.h. at the start and a bit harder later. There was a lively wind chop but no real sea, and the course was windward-leeward.

Mann put the challenger over the starting line with full way on and a length off *Columbia's* weather beam—a fine start. But in just four minutes *Columbia* had worked up under *Sceptre's* bow and ahead of her, feeding her a dose of backwind that made the challenger tack. They made a score of tacks in the six miles to windward but *Columbia* covered every time and kept edging out to windward. About an hour after the start she rounded the mark tug with a lead of 2:23.

They roared downwind at 10 knots under spinnakers. *Sceptre,* using her huge tri-color kite again, chose to reach off to the northward, jibe over and reach in again, while Cunningham held straight for the mark. In that strong breeze it made little difference which way they played it. *Sceptre* lost only six seconds on that run, rounding 2:29 after *Columbia.*

The second weather leg was like the first except that they made fewer tacks and *Sceptre* lost more ground. She turned the weather mark this time 7:45 behind which, at the pace they were travelling, was about a mile and a quarter. She lost another half-minute on the final run to finish a loser by 8:20. Elapsed times for the 24 miles were the fastest of the series:

Columbia, 2:59:07; *Sceptre,* 3:07:27.

The observers watched closely for the answer to the usual flag signal from the committee boat, "Do you consent to race tomorrow?" *Sceptre* might have prolonged the series for a day, but there was obviously nothing they could do in a day to make her a match for *Columbia.* She'd had her long-talked-of heavy weather day, and lost. They hoisted the "Affirmative" signal.

The Last Race

The final race was notable mainly as the day *Sceptre's* gremlins came aboard. That she finished at all took seamanship and courage. Of the once-great spectator fleet, fewer than 200 came out, partly because warnings of a hurricane off the Carolinas had sent a lot of skippers off to their home moorings. The breeze was again sou'west, about 15 m.p.h. at first, easing a bit later. There was less wind-chop but a slightly larger rolling sea than the day before and, surprisingly, *Sceptre's* usual heavier pitching, compared to *Columbia,* was less noticeable under those conditions.

It looked as if Graham Mann would have the better of the start as they came up to the line with *Columbia* squarely astern of *Sceptre* and eating her backwind. But the challenger was a couple of seconds early. Her recall number went up on the committee boat along with the starting signal, and the few seconds it took her to dip back over the line lost her a position in which she might have held *Columbia* back for a while. With her wind clear, the defender climbed out to windward as usual. They made 18 to 20 tacks in the eight-mile beat, *Columbia* staying between *Sceptre* and the mark all the way and rounding the tug 5:33 ahead.

On the next-to-last tack *Sceptre's* gremlins got to work. Her jibsheet fouled a cleat (for the first time in a season's sailing) and held the big genoa aback on the new tack until they could cut the wire sheet. On the next leg, in quick succession, her spinnaker guy parted, the end broke off the pole, and she broke her main boom. The latter mishap was caused by the sheet of the spinnaker (after it was re-set on the spare pole) catching under the main boom and lifting it against the downpull of the boom vang near its forward end. The vang proved stronger than the boom—an inverted U-section aluminum spar—and the boom broke into two parts held together only by the steel sailtrack.

The prospect of a jagged-ended metal spar thrashing around overhead is a fearsome thing to contemplate, especially with a jibe coming up in a lively breeze. The British crew considered dropping out—but decided to carry on, and fished the broken boom with the broken spinnaker pole—a real sailor's job under the conditions. With all this, it was remarkable that *Sceptre* lost only 2:40 more on that leg, jibing around the second mark 8:13 after *Columbia*. And on the final reaching leg the challenger actually picked up over a minute.

It must be admitted that *Columbia* wasn't trying too hard in those last eight miles. They coasted down to the finish with the crew loafing on deck, eating cookies and listening to radio accounts of the yacht race—from which they learned about *Sceptre's* broken boom. She'd been too far back for them to see it happen. The final time difference was 7:05, the elapsed times *Columbia*, 3:04:22; *Sceptre*, 3:11:27.

The two sloops ranged abeam and exchanged three cheers, and the Coast Guard and Naval vessels of the official fleet broke out a flag signal which Commodore J. Burr Bartram of the New York YC had suggested as highly appropriate. It was a quotation from British naval history; a message sent Admiral Lord Nelson by his commanding officer Admiral Lord St. Vincent after Nelson's failure to capture Teneriffe in 1797. It read, "To mortals it is not given to command success, but you and your gallant companions have done even more, you have deserved success."

So ended a campaign that, while disappointing from a competitive standpoint, was marked throughout by a spirit of warm, friendly sportsmanship on both sides, a feeling that had been regrettably lacking in some past *America's* Cup matches.

A few comparative figures are enlightening. The total of winning margins in all 12 match races of the final American trials had been 29 minutes, 19 seconds; in only four Cup races *Columbia* had beaten *Sceptre* a total of 34:51. The closest margin in a trial race had been 10 seconds, the widest 5:56; in the Cup match the closest was 7:05, the widest 11:42. The conclusion is inevitable—mathematically, any one of the four American candidates was capable of defending the cup against *Sceptre*.

Chapter XXI

THE FIRST AUSTRALIAN CHALLENGE—"WEATHERLY" LOSES A
RACE BUT WINS AN EXCITING SERIES OVER "GRETEL"

DISAPPOINTMENT over the *Sceptre* fiasco could have brought
another hiatus in *America's* Cup activity as long as that for
World War II, but fortunately a new element was soon injected
into the picture, and the most exciting and interesting challenge,
at least since 1934, if not in the history of the series, resulted.

Australia, anxious to prove itself in world competition from
its far-off location in the Antipodes, emerged as a potential challenger soon after the 1958 series ended. The Aussies had long
held their own in tennis, cricket, swimming, and track and field,
despite their location and small population, but they were not
as well known to the "other side of the world" as international
sailors. The general impression was that they enjoyed sailing
over-canvassed dinghies in heavy air for cash prizes and wager-
ing, and that they were also rugged offshore seamen, but that was
about all.

At Newport in 1958, two bachelor brothers, slightly eccentric
and apparently wealthy sheepherders named Frank and John
Livingston, had been very much in evidence, talking to all and
sundry about the problems of an *America's* Cup challenge.
They owned the largest racing yacht in Australia, *Kurrewa IV*,
about the size of a Twelve, and they expressed a strong interest
in becoming involved in future competition. As they talked to
more and more people, however, they became more and more
disillusioned about the realities of staging a challenge from their
isolated homeland, and they departed in October, leaving the
impression that they had given up the idea and that Australia

256

was only a talking possibility, not an actual one.

There was great surprise, therefore, in October 1959, when those interested in the Cup matches, wondering which of several British yachtsmen would be the first to renew the series, suddenly learned that *Vim,* the underdog heroine of the 1958 trials, had been chartered for four years, with an option to buy, by the Australian publisher Sir Frank Packer. Australian Olympic Finn sailor Colin Ryrie, in the United States for some Finn competition, had quietly negotiated with Capt. Matthews on Packer's behalf, and before anyone was aware of this interest, the graceful "superboat" of 1939 was on her way Down Under. All of this had nothing to do with the Livingstons.

This was followed in January by a visit to the United States by Alan Payne, Australia's most successful designer of ocean racers, and its only full-time practicing yacht designer. He visited with New York Yacht Club officials and with the towing-tank crew at Stevens Institute in Hoboken and quietly and efficiently established a working arrangement "in case" he was selected to design a challenger. It was agreed that he would be able to use the facilities at Stevens, which had played such a vital part in the two most recent defense efforts, and which had never been used by a challenger before. Payne pointed out that there were no similar facilities in Australia, and that a Twelve-Meter had never been designed or built there. *Kurrewa IV,* which Packer had once owned when she was called *Morna,* was an old Scottish-built Fife design.

Rumors began to fly concerning an "Empire challenge," with the Duke of Edinburgh as coordinator. Supposedly, he was to try to pull various Commonwealth nations together into a common effort that would produce several candidates, a sail-off, and an eventual challenge that would have a stronger competitive background than the ill-fated *Sceptre* effort.

While these rumors were flying about, New York Yacht Club officers were startled to receive, on April 20, a direct challenge from the Royal Sydney Yacht Squadron for a series in 1962. Evidently word had come through to Packer that the Duke's letter was being formulated, and the Royal Sydney Yacht Squadron challenge was quickly sent off before receipt of any royal communication. After careful consideration by New York Yacht Club officers, Commodore George Hinman announced on April 28 that the Australian challenge had been accepted. At first it was thought that the Australians might cooperate with possible British candidates, but this notion was soon brushed aside, and the yachting world looked forward eagerly to an entirely new chapter in the *America's* Cup history.

The 40-year-old Payne, quiet, earnest and self-effacing, promptly became one of the world's busiest men as he tackled the monumental task of creating a Twelve-Meter from absolute scratch in a country of ten-million population, where no one had ever before attempted the building of a sailboat anywhere close to the complexity of a Twelve. In one great leap he had to investigate the industrial potential for making such items as masts and winches as well as sails and all sorts of sophisticated fittings. And he also had to try to catch up to the acknowledged genius of Olin Stephens, who had first designed a Twelve-Meter over 20 years before, and of other designers who had the benefit of the availability for study of the U.S. Twelve-Meters that had been built.

The question of sailcloth had not come up before and was therefore never spelled out in the conditions governing the boats, but in order to make sure that the Aussie challenge was competitive, it was interpreted that sails were not an item that had to be "built in the country of origin" of the challenge. It was agreed that the Australians could use American-made sails if they felt the need, and of course the Stevens Institute tank had been made available to tank-test designs. These two concessions literally made the Australian challenge a practical possibility.

While Alan Payne bustled, and the brash, cocky Australian character bristled with pride, there was little early reaction by way of defense candidates in the U.S. In 1959 it developed that the Shields brothers, well-known senior sailors from Larchmont, N.Y., would be taking over *Columbia*, with Paul as owner and Cornelius, who had been called in to help *Columbia* in 1958, as advisor, and Corny, Jr., better known as Glit, as skipper. Doctor's orders kept Corny, Sr., out of the cockpit, but he was a strong, key figure in the effort. The boat had been given a new veed keel shape and less ballast.

The Henry Mercer syndicate decided to rejuvenate *Weatherly*, altering her according to some ideas arrived at by her builder, Bill Luders, and her original designer, Phil Rhodes. When Bus Mosbacher was announced as her skipper, she immediately became a formidable contender. She was being lightened a great deal, including having her stern bobbed, her underbody was altered to reduce wetted surface, and ballast had been added to her keel. *Easterner*, slightly modernized and modified, was to be sailing again, but was still a family affair, without the high-pressure effort expended on the other boats.

The only new contender for this campaign aroused a great deal of interest when announced. Sponsored by a syndicate headed by Boston yachtsman Ross Anderson, she was built in considerable secrecy, even unto her name, in Graves' Yard in Marblehead, Mass. The brainchild of sailmaker F. E. "Ted" Hood, she embodied a sailmaker's ideas of an efficient sail-carrying platform. He had only designed a few ocean racers, but, with his father Steadman, known as "The Professor," as astute adviser, and with his reputation for success as a sailor and as the key man in Twelve-Meter sailmaking, the laconic Ted's boat was considered a formidable front-runner for the defense berth even before she was launched in late May.

In a late evening ceremony under a full moon, to get the benefit of the highest tide, she slid down the ways and her name was finally revealed as *Nefertiti*. (The name ever remained a controversial one and the subject of continual parady.) The stage was now set for the defense campaign.

Meanwhile, cautious optimism was growing on the other side of the world as the new Aussie yacht took shape. Named for Packer's late wife, *Gretel* was beautifully built by the Lars Halvorsen Yard, run by brothers with a top reputation in ocean racing. *Gretel* hit the ways in February 1962. By early March, her gear and sails had been assembled, and she was taking short trial spins around Sydney Harbor. The tough, eager sailors who, as two rival crew units, had been working out on *Vim* for almost two years, itched for a chance to try her in action.

Their chance came unexpectedly on a cloudy Sunday in March. Packer, a large, forceful man famous for his business methods, and complete dictator of the *Gretel* campaign, had given orders up until then that she and *Vim* were under no circumstances to sail in the same water at the same time; but with a group of luncheon guests assembled on the lawn of his waterfront house, he decided on the spur of the moment to put on a show. It was only *Gretel's* fifth shakedown sail, but he ordered the two boats to stage a brush in the eastern arm of the harbor just inside its entrance at The Heads.

In an atmosphere electric with excitement and anticipation, they headed south on a close, port tack reach. *Vim* was to windward and about a half length astern, and both boats had their wind clear in a 12-knot breeze. At first they seemed tied together, but, gradually, inch by inch, *Gretel* began to move ahead. She was moving smoothly, with a noticeable absence of quarter wave, and standing up a bit stiffer than the older boat. When they reached the end of the three-mile straightaway in the vicinity of Packer's house, *Gretel* had moved out by about 100 yards. On the strength of this, no one could exactly claim that the Cup was as good as won, but there were broad smiles all around, and, as the boats moored for a lunch break, the remark

"At least she's no *Sceptre!*" was heard repeatedly. From that moment on, there was a real undercurrent of optimism and excitement in the Aussie campaign.

It carried right on to Newport, where the colorful *Gretel* contingent practically took over the town. Despite the tremendous hours of hard work they put in, as much in altering *Gretel* as in sailing her in rather meaningless practice starts and buoy roundings against *Vim* under orders that Packer boomed over the voice radio, they made friends all over town. Bars became "pubs" and their infectious enthusiasm lent a gaiety and a great sense of anticipation to the summer as the four American boats went through their eliminations.

At first these promised to be wide-open battles, potentially as exciting as the *Vim-Columbia* set-to in 1958. *Nerfertiti* took some early races and became the darling of New England, but gradually a pattern emerged that took most of the suspense out of the summer. *Easterner* again showed flashes of natural speed, but she never developed into a truly serious contender. *Columbia's* gang was never able to settle down, as personnel changes became more and more frequent in a belated attempt to find a winning combination, and the lack of previous Twelve-Meter experience showed up in her handling. At times she was dangerous, but too often she took herself out of contention with mistakes.

This left it to *Weatherly* and *Neffy,* and it soon became apparent that Hood's creation was great on some points but was not a well-rounded boat. Her sail-carrying power really told in a blow, especially on reaches, and sometimes no one could hold her, but she paid for her beamy power with too much wetted surface and she was ineffective in light and moderate airs to windward and on runs.

Mosbacher, with by far the most hours at a Twelve-Meter helm of anyone in the competition (he had sailed *Easterner* for one summer after all the time spent on *Vim* in 1958) and with

a demonstrated genius for molding a highly efficient, loyal
crew that knew collectively that each job was secure, barring
a monumental lapse or loss of enthusiasm, was soon demonstrating his ability to dominate any given match race. In the
selection series in August, *Easterner* and *Columbia* were soon to
be eliminated, and only one heavy weather loss to *Nefertiti*,
when she broke two spinnaker guys and blew out two spinnakers, kept *Weatherly* from being undefeated.

This came after four wins, and matched her 4–1 against
all comers with *Neffy's* 3–2. Each added a victory that eliminated the other two, *Weatherly* soundly trouncing *Columbia*
in a fresh breeze to dramatize how much better in a blow
her changes had made her, and then, with the choice down
to the last two boats, *Weatherly* ran off three straight wins in
moderate air. Mosbacher controlled the starts when it counted,
and the blue-hulled Mercer boat was even able to hold off
Nefertiti when a windward-leeward course turned into an all-
reaching one in freshening breezes. On August 25, with the
score 4–1 for *Weatherly* in their own series, after a 5-minute,
39-second win, Commodore Henry Morgan and his committee
came alongside *Weatherly's* berth in the fading twilight to in-
form Bus and his happy crew that *Weatherly* would be the
defender.

All this time, Packer had been switching crews, failing to
pick a helmsman (much less a "skipper" who could mold his
own crew à la Mosbacher) and running odd, sketchy drills
between the two Aussie boats. Never once did they stage a
formally simulated full race over a Cup-type course. Payne,
slaving day and night on the fantastic number of details to
bring a Twelve-Meter to top racing pitch, had almost worked
himself into a state of exhaustion, and the crew was beginning
to tire of the meaningless sailing drills and a rugged physical-
education regime that had been clamped on it. But not much
of this was visible to the Newport townspeople and the yachts-

men crowding into the narrow, hilly streets of the town.

Over Labor Day weekend, the Aussies did something which startled everybody, including some of their own syndicate members who arrived in town for the first time and found *Gretel's* mastless hull lying in her slip almost completely gutted. To correct a weather helm, Payne had finally convinced Packer that the mast had to be moved forward 19 inches (the maximum the frame structure would allow), and the boat was virtually rebuilt amidships and completely rerigged in less than a week. It was a monumental effort and typical of the dedication of *Gretel's* personnel.

Finally Packer named Jock Sturrock as helmsman for the Cup series. Sturrock, a bluff, fun-loving man in his mid-40's and a proven winner, still had no power over crew selection or other policies and was therefore one of the most relaxed men in Newport as the September 15 starting date approached. "It's just another boat race," was his grinning comment when asked for his reaction. Packer's dictatorial policies reached a climax the morning of the opener, when he removed the navigator, put in his alternate helmsman, aging Archie Robertson, as a cockpit observer, and gave navigational duties to Magnus Halvorsen in the cockpit crew.

Sturrock therefore had to face the world's most experienced Twelve-Meter helmsman, in point of hours of actual racing, and a crew that had been virtually intact since the spring through two dozen tough races, with a crew that had never before sailed in the same combination, and he himself never having once sailed a Twelve-Meter race "in anger."

That *Gretel* made it close is a remarkable tribute to the effort that produced her out of nothing; to Payne's design, which made it possibly the fastest Twelve in the world at that time; and to the enthusiasm and fighting spirit of the crew. To beat this combination would take an equal amount of fighting spirit, cool control and skill, and fortunately for the defense of the Cup, *Weatherly* had all these.

The tremendous interest that the build-up had aroused was made all too evident on the bright, clear, breezy morning of September 15 when a spectator fleet that dwarfed the impressive opening-day assemblage of 1958 swarmed all over Rhode Island Sound. Unfortunately for the Coast Guard in its attempts to handle this mammoth armada, the wind was northwest, off the land, which meant that the course had to be laid out toward the direction from which the spectators were coming. If the breeze had been from the sea, the fleet would have been behind the course, but as it was, they formed a massive clutter all over it, and the start had to be delayed as Coast Guard cutters dashed hither and yon, sirens screaming and bullhorns roaring, trying to clear the area. The sea would have been quite smooth if it hadn't been for the bobble created by the wakes of this fleet that was estimated as close to 2,500 boats, ranging from cruise liners jammed with passengers to outboards and small day-sailers.

Finally, at 1:10, over an hour late, the race got underway over a twice-around windward-leeward course of 24 miles. Under mainsails only, with jibs ready to break out, the adversaries circled like wary dogs in Mosbacher's favorite starting pattern for most of the ten-minute preliminary period. Bus came out with the advantage, at just the right moment, of what had appeared to be standoff, forcing *Gretel* over the line just before the gun, so that Sturrock had to tack back for the line and was late. As the gun sounded, *Weatherly* was away and winging, with her wind clear, a telling demonstration of the gap in combat experience between the two skippers.

The advantage of several lengths she gained in this way was gradually increased as the wind backed to the west a bit and allowed *Weatherly* to reach the lay line after two tacks. She had a lead of 1 minute, 28 seconds at the stake boat, and this was the race to all intents and purposes. *Gretel* did close the time gap a

Left,
Weatherly (top) fights
off *Gretel's* challenge
on exciting last leg of
fourth race, closest
finish in Cup history.

Below,
the 1962 series
brought a fantastic
outpouring of specta-
tor boats.

The second 1962 race started with a slam-bang tacking duel, with *Weatherly* to windward.

Designer Alan Payne developed special gear for *Gretel,* much of which was scrapped after early trials.

bit as they ran back to the start in a freshening breeze, both with blue-topped spinnakers. On the next heat, with the breeze increased from the eight knots that prevailed at the start to a fresher 15–18 knots, *Gretel* suffered from sailing with a light weather main, and also from some internal troubles resulting from her makeshift crew setup. Without a full-time navigator, she overstood the mark a bit, and slow reactions by her un-coordinated cockpit crew caused a backstay fitting to fail, calling for a quick, unnecessary tack to take the strain off it while it was being replaced.

The result was a 3 minutes, 43 seconds victory for *Weatherly* as the huge gathering gave her a thunderous ovation of whistles and sirens, and it almost looked like the same old story as the boats headed for port in the slanting late-afternoon light. *Gretel* signaled for a layday, which was to be her calculated policy after every race. Payne later explained that this was decided upon to give the maximum time after each race for making adjustments according to lessons learned in combat. After all, this was her first formal competition of any kind.

A very different complexion on the series emerged with the second race, which wasn't until Tuesday, since Sunday was not a scheduled day and Monday counted as the layday. The week-day spectator fleet was perhaps 700–800 boats on a sunny, breezy day, with a 15-knot W by N breeze kicking up a lump of sea and freshening to more than 20 before the race ended.

What developed became one of the great races of Cup his-tory, beginning with the usual merry-go-round start that put *Weatherly* into what has emerged over the years as Mosbacher's favorite spot, a safe leeward with wind clear.

Soon the close-winded American boat was feeding bad air back to *Gretel* and Sturrock had to tack. *Gretel* had a flatter Hood sail than her loose, opening-day main and was going well, but Mosbacher was still gradually eating up to windward as they stood off on a long port tack. Then came one of the most concentrated periods of action in all the years back to 1851, when Sturrock began a short-tacking duel. Within ten minutes, there were more than a dozen tacks, as the crews belted into the coffee-grinders like football linemen blocking out opposing tackles. It was a slam-bang affair, with the Aussies working themselves into a competitive frenzy as they flipped their boat about and whanged her flailing genoa home time after time. The yoked winches Payne had developed were paying off, and *Gretel* had almost halved the distance between the boats when Mosbacher decided not to play the Aussie game in quite the same way and broke off into a loose cover. It kept him ahead by a boat length at the first mark of the eight-mile-legged triangle, 12 seconds on the clock, and the margin remained exactly that as the boats roared southeastward on a reach as though yoked together.

At the turning mark, the already exciting race erupted into one of the great moments of Cup history as they jibed around the tug and squared away for a run almost directly downwind to the finish. *Weatherly* was a bit slow in breaking out her heavy weather chute, a blood red affair, and Mosbacher allowed Sturrock to shoot up on his weather quarter during the rounding into a position that cast *Gretel*'s wind shadow over the leader. *Gretel*'s spinnaker was the first to fill, a pure white orb that burst instantly, without a flutter, into sculptured marble. Just as it did, her long lean hull surged up onto a big Point Judith roller, and suddenly the deep-displacement hull was surfing like a planing dinghy. Sturrock felt the wheel quiver and go slack as the boat surged forward, and the whole boat began to vibrate, her bow soaring into space as she rode the crest. Standing at *Gretel*'s mast, just having secured the spinnaker halyard, burly Norm Wright, whose early sailing had been in the hotly competitive 18-foot dinghies, couldn't resist an old custom of eighteen-sailors, a blood-curdling war-hoop they always let fly when they feel a boat pick up on a plane.

His exultant "Yeeee-hooooo" almost frightened Sturrock out of the cockpit, as he thought the mast must be going, and the cry also froze *Weatherly*'s crew for an instant as it hurtled down the breeze to them. *Weatherly*'s chute was just filling as *Gretel* surged by, but it was too late, and the Aussie boat took the lead in this one swift instant.

Just as *Gretel* swept by, *Weatherly's* spinnaker guy chose to part, and her pole whanged forward against the headstay and buckled like a broken lance, ruining any chance she had of fighting off the flying *Gretel*. They paraded to the finish, where the Aussie margin was 47 seconds, to a tumultous ovation, and the series stood at 1–1.

It was at this moment that the critical decision was made to stick to the layday-after-every-race policy, creating one of the great "might-have-beens" of the *America's* Cup story. The next day brought a carbon copy of the fresh westerly, and *Gretel,* now a proven performer, might have once again beaten the shaken Americans, but this was not to be. Instead, after one of the most riotous celebrations in the history of yacht racing, the the next day was spent puttering in port. The night before, the Aussies had taken over their favorite waterfront "pub," the Cameo, which they dubbed the Royal Cameo Yacht Squadron, and staged an all-out bash that will never be forgot-by those hundreds of celebrators who managed to wedge through the doors. "Waltzing Matilda" rang from the rafters time after time, along with many less-printable ballads; beer flowed down throats, over heads and cascaded along the bar and across the floor; and the decibel level was unbelievable.

As it turned out, this was the high point, although there was one more splash of drama before the series ended. The third race didn't provide it. The westerly had faded to a whisper and veered to N by E at about 6–7 knots on a warm, quiet day, and the only excitement was at the start. Sturrock seemed to have the ring-around-a-rosy advantage and forced *Weatherly* to

tack away just before *Gretel* started on the port tack at the
leeward end of the line. Mosbacher was late but had his wind
free on starboard, then tacked to port, and when Sturrock
tacked over to cover, he crossed *Weatherly*'s bow and tacked
back on top of her, losing his advantage, as Mosbacher still had
his wind free. This was all he needed to work out ahead in a
faltering breeze, and the long twice-around windward-leeward
race degenerated into a drifting match, with the last two legs
becoming reaches as the wind turned fluky. *Weatherly* ate it
up, *Gretel* wallowed, and the margin was as much as 23 minutes
halfway through the race. As the breeze freshened late in the
day, and the boats began to move faster, *Gretel* cut down some
of the distance and also the time margin so that it was 8 minutes, 40 seconds at the end, a far cry from the exhiliration of the
second race. Again the layday request went up, and again the
Aussies missed a fine sailing breeze by so choosing.

This put the fourth race on Saturday, a week after the start,
and another big fleet came out to watch a triangular race in a
moderate southerly that filled in nicely as the afternoon went
on. *Weatherly* took another safe leeward start after the preliminary circling and worked steadily out to a windward advantage during the whole leg, with Mosbacher refusing to
respond to Sturrock's attempts at a tacking duel, maintaining a
safe, loose cover. He had a 1-minute, 31-second margin at the
mark, and the rest of the race was a thrilling cliff-hanger as
Gretel, slightly faster off the wind, tried to close the gap. On
a spinnaker reach she whittled it to 55 seconds at the second
mark, and then kept coming on as they jibed and squared away
for the finish on the port tack. At first they both flew spinnakers, but, with *Gretel* inching up on his quarter, Mosbacher
sailed higher and shifted to a genoa. *Gretel* followed suit, and
many thought that she had been "psyched" into dropping
an effective sail. She stopped gaining and soon shifted back to
spinnaker, driving off to leeward until she was almost abeam

of *Weatherly*. Before she could break through, however, *Weatherly* put her spinnaker back up and also began to drive off on a slightly lower course for the line. This gave her enough of a better sailing angle to keep her ahead by 26 seconds, which is the closest official time margin in Cup history, though some boat-for-boat finishes were closer in the days when handicaps determined the time margin. When she finally made it, tension released in *Weatherly*'s crew like a kettle blowing its top.

Unfortunately, after another two-day layday brought on by an intervening Sunday, the fifth race was a distinct anti-climax before a greatly diminished spectator fleet. This was another twice-around windward-leeward, the last one to be used in Cup competition, on a hazy day, in a moderate southerly. This time Sturrock took the safe leeward, but it availed him naught, as Mosbacher worked up from his trailing windward position until Sturrock tacked first and Mosbacher flipped to a safe leeward on port that soon had command. That was the race and the series, as he built on the lead with a loose cover, with the long, lean, light-blue hull loping easily over the ground swell. Nothing *Gretel* tried produced any significant gain, and the two-minute lead the defender had at the first mark increased slowly to a final one of 3 minutes, 40 seconds.

Although this series ended more with a whimper than a bang, it had been a lively, relatively dramatic one and it restored some semblance of competitive interest to the *America's* Cup. It also aroused dreams of possible glory in the heads of many potential challengers and no doubt assured a good future for the competition in Twelve-Meters. If the far-off Aussies could come this close from scratch, couldn't others feel that they might do even better?

Chapter XXII

"CONSTELLATIONS'" LATE SURGE GAINS BERTH OVER "AMERI-
CAN EAGLE"—"SOVEREIGN" BEATEN BADLY IN FOUR RACES

IT HAD BEEN agreed that the British, forestalled by the quick
Aussie maneuvering in putting in the challenge for 1962, would
have next crack at the Cup. They already had a new challenge
candidate, Anthony Boyden's *Sovereign,* designed by David
Boyd, who had been responsible for *Sceptre.* Boyden, champ-
ing at the bit, wanted a 1963 series, but this was too soon for
the New York Yacht Club, whose committee members and officials have to give up so much time over a summer's campaign;
and it was agreed that the challenge from the Royal Thames
Yacht Club would be contended in 1964.

There were a few interesting innovations for this series.
One of the most important concerned the type of course.
Finally, slavish observance of the outmoded tradition of windward-leeward courses was scrapped, and no longer would a
mid-afternoon wind shift, so common off Newport when the
breeze steadies and veers from southerly to southwest, mean a
succession of pointless reaches in which a trailing boat would
have no chance to catch up. Instead of alternating this type of
course with once-around triangles, a decision was reached to
use an Olympic-type course of a triangle followed by beat, a
run and a final beat back to the finish, totalling 24.3 miles.
Tactically this would provide more windward work, more
mark roundings and, theoretically, closer action. A boat with
superior windward ability could not build quite such a lead,
and would be more vulnerable to attack on the reaches and
runs.

The other big innovation was a selection series run in American waters to pick a challenger, another first in Cup history. Royal Thames had belatedly come up with another challenge candidate to test *Sovereign* when a rather unusual syndicate was formed. Owen Aisher, whose *Evaine* had been used as a trial horse for *Sceptre* in 1958, and who had had a great deal to do with *Sceptre's* crew selection and training, joined forces with the Australian Livingston brothers, who had not been in evidence since their visit to Newport during the 1958 series. Since this new group had made a late start, it was decided that the only way to get a boat in being was to use Boyd's design for *Sovereign* and have her built in the same yard, Robertson's in Scotland. The new yacht was called *Kurrewa,* for the Livingston line of yachts. She was to be rigged a bit differently from *Sovereign,* and her keel shape was altered. Each camp went about crew organization in its own way, but the boats were basically sisters.

After a series of 19 shakedown races in England, which were not counted officially for selection, the boats and entourages arrived in Newport in mid-summer and staged their historic first, a challenge selection race in American waters, on August 10, a beautiful sailing day with a fresh southwester. It was a close affair with the lead changing hands several times, evidence that the new-type course could produce better action. *Sovereign,* with Peter Scott at the helm, finally gained a victory of several lengths after pulling some clever match race tactics at the last mark, forcing *Kurrewa* to the outside and into *Sovereign's* backwind when they finally rounded up. If all *America's* Cup races were as close and exciting as this one, a challenge would have the whole sailing world holding its breath.

Gradually, over the series, *Sovereign* proved the better-organized boat, better-sailed and with better sails, and was selected after six victories. Scott was one of the world's most experienced sailors, a champion in small boats such as the International Fourteen, a famed ornithologist, a painter, author, and an influential racing official as president of the International Yacht Racing Union. He had a husky crew of athletes with him, but among those who had observed this series, there were still strong doubts concerning the total British preparedness for the Cup series. The sails did not look right, rigging and spars were much cruder and heavier than those on the American boats, and many other refinements in gear and equipment that had been developed on the defense candidates had not been matched. Also, the twin hulls did not appear completely at home in Newport's notorious long ground swell and surface chop.

While all this was going on, the American campaign to pick a defender was running an unusual course. Two old boats were out, *Columbia* and *Nefertiti*. *Columbia* had been acquired by West Coast yachtsman Pat Dougan, who was not previously known beyond his local waters and had as helmsman California Ten-Meter skipper Walter Podolak. *Nefertiti*, again with Ted Hood and the Ross-Anderson syndicate, was somewhat altered in ballast and underbody from 1962.

There were also two new boats. *Constellation*, Olin Stephens' third Twelve-Meter, was designed for a large syndicate headed by Walter Gubelmann and Eric Ridder of Long Island and built at Minneford Yacht Yard at City Island, N.Y. The other was *American Eagle*, whose syndicate was headed by Pierre S. duPont III, and she had been designed by Bill Luders and built in his yard at Stamford, Connecticut, embodying many ideas learned from *Weatherly's* alterations in 1962. *Weatherly* had been retired to the Merchant Marine Academy at Kings Point, Long Island. *Easterner* came out again for a while but did not make a serious effort.

In the two earlier series, on Long Island Sound, known as Preliminary and Observation, *Eagle,* of Newport, with cham-

The summer-long battle for selection between *American Eagle* and *Constellation* (covering here after start of next-to-last trial race) was a tension-filled feature of 1964 campaign.

Most exciting moment of 1964 series was Bob Bavier's decision to take *Constellation* to windward of *Sovereign* at start of first race.

Sovereign showed her tendency to hobby horse in the swells off Newport.

pion small-boat sailor Bill Cox as skipper, ran up an impressive string of victories over all comers and was touted by many as a shoo-in for the defender's berth. Her crew and equipment seemed to be well set and she was operating smoothly, while *Constellation* was having all sorts of trouble. Many experts kept saying that a Stephens production should not be counted out too quickly, but she definitely wasn't winning. Ridder was acting as skipper, and while he had a good record in Six-Meters and ocean racers, he obviously had not yet gotten the feel of a Twelve.

With Olin and Rod Stephens working hard on every detail and problem, *Constellation's* performance gradually began to improve. A first inkling of the improvement came in one of the late Observation Series races, when her relief helmsman, Bob Bavier, was given a chance to see what he could do. On a windward leg in typical smoky sou'wester conditions off Newport, Bavier got *Connie* in the groove, outmaneuvered Cox at the start and had a good lead at the first mark. At this point, fog, which plagued the boats all summer, rolled in to cancel the race, and it was not an official part of the record. But optimism suddenly awoke in the *Connie* camp. Ridder graciously ceded the helm to Bavier for starts and windward work while continuing as captain and in charge of the crew.

However, the new optimism in the *Constellation* crew was frustrated for the rest of the scheduled days for the Observation Series, as each morning saw fog and more fog blanketing the course accompanied by an almost total lack of wind. No more races could be held and the official score was *Eagle* 5–0 over her rival, with the other boats outclassed.

And so the big question still hung in the air as the yachts gathered for the New York Yacht Club Cruise, a mid-summer fixture that split the Cup trials. Was that good windward leg of *Connie's* just a fluke (there were murmurings that *Eagle* had had the wrong sails for the weather), or had she really come alive? The first day of the cruise was a run from New London to Block Island in a blustery northeaster, and *Connie* lost her titanium-topped stick when a clevis pin let go in a shroud turnbuckle, so *Eagle* swept to her fifteenth straight official victory.

Then the spell broke. In the *Caritas* Cup around buoys off Newport, with Bavier at the helm, *Connie* moved to a commanding lead of one minute, 8 seconds at the first mark and held on in freshening breezes in the reach and run that followed, to win by 29 seconds, a significant moment in her career. She was over early at the next start and never recovered, but she then won three consecutive squadron runs in light-to-moderate air, all of them close and exciting, including a come-from-behind thriller after losing a jib early in the race on the final day's triangle in Buzzards Bay.

Results on the cruise don't count toward selection, but their morale factor was inestimable. From then on, *Connie,* whose battle cry was "Beat the Bird," was sailed with increasing confidence, while *Eagle* was, more and more, "running scared." The dominant role had changed, and now *Eagle's* crew, which had been feeling all through the course of their fifteen wins that they had hit the right combination and didn't have to experiment, suddenly lost confidence in sails that had seemed fine and began to make too many changes, losing more confidence with each change.

Rod Stephens joined the *Constellation* cockpit gang for the cruise and thereafter became a permanent member of the afterguard. With his vast knowledge, experience, analytical ability and physical prowess as a racing sailor, he added a real lift to her effort.

The two weeks between the cruise and the Selection Trials, also known as the Final Trials, were spent in long hard hours of analyzing and improving every item of equipment on the boats, along with arduous hours of sail drill. The trials started on August 17, pairing the two new boats with the old ones, and they soon showed that it was truly a two-boat battle when *Connie* beat *Columbia* by more than five minutes, and *Eagle* took *Nefertiti* by a slightly larger margin.

The first showdown between *Connie* and *Eagle* started tensely, with Bavier gaining a slight advantage with a safe leeward berth at the gun. The boats were very close until *Eagle* dropped a jib when the luff wire of the light, hankless sail parted. She never could come back and lost by a big margin, 11 minutes, 42 seconds. In the third race the two new boats eliminated the older ones with convincing victories and squared away for the final confrontation for which they had been preparing all year. This was the most dramatic race of the campaign, and one of the really exciting ones in match-race history. *Connie* took the start by a whisker of margin in safe leeward after eight minutes of wary circling, lost the lead by tacking in a soft spot, and finally got it back on a slam-bang last windward leg. A monumental tacking duel ended with her breaking through after inexorably closing the gap five to ten yards at a time as the big jibs slashed across and the crews whirled the coffee grinders like mad dervishes.

This breakthrough put *Eagle* thoroughly on the defensive thereafter, and instead of tuning up what should have been a thoroughly tested boat, her crew went through all kinds of experimentation with new sails. Nothing worked for her as *Connie* took three more races by Bavier's favorite move of gaining a safe leeward start and then squeezing up gradually, feeding backwind until the opponent had to tack.

Although there was speculation that this would put *Connie* in, the committee called for another look, and *Eagle* gained her first victory over *Connie* since early in the cruise when she was first to catch a 90° wind shift while trailing, but this was classed as a fluke, and a 4 minute, 27 second win in a good sailing breeze on August 27 was the clincher for *Constellation*. The commit-

tee, with Commodore Morgan again the spokesman, made the
announcement on its traditional visit to the boats at their
berths, *Eagle* first, then *Connie*. The long uphill fight was
ended and now thoughts could turn to the British.

Unfortunately, all the speculations about the lack of basic
preparation in the British camp were extremely accurate. One
observer from Australia (there were hundreds of Aussies "observing" and swarming all over Newport in anticipation of
coming back) looked at *Sovereign's* heavy mast section and
said, "I say, mate, do you always sail in a bloody hurricane
over there? You must with a walloping big mast like that."
This somehow summarized the British problems. Many of
their fittings and techniques were duplicates from the losing
1958 effort, and little effort had been made to keep up with
the advanced sophistication of Twelve-Meter gear and the techniques for handling it. The problem of weight aloft, attacked
on *Constellation* with painstaking attention to every ounce
that could be removed topsides, was never adequately solved,
and the British sails were, for the most part, baggy and ill-
fitting.

The social build-up for the two-week period before the
September 15 start of the series saw Newport a-whirl with
parties and receptions at which the crews made token appearances before going home for their conservative mid-evening
curfews at the big estates they had rented for the summer. The
Connie gang took a few days off completely before returning
to practice sessions with Mosbacher, Cox and Hood all lending
a hand for practice maneuvers and on-board analysis.

Tuesday, September 15 was a beautiful day with a good
west-southwest breeze that was about eight knots at the start
and building. The spectator fleet only numbered about 300
boats and was long on quality, if short on the exhibitionists
who had been out for the opening days in 1958 and 1962. It
was relatively easy to control as the Twelves dropped their tow-

lines near the *America's* Cup buoy and began pre-race maneuvers.

As it turned out, these next few moments contained the only element of drama in the whole series. The maneuvering before the start of a first meeting between two boats is always an exciting time, and Bavier quickly clamped a "tail" on Peter Scott by feigning lack of preparation as the boats passed for the first time, then quickly tacking onto *Sovereign's* stern before the latter reacted. Bavier was more interested in preventing Scott from controlling him than in gaining direct control himself, and with two minutes to go, he broke away from the circling, which Scott laughingly said later had made him "quite giddy," and reached away from the line gathering speed.

Timing his turn he jibed back and reached for a spot at the windward end of the line, which seemed slightly favored, building to nine knots as the seconds ticked away. Meanwhile, Scott was working *Sovereign* toward the windward end by tacking to port for a while and then coming over onto starboard in a spot that should have put him to windward of the defender. All this maneuvering slowed the dark-blue challenger to about six knots while Bavier had *Connie* charging in with great momentum. To everyone watching and to the crews of both boats, it seemed obvious that he was going to use his greater speed and momentum to try to break through to leeward into his favorite spot. Then, with the defender's white bow almost overlapped to leeward, he made a split-second decision to swing to windward as he saw a big hole opening up between *Sovereign* and the committee boat. Calling "trim," which was all the instruction his crew needed, he swung *Connie's* bow to weather, clearing *Sovereign's* stern by a mere 20 feet, and the sails barely luffed once as the crew adjusted them to this move.

As the gun boomed, *Connie's* charging bow was only a few seconds away from the line. The white hull was a length to windward of the blue one and 30 feet ahead, completely

blanketing the other. It was one of the most masterful starts in
Cup history, arrived at by split-second improvisation to take advantage of a sudden opening, and it was, to all intents and
purposes, the end of the series.

As in every other Twelve-Meter series except 1962, the end
result became perfectly obvious after the first ten minutes of
the first race. Just as *Sceptre* had revealed how outclassed she
was the first time her bluff bow lifted over a long swell and
plunged into it, now *Sovereign's* motion and actions gave her
away on this first leg, and the same thing was to happen again
in 1967.

For this first leg, *Sovereign,* aided by a wind shift to the
westward near the end of the leg, was only one minute, 49
seconds behind at the mark, and this was actually her best
windward leg of the four races. The final margin for this race
was 5 minutes, 34 seconds. The other race margins tell the
rest of the story. All were sailed in fresh breezes, after an attempted second race was called off for lack of air. *Connie* won by
20 minutes, 24 seconds; 6 minutes, 33 seconds; and 15 minutes
40 seconds, a bigger total time margin than that in the beating
handed *Sceptre* by *Columbia.* By the end, the series the boats
were sailing before a much smaller spectator fleet than many
of the trial races had attracted, and the races almost became
the same type of formality as the matches played to complete a
Davis Cup round after the victory has been clinched.

Each race followed a similar pattern. Once *Connie's* superiority in every department became so clearly established,
with faultless jibes and tacks carrying her through all her
maneuvers, Bavier merely made sure he had his wind free at
the start and let the powerful white hull settle in a groove and
work gradually up to windward. *Connie* swept evenly over the
surface chop and large groundswells pushed up by a hurricane
far offshore, never halting or hobby-horsing, while *Sovereign*
reared and plunged like a recalcitrant mare. Her heavy mast

plunged forward and aft like a pendulum, and her bow threw its wash forward as she plunged haltingly into each sea.

The end of the long campaign for *Constellation* and her big entourage came as her crew drove her to windward through the last leg of the last race with all the snap and precision that had seen them through their tensest moments. As she crossed the line amid whistles, cheers and sirens, Rod Stephens and Bob Bavier spontaneously reached over the side and affectionately patted the "flanks" of this remarkable marine racehorse, a thoroughbred brought to a pitch of perfection by the intense effort of a great many people.

Chapter XXIII

"INTREPID" DOMINATES TRIALS AND HANDLES AUSTRALIA'S
"DAME PATTIE" WITH EASE

ENCOURAGED by their showing in 1962, the Australians were
eager to get back into competition, and during the 1964 campaign they had been almost more in evidence in Newport
than had the British. Sir Frank Packer, Alan Payne and Trygve
Halvorsen were on hand, ostensibly to observe on behalf of a
new boat to be built for Packer. Also in Newport was Payne's
former assistant, Warwick Hood, who had worked with him
closely in the *Gretel* effort. Hood had been signed up by a
rival syndicate headed by Melbourne industrialist Otto Meik,
which had also selected Jock Sturrock as skipper. Jock had
quickly separated himself from the *Gretel* group after the 1962
campaign.

Even before the *Constellation-Sovereign* match was over,
many of the Australians had gone home, so convinced were
they of *Connie's* superiority after observing both the defense
and challenge trials. But before leaving, Packer had entered a
challenge in the name of Royal Sydney Yacht Squadron. By
this time, New York Yacht Club had established the policy
which provides for an interval of at least three years between
America's Cup challenges, and it also had a policy of considering all challenges received within 30 days after the conclusion
of a series as having been entered simultaneously.

No further challenges were made, so on November 5 Com-
modore Chauncey Stillman announced that the Royal Sydney
Yacht Squadron challenge had been accepted for a 1967 series.
Nearly everyone had had enough of the high-pressure atmos-

phere surrounding the *America's* Cup, and there was a quiet period of a few months. But not for Payne and Hood; they had gone to work immediately. Payne was working with Halvorsen, but Hood's program received a setback when Meik decided not to go through with his plans. But it wasn't long before a group of Melbourne yachtsmen formed another syndicate. The feeling between Sydney and Melbourne is something like the old Dodger-Giant baseball rivalry in New York, and Melbourne did not want to be left out this time. The new syndicate, headed by Emil Christiansen, a retired ice-cream tycoon, gave the go-ahead to Hood and Sturrock, and the Aussie pot began to boil well before the Americans became active again.

Back in the United States, a hard look was being taken at the conditions by the New York Yacht Club *America's* Cup Committee. To make the Australians' challenge acceptable in 1962, all sorts of concessions had been made on the subject of equipment, sails, spars, etc., and sails were not classed under the "made in country of origin" provision that applied to the boat. But the scare that *Gretel* threw into the American camp changed the thinking on this, and it was decided to establish sails and sailcloth under the same restriction as the designer and the boat itself. They all had to be home-grown.

With characteristic optimism, the Aussies took this in stride and were soon deep in programs to develop their own synthetic sailcloth. Australian sailmaker Joe Pearce, who was to become Hood's Australian agent after the 1967 series, spent the entire summer of 1964 working in Ted Hood's loft, recutting and repairing Twelve-Meter sails. He was thoroughly familiar with Hood's methods and thinking. Australia's textile industry produced a cloth that was eventually dubbed KAdron (KA are Australia's international sail-identification letters). It was said to be as good as Dacron, and of lighter weight-to-strength ratio. Aussie yachting writers soon came out with learned articles about woof and weft and bias stretch, and the problem of sailcloth was supposedly solved.

It was also decided to bar challenger's tank-testing in the U.S., thus cutting off the kind of assistance Payne had received in this department in the early 1960's. But both Payne and Hood had been developing facilities for towing-tank tests at Sydney University and now had a place to work. They knew *Gretel's* comparison to the American Twelves that had been tested by 1961, and they could also use *Vim's* lines if they wished to. Hood, having worked on *Gretel,* was thoroughly familiar with her characteristics, and he had studied *Constellation* intensively at Newport in 1964. They would not be too severely handicaped at being cut off from the Stevens Institute facility.

Christiansen's syndicate commissioned builder Bill Barnett for Hood's creation. Barnett, whose simple shed perched high on a bank over one of the many coves in Sydney Harbour, had never built a racing yacht bigger than a Six-Meter before, and he worked with a very small staff on this project. An expert sailor, he also signed on as a crew member.

Things were less definite in the Packer camp, and gradually it emerged that he was not going to build a new boat after all. Based on the studies by Payne and Halvorsen, *Gretel* was to be completely re-designed and rebuilt as a single-planked boat. Actually, with very little left from her original structure, she virtually became the new boat that they would have built, but by remaining technically an old boat, she had the benefit of an agreement that any gear she carried in 1962 could be used again, including some American sails made by Hood.

In the United States, the name of the game became "Who wins Olin Stephens?" Several potential syndicates and individuals were talking with him. Everyone tacitly agreed more or less that whoever commissioned him would have the leading contender, as he would only work actively on one boat, and would set a cutoff date for consulting on his previous boats when he started on the new one. Thus, when it was announced that a syndicate formed by William Strawbridge of Philadelphia, with former New York Yacht Club Commodore Burr Bartram as its head, had commissioned Stephens for the 1967 campaign, it was the end of any Stephens plans for other new boats. Strawbridge had worked with the *American Eagle* syndicate in 1964, helping with operation of the tenders and other practical details while quietly collecting ideas and observations on how a syndicate should be formed, handled and operated, and he used this experience to very good effect in the 1967 campaign. The new syndicate, which was known as the Intrepid Syndicate, though this name was not announced as that of the new boat, arranged to work with a group that had chartered *Constellation* from her European owners, who had bought her after the 1964 campaign. They also had bought *Sovereign* and *Kurrewa,* and were working on a long-range program to get into the *America's* Cup campaign. French ball-point pen manufacturer Baron Marcel Bich headed this effort and had the cooperation of some French and Dutch industrialists.

Bob McCullough, a successful ocean-racing skipper in his 48-foot yawl *Inverness,* was in charge of the *Constellation* charter group, and they ended up working with the Strawbridge syndicate. The original idea was to use *Connie* for training and trial-horse purposes only, but eventually she became a full-fledged candidate in her own right, albeit a slightly "second class citizen," to keep her crew morale up, and also to provide an even number of boats for the trial series.

Coming out again were *American Eagle,* under a new syndicate of Long Island Sound yachtsmen and with former Commodore George Hinman as skipper; and an extensively rebuilt *Columbia,* owned by Pat Dougan with Briggs Cunningham, inactive since 1958, back in action as her skipper. The new Stephens design, *Intrepid,* was the only new boat, a situation similar to that of *Nefertiti* in 1962. She and *Easterner* were

completely out of campaign; *Easterner* was sold to the West
Coast and renamed *Newsboy,* and *Neffy,* chartered to the
Aussies for a while, was sold in late 1967 to Greek yachtsman
John Theodoracopulos. For a while there was talk of a
Florida syndicate building a boat to designs by Charles Morgan,
a young St. Petersburg sailmaker, designer, builder and racing
skipper, but financing did not materialize in time.

Crew work began early in Australia. Packer still owned *Vim,*
and he had candidates for his team working out on her con-
tinuously while *Gretel* was being rebuilt. The Hood-designed
boat was to be named after Dame Pattie Menzies, wife of the
the Australian Prime Minister, and her launching was scheduled
for late August. It was a great day, August 22, when the boat
was lifted from Barnett's shed by a crane and gently placed in
the water. It was immediately apparent that she owed a great
deal to *Constellation* in layout and general aspect, that she had
short, weight-saving ends, sophisticated yoked coffee grinders
and a rudder—the subject of much secrecy and conjecture while
she was a-building—that was broader at the top than at the
bottom.

In answer to a flood of inquiries about her characteristics,
Hood officially described the boat in the following terms:
"*Dame Pattie* is a yacht of heavy displacement with a long
waterline length, minimum beam and low-wetted surface combined with a small keel area, a short overall length to save
structure weight, and a correspondingly reduced sail area to
compensate for her greater length waterline.

"She has a relatively high degree of stability because of the
way we have controlled hull weight and positioned ballast. The
hull form shows a very slack section amidships with a wall-sided
bow above the water and distinctly U-shaped below the waterline forward. Towards the stern, aft of the waterline, the bottom is flat, and she has a very soft bilge and wall sides. Later
alterations to the underwater part of the stern carried the V

of the midships section aft almost to the end of the waterline, and it picked up her windward performance significantly, as well as resulting in a reduction in the upright resistance, giving better downwind performance."

An eager, extrovert in sharp contrast to the quiet, soft-spoken Payne, Hood became even busier, if possible, than Payne had been in 1962 as he bustled about Sydney from towing tank to yacht club to boat yard to his office in the appropriately named suburb of Crow's Nest, and somehow found time for an occasional game of squash or a sail with his wife and small daughters. Payne had married since his bachelor days of 1962, and, with Halvorsen to help in the work load, did not seem so frantically busy this time.

The early Aussie shakedowns were marred by a rash of dismastings. *Gretel* lost a spar in August, and the *Dame,* which had a sprig of wattle, the Australian national flower, painted on the bow of her light-blue hull, lost her stick on her maiden spin on September 7.

There was much political by-play in setting up Australian trials, as Packer tried to dictate arrangements to suit his plans. Finally, a first series off Sydney Heads in January resulted in smashing victories for *Dame Pattie,* before she was again dismasted. Packer tried several helmsmen for *Gretel* but saw most of them leave in a huff over his high-handed tactics, and she was continually bothered by bickering over personnel. Sturrock had followed Mosbacher's system of picking a crew early and sticking with it and had been given complete operational control by the syndicate.

When the dismasting halted the January trials, Packer ordered another complete rebuilding of *Gretel,* probably the world's most altered yacht by this time, causing a delay in the second set of trials which had been scheduled for early March. *Gretel* finally emerged from her latest face-lifting with a sharper entry forward, a more deeply-veed after underbody, slacker

bilges and greater beam on deck than she had in 1962. Not a
single frame station remained the same shape as it had been
originally in 1962, and only her deck (widened) and rudder-post
remained from the original boat. On her first trial spin off
Sydney Heads, an unofficial brush with the *Dame,* she seemed
to have an easier motion in the waves than previously, throwing
less spray. She appeared to hold her own, but when the next
set of formal trials came, the *Dame* again walked away by wide
margins. Supposedly both boats were to go to the United States
for final trials, but Packer decided not to undergo the expense
and retired *Gretel,* leaving *Dame Pattie* to spend a lonely, fruitless summer without real competition in Newport. They
chartered *Nefertiti* but didn't use her much for practice brushes
as she was no longer effective against the new boat.

The average Aussie-in-the-street was wildly confident that
the *Dame* would bring the *America's* Cup home at last ("and
you Yanks can have the Davis Cup for a while, we don't mind"),
but the insiders in the Cup boat program were not quite so
confident. There were still nagging doubts about the Aussie-
made sails, and the lack of competition was sure to hurt her.

There was also great conjecture about what the new Stephens
creation would look like. *Intrepid* was being built at the Minneford Yard on City Island amid great secrecy and heavy
security measures, but doodling at his desk in Crow's Nest,
Hood was able to sketch out a fairly accurate idea of her profile in March, as rumors began to get around. British journalist
Jack Knights caused a furor by jumping a release deadline after
inspecting the new boat, with articles in a British and an American magazine revealing many of her features, including that she
had a rudder separate from her short keel, linked by a skeg or
"kicker," and a trimming rudder. The other writers observed
release dates and sat on their knowledge of these features, but
there were still plenty of surprises when *Intrepid* was launched
with great fanfare in May.

Olin Stephens looking at *Intrepid's* profile, a radical change for 12-Meters.

Dame Pattie had a "bustle" added aft of rudder following early trials.

Intrepid's deck presented new, uncluttered look with winch-grinders relegated below decks.

Construction shot reveals *Intrepid's* two rudders and skeg or "kicker" in front of after one.

She showed short, stubby ends and a powerful, U-shaped hull as she slid into Long Island Sound, and on her deck were canvas covers over protuberances that looked like coffee grinders. It wasn't until she started sailing that it was discovered that her winches were actually below decks, a radical innovation to keep weight down low. And the syndicate had not only commissioned Olin Stephens to design her. They also, after a period of indecision, persuaded Bus Mosbacher to return to the wars. Although on *Vim* in 1958, he had never been connected with a new Stephens boat, and this high-powered combination looked a formidable one for the other boats to contend with.

It turned out that this was very much the case, and *Intrepid* made a shambles of the trials in a manner as devastating as *Ranger's* foray through the J-boat ranks in 1937. Mosbacher once again followed his practice of selecting a set crew early in the game and then training it to achieve perfect teamwork. This was a very business-like, hard-nosed effort with even less of the horseplay and touches of light-heartedness than in the serious-enough campaigns of previous years, and the public-relations pressure became so heavy during the summer that the syndicate hired professional public-relations men to deal with the demands for interviews, photographs and feature material that flooded in.

Never before had a Twelve been the object of such pains-taking concern with reduced wetted surface, weight-saving and sophistication of gear and sails. For example a deeply-routed cove stripe below her rail was for weight-saving, not decoration, and all these refinements really added together to increase her speed. *Intrepid* emerged so early and so obviously as the boat to beat, that there was little of the suspense and drama that had featured the other trial campaigns. In early brushes against *Connie,* she proved herself measurably faster than the 1964 champion. Bob Bavier, sailing *Constellation* in these brushes, was amazed to find that *Intrepid* was closer winded than his old love, accelerated noticeably faster, and had better maneuverability due to her separate rudder and extra trimming rudder on the trailing edge of her keel.

Stephens had already designed a "bustle" (skeg or kicker) but not a separate rudder for the rebuilt *Columbia* before turning all his efforts to *Intrepid,* and all the boats thereafter had some form of alterations done to their underbodies aft, in keeping with this thinking.

Intrepid's weight-saving snub bow and cut-off stern, her flat sheer and utilitarian deck and cockpits did not make her a thing of conventional beauty, and it was interesting to compare her with the graceful long-ended creations of just nine years before, when the class was revived. A lot had been learned about what weight in the ends of a boat does to her seakeeping ability, especially in the distinctive conditions off Newport. Those who like to see a boat moving really well soon found a different kind of beauty in *Intrepid's* performance.

She only lost one trial race all summer, and that was actually as the result of a ridiculous mistake that merely went to prove that the men of the "superboat" were only human after all. In one of the early races on Long Island Sound in June, using government marks rather than racing buoys, *Intrepid* built a long lead over *Eagle* on a windward leg, only to sweep right past the leeward turning mark, a buoy most of her crew had raced around all their lives, heading for the wrong mark. *Eagle,* coming along several minutes later, took the correct mark, and only then did *Intrepid's* crew realize the error. She had to down spinnaker and beat back, and even though she gained some time back, it was too late to recoup. Her crew took a ribbing the rest of the summer, but it was about the only thing she could be faulted for in the entire campaign. *Columbia* emerged as her closest threat, mainly because she was beating the other two boats most of the time, but she never could handle *Intrepid.* Once, when she still appeared to be a threat after winning the *Caritas* Cup on the New York Yacht Club Cruise, as the result of the best start in an unprecedented fleet of seven Twelves, the next meeting in a trial race generated a little advance excitement. Mosbacher, who had not been using much infighting, preferring to rely on *Intrepid's* obvious speed superiority, therefore changed tactics. He forced the California boat away from the line for over three minutes after the gun had sounded, wiped her off and dumped her back there, and then headed back for the starting line with a commanding lead that increased all day.

The Selection Committee had no problem in making the decision this time, and only prolonged the series to make sure there could be no intimation that the West Coast boat hadn't been given a fair chance. *Intrepid* ended up with a 6–0 record in the Final Trials, and her shakiest moment all season came in a dismasting on breezy Buzzards Bay during the cruise. Her titanium-topped bendy mast shattered in a breeze heavier than the Twelves usually race in, as did *Constellation's* on the same day, a black one for the syndicate (and a red one for its finances).

The Australians had been a lot quieter and much less in evidence than in 1962, and somehow, they didn't seem to have the same old bounce. No doubt the sight of *Intrepid* romping away from her well-sailed, well-found rivals day after day put a damper on their natural optimism, and there was some dissension in the camp over Sturrock writing a series for an Australian newspaper. Still, there was an element of drama and a natural build-up as the start of the Cup series approached, based mainly on memories of the colorful campaign in 1962.

Many Australians came to Newport as tourists, having made their bookings back in the days when the *Dame* was whomping *Gretel* in home waters and optimism had been at its peak. They made a colorful addition to the crowded Newport scene and they gamely put up a brave front on the eve of the races.

Once again, though, it didn't take long to establish a convincing picture of the relative abilities of the two boats as soon as they confronted each other in actual combat. The first ten minutes told the story as it had in 1958 and 1964, although *Dame Pattie* was stiffer competition than the two British boats had been.

The series once again began on a Tuesday, September 12, to avoid the spectator-fleet crush, and the weather played a vital part in the story of this twentieth defense. Warwick Hood had played a calculated gamble with *Dame Pattie's* design and had aimed her to be at her best in 10–12 knots of breeze. Careful study of weather data over many years for the Newport area in September revealed a pattern of winds averaging in this range, and he decided to play for the averages. Part of his reasoning was that Americans could not afford a "one-sided" boat, designed for a specific wind range, because defense candidates had to be effective over a variety of conditions in the summer-long selection trials. *Nefertiti,* for example, had revealed that a limited boat, one with some strong points but weaknesses in other areas, could not build up a winning record against better-rounded boats. Why not, therefore, develop a boat that would be at her absolute best in the expected conditions, which would give her perhaps a bit of edge on a boat designed to handle a wider range? He hadn't made *Dame Pattie* poor in light or heavy breezes by any means, but her optimum was to be in the narrow range of moderate air the records called average.

Just as a fisherman always says "you should have been here yesterday," *Dame Pattie,* unfortunately for Hood's theory, should have been at Newport some other mid-September. The night before the first race, a large high-pressure area moved into southeastern New England. Ordinarily, it would have moved on through after one day of brisk northwest breeze with a mild southwesterly 10–12-knot return flow behind it, but this one stalled with its leading edge just offshore, blocked by two hurricanes acting strangely further out to sea. The result was three days of bright, sparkling weather, ideal for cruising and for most kinds of racing, but bad news for the Aussies. It blew a steady 14–20 knots, with higher gusts, and rolling whitecapped seas surged across Rhode Island Sound. Conditions served to hold down the spectator fleet, and those who came out had a bouncy time, making a splashy, colorful spectacle themselves.

The four races followed a remarkably similar pattern that was revealed with the first start. Sturrock, who might have been expected to use aggressive tactics, as an underdog should, showed little inclination to mix or play ring-around-a-rosy, perhaps discouraged by the way *Intrepid's* two rudders allowed her to turn inside the *Dame's* turning circle, and also to brake when necessary by being set hard against each other.

Sturrock went for a safe leeward start in each of the first three races, a good move when, like *Weatherly* in 1962 or *Constellation* in 1964, one's boat is obviously closer-winded and/or faster. By squeezing up, throwing bad air back, and forcing the other boat to tack, one is in command. When the boat on the windward quarter is faster and closer-winded, however, the safe leeward doesn't stay safe very long, and this is what happened in each of the first three races. As it turned out, *Intrepid* averaged an advantage of 11 seconds per mile faster over the 97.2 miles (rhumb line) of racing, and all she needed was her wind clear to start applying this advantage.

In the first race, this was helped by the fact that the *Dame's* mainsail soon "went to pieces" shivering like jelly, bulging and wrinkling and obviously not driving her. The natural reaction was to blame this on the KAdron cloth, but in truth, because of some internal friction in her crew, the mast was not set up for the cut of that particular sail, and a horrendous mis-match resulted. In the remaining races, rig and sails were correctly matched and the Aussie sails could not be seriously faulted.

Intrepid's superiority was obvious as she moved out on the
first two tacks, standing a bit straighter and taking the big
ones better, and built steadily to a 5-minute, 58-second margin,
the largest of the series. The *Dame's* shaky sail and a fruitless
gamble by Sturrock on tacking downwind on the last run helped
to add to *Interpid's* lead.

Each night, the weather forecast was for more moderate wind
the next day, and remembering *Gretel's* misfortune with too
many laydays in 1962, Sturrock did not ask for one after the
first or second races, only to find the same blustery northeaster
dusting the big swells as the boats towed out the next morning.

The second race produced the closest thing of all of them to
real combat. Sturrock started to leeward again, and *Intrepid*
seemed well on her way to working up to a commanding spot
right after the start, when a slight header dropped her back almost into *Dame Pattie's* wake. Mosbacher tacked away first, virtually an admission of being behind, but the wind swung back as
he did and, when Sturrock tacked to cover, this new header on
port tack put him at a disadvantage. They held this tack for 16
minutes as *Intrepid* gradually consolidated the slight advantage,
and when she came back to starboard, almost amid the spectator
boats, *Intrepid* crossed the *Dame* by two lengths. Here Sturrock decided to try a tacking duel, but this was nothing like
the *Weatherly-Gretel* slam-banger in the second race of 1962.
For a few tacks there was no obvious gain or loss, as he never
succeeded in getting out of phase, and *Intrepid* was on top without fail each time the boats flipped. Then Jock tried a ploy
that has been hailed as a good trick in match racing, but not
against as alert a combination as Mosbacher, George O'Day
and Vic Romagna, *Intrepid's* cockpit crew. Sturrock put *Dame
Pattie* into the wind, but instead of swinging over, he fell
away again on the same tack. *Intrepid* made one flicker of response to the false tack, but the deception had been detected

In every race *Intrepid* quickly took **controlling** position over *Dame Pattie,*
as in third race here.

immediately, and she then bore off again on the same tack under a full head of steam, and several more lengths had been added to the lead by the time the *Dame* gained speed again. The maneuver was so unsuccessful that some observers thought that the Aussies must have had some sort of jam on a genoa sheet, forcing her to fall back on the same tack, but it was admitted afterward that it had been a calculated false tack.

That ended that contest, and *Intrepid* went on to a 3-minute, 36-second margin. The third race started in carbon-copy conditions and situation, but this time Sturrock was at a disadvantage from the start, and even one of the weirdest encounters ever to take place on a race course failed to halt *Intrepid's* relentless piling on of that 11 seconds per mile. Mosbacher reached the lay line on the first starboard tack, aided by a lift, tacked to port with *Dame Pattie* well tucked away, and was storming along for the mark, when he suddenly was confronted with the spectacle of a Coast Guard helicopter hovering close to the water directly on his course. Two lads in a 12½-foot Beetle Cat from Sakonnet, R.I., had wandered onto the course, attempting to get from one side of the spectator fleet to the other, and the helicopter, in trying to shoo them away, capsized the little sailboat with its downdraft. The 'copter was in the process of lifting the boys from the water when *Intrepid* happened along, and only a quick slacking of sheets and bearing away saved the Twelve from a possible dismasting in the vicious blasts from the helicopter blades. If the race had been close, this could have been a deciding factor, but nothing short of a dismasting could have stopped *Intrepid* by then. She lost perhaps 30 seconds, but her ultimate margin was 4 minutes, 41 seconds, and Sturrock finally decided to ask for a layday for Friday.

The offshore hurricanes had been acting strangely, and the nearer one, Dora, had actually backtracked from east of Nantucket to North Carolina, so Saturday's race was cancelled

Friday night to give the weather a chance to settle down, which it did, the storm moving offshore again. An attempt to hold the first Sunday race in Cup history was thwarted by fog, and the fourth race finally came off on Monday. Fog again lay over the course, but it began to blow away just before the start in a moderate southwester. Confusion over whether there was going to be a start in the poor visibility kept the Twelves from any radical maneuvers, and they were actually on opposite tacks when the gun went off. *Intrepid* started on port and was already well ahead when they converged after tacking back, and the series ran out with a leisurely parade as she worked out her final margin to 3 minutes, 35 seconds under clearing skies. This was the smallest of the series by one second, as *Dame Pattie* tacked downwind on the last run and moved into a fresher breeze, improving her time a bit from the last mark; but this was small consolation for the disappointed Aussies, who had found "their breeze" and still had lost.

It was not much help to them to realize that the second Twelve they had ever built was probably the second-fastest one in the world, but that she had run into one of the most potent combinations to this point in *America's* Cup history: Olin Stephens, Bus Mosbacher and a well-organized crew and syndicate. This effort should set a standard for years to come in Cup campaigns.

RECORD OF THE AMERICA'S CUP MATCHES

Date	Name	Rating	Course	Allows	Elapsed Time	Corrected Time	Wins by
		†Tons.		M. s.	H. M. S.	H. M. S.	M. s.
Aug. 22, 1851	America	170.	Cowes, around the Isle of Wight. 58 miles (Second.)	—	10.37.00	10.37.00	8.00
	Aurora	47. Water-line Area.		—	10.45.00	10.45.00	
Aug. 8, 1870	Magic	1680.0	N. Y. Y. C. course. 35.1 miles (Tenth.)	14.7	4.07.54	3.58.21.2	39.17.7
	Cambria	2105.8 Displacement.		—	4.34.57	4.37.38.9	
Oct. 16, 1871	Columbia	1694.	N. Y. Y. C. course. 35.1 miles	1.41	6.17.42	6.19.41	27.04
	Livonia	1881.		—	6.43.00	6.46.45	
Oct. 18, 1871	Columbia	1694.	*20 miles to windward from Sandy Hook Lightship and return. 40 miles.	6.10½	3.01.33½	3.07.41¾	10.33¾
	Livonia	1881.		—	3.06.49½	3.18.15½	
Oct. 19, 1871	Livonia	1881.	N. Y. Y. C. course. 35.1 miles (Partially disabled.)	—	3.53.05	4.02.25	15.10
	Columbia	1694.		4.23	4.12.38	4.17.35	
Oct. 21, 1871	Sappho	1957.	20 miles to windward from Sandy Hook Lightship and return. 40 miles.	—	5.33.24	5.36.02	33.21
	Livonia	1881.		2.07	6.04.38	6.09.23	
Oct. 23, 1871	Sappho	1957.	N. Y. Y. C. course. 40 miles.	1.09	4.38.05	4.46.17	25.27
	Livonia	1881. Cubical Contents.		—	5.04.41	5.11.44	
Aug. 11, 1876	Madeleine	8499.17	N. Y. Y. C. course. 32.6 miles	1.01	5.24.55	5.23.54	10.59
	Countess of Dufferin	9028.40		—	5.34.53	5.34.53	

* Distance approximate; yachts reached round the course.   † No time allowance.

RECORD OF THE AMERICA'S CUP MATCHES—*Continued*

Date	Name	Rating	Course	Allows	Elapsed Time	Corrected Time	Wins by
		Cubical Contents.		M. s.	H. M. s.	H. M. s.	M. s.
Aug. 12, 1876	Madeleine ...	8499.17	20 miles to windward from Sandy Hook Lightship and return. 40 miles.	1.01	7.19.47	7.18.46	27.14
	Countess of Dufferin ..	9028.40		—	7.46.00	7.46.00	
Nov. 9, 1881	Mischief	3931.90	N. Y. Y. C. course. 32.6 miles	—	4.17.09	4.17.06	28.20¼
	Atalanta	3567.60		2.55¼	4.48.24½	4.45.29¼	
Nov. 10, 1881	Mischief	3931.90	16 miles to leeward from Buoy 5 off Sandy Hook and return. 32 miles.	—	4.54.53	4.54.53	38.54
	Atalanta	3567.60		2.55	5.36.52	5.33.47	
		Length & Sail Area.					
Sept. 14, 1885	Puritan	83.85	N. Y. Y. C. course. 32.6 miles	—	6.06.05	6.06.05	16.19
	Genesta	83.05		0.28	6.22.52	6.22.24	
Sept. 16, 1885	Puritan	83.85	20 miles to leeward from Sandy Hook Lightship and return. 40 miles.	—	5.03.14	5.03.14	1.38
	Genesta	83.05		0.28	5.05.20	5.04.52	
Sept. 9, 1886	Mayflower ..	87.99	N. Y. Y. C. course. 32.6 miles	—	5.26.41	5.26.41	12.02
	Galatea	86.87		0.38	5.39.21	5.38.43	
Sept. 11, 1886	Mayflower ..	87.99	20 miles to leeward from Sandy Hook Lightship and return. 40 miles.	—	6.49.00	6.49.00	29.09
	Galatea	86.87		0.39	7.18.48	7.18.09	
Sept. 27, 1887	Volunteer ..	89.10	N. Y. Y. C. course. 32.6 miles	—	4.53.18	4.53.18	19.23¾
	Thistle	88.46		0.05	5.12.46¾	5.12.41¾	

RECORD OF THE AMERICA'S CUP MATCHES—*Continued*

Date	Name	Rating (Length & Sail Area)	Course	Allows (M. S.)	Elapsed Time (H. M. S.)	Corrected Time (H. M. S.)	Wins by (M. S.)
Sept. 30, 1887	{ Volunteer { Thistle	89.10 88.46	20 miles to leeward from Sandy Hook Lightship and return. 40 miles.	— 0.06	5.42.56¾ 5.54.51	5.42.56¾ 5.54.45	11.48¾
Oct. 7, 1893	{ Vigilant { Valkyrie II	96.78 93.11	15 miles to leeward from Sandy Hook Lightship and return. 30 miles.	— 1.48	4.05.47 4.13.23	4.05.47 4.11.35	5.48
Oct. 9, 1893	{ Vigilant { Valkyrie II	96.78 93.11	Equilateral triangle, from Sandy Hook Lightship. 30 miles.	— 1.48	3.25.01 3.37.24	3.25.01 3.35.36	10.35
Oct. 13, 1893	{ Vigilant { Valkyrie II	96.78 *93.57	15 miles to windward from Sandy Hook Lightship and return. 30 miles.	— 1.33	3.24.39 3.26.52	3.24.39 3.25.19	.40
Sept. 7, 1895	{ Defender { Valkyrie III	100.36 100.49	15 miles from mark, 3 miles N. E. of Seabright, N. J., and return. 30 miles.	0.29 —	5.00.24 5.08.44	4.59.55 5.08.44	8.49
Sept. 10, 1895	{ †Valkyrie III { Defender	100.49 100.36	Equilateral triangle, from Sandy Hook Lightship. 30 miles.	— 0.29	3.55.09 3.56.25	3.55.09 3.55.56	.47
Sept. 12, 1895	{ Defender { ‡Valkyrie III	100.36 100.49	15 miles to windward from Sandy Hook Lightship and return. 30 miles.	0.29 —	4.44.12 Did not finish	4.48.43 finish	
Oct. 16, 1899	{ Columbia { Shamrock	102.135 101.092	15 miles to windward from Sandy Hook Lightship and return. 30 miles.	— 0.06	4.53.53 5.04.07	4.53.53 5.04.01	10.08
Oct. 17, 1899	{ Columbia { aShamrock	102.135 101.092	Equilateral triangle, from Sandy Hook Lightship. 30 miles.	— 0.06	3.37.00 Did not finish	3.37.00 finish	

* Remeasured. †Disqualified for fouling Defender. ‡ Withdrew on crossing the line. a Carried away topmast and withdrew.

RECORD OF THE AMERICA'S CUP MATCHES—*Continued*

Date	Name	Rating	Course	Allows	Elapsed Time	Corrected Time	Wins by
		Length & Sail Area.		M. s.	H. M. S.	H. M. S.	M. s.
Oct. 20, 1899	Columbia ...	102.135	15 miles to windward from Sandy Hook Lightship and return. 30 miles.	0.16	3.88.25	3.38.09	6.34
	Shamrock ...	*102.565		—	3.44.43	3.44.43	
Sept. 28, 1901	Columbia ...	102.355	15 miles to windward from Sandy Hook Lightship and return. 30 miles.	0.43	4.31.07	4.30.24	1.20
	Shamrock II.	103.79		—	4.31.44	4.31.44	
Oct. 3, 1901	Columbia ...	102.355	Equilateral triangle from Sandy Hook Lightship. 30 miles.	0.43	3.13.18	3.12.35	3.35
	Shamrock II.	103.79		—	3.16.10	3.16.10	
Oct. 4, 1901	Columbia ...	102.355	15 miles to leeward from Sandy Hook Lightship and return. 30 miles.	0.43	4.33.40	4.32.57	.41
	Shamrock II.	103.79		—	4.33.38	4.33.38	
Aug. 22, 1903	Reliance ...	108.41	15 miles to windward from Sandy Hook Lightship and return. 30 miles.	—	3.32.17	3.32.17	7.03
	Shamrock III.	104.37		1.57	3.41.17	3.39.20	
Aug. 25, 1903	Reliance ...	108.41	Equilateral triangle from Sandy Hook Lightship. 30 miles.	—	3.14.54	3.14.54	1.19
	Shamrock III.	104.37		1.57	3.18.10	3.16.12	
Sept. 3, 1903	Reliance ...	108.41	15 miles to windward from Sandy Hook Lightship and return. 30 miles.	—	4.28.00	4.28.00	
	Shamrock III.	104.37		1.57	Did not finish	Did not finish	
		Sail Area: Limits & Penalties					
July 15, 1920	Shamrock IV.	93.8	15 miles to windward from Ambrose Channel Lightship and return. 30 miles.	6.42	4.24.58	4.24.58	
	†Resolute ...	83.5		—	Did not finish	Did not finish	
July 20, 1920	Shamrock IV.	*94.4	Equilateral triangle from Ambrose Channel Lightship. 30 miles.	7.01	5.33.18	5.22.18	2.26
	Resolute ...	83.5		—	5.31.45	5.24.44	

*Remeasured. †Throat halyard rendered on winch drum—withdrew.

RECORD OF THE AMERICA'S CUP MATCHES—*Continued*

Date	Name	Rating	Course	Allows	Elapsed Time	Corrected Time	Wins by
		Sail Area: Limits & Penalties		M. s.	H. M. S.	H. M. S.	M. s.
July 21, 1920	Resolute	83.5	15 miles to windward from Ambrose Channel Lightship and return. 30 miles.	—	4.03.06	3.56.05	7.01
	Shamrock IV.	94.4		7.01	4.03.06	4.03.06	
July 23, 1920	Resolute	83.5	Equilateral triangle from Ambrose Channel Lightship. 30 miles.	—	3.37.52	3.31.12	9.58
	Shamrock IV.	*93.8		6.40	3.41.10	3.41.10	
July 27, 1920	Resolute	83.5	15 miles to windward from Ambrose Channel Lightship and return. 30 miles.	—	5.35.15	5.28.35	19.45
	Shamrock IV.	93.8		6.40	5.48.20	5.48.20	
		Sail Area: Limits & Penalties†	Races of 1930, 1934 and 1937 started and finished at a mark anchored nine nautical miles S. E. (Magnetic) from Brenton Reef Lightship.				
Sept. 13, 1930	Enterprise ..	76.	15 miles to leeward and return. 30 miles..	—	4.03.48		2.52
	Shamrock V..	"		—	4.06.40		
Sept. 15, 1930	Enterprise ..	"	Equilateral triangle. 30 miles............	—	4.00.44		9.34
	Shamrock V..	"		—	4.10.18		
Sept. 17, 1930	Enterprise ..	"	15 miles to windward and return. 30 miles.	—	3.54.16		—
	‡Shamrock V.	"		—	Did not finish		
Sept. 18, 1930	Enterprise ..	"	Equilateral triangle. 30 miles............	—	3.10.13		5.44
	Shamrock V..	"		—	3.15.57		
Sept. 17, 1934	Endeavour ..	"	15 miles to windward and return. 30 miles.	—	3.43.44		2.09
	Rainbow	"		—	3.45.53		

* Remeasured. † Built to Rating; no allowance. ‡ Parted main halyard at masthead sheave: withdrew.

RECORD OF THE AMERICA'S CUP MATCHES—*Continued*

Date	Name	Rating Sail Area: Limits & Penalties†	Course	Allows M. S.	Elapsed Time H. M. S.	Corrected Time H. M. S.	Wins by M. S.
Sept. 18, 1934	{ ENDEAVOUR { RAINBOW	76. "	Equilateral triangle. 30 miles..........	— —	3.09.01 3.09.52		.51
Sept. 20, 1934	{ RAINBOW { ENDEAVOUR	" "	15 miles to leeward and return. 30 miles..	— —	4.35.34 4.39.00		3.26
Sept. 22, 1934	{ RAINBOW { ENDEAVOUR	" "	Equilateral triangle. 30 miles..........	— —	3.15.38 3.16.53		1.15
Sept. 24, 1934	{ RAINBOW { ENDEAVOUR	" "	15 miles to leeward and return. 30 miles..	— —	3.54.05 3.58.06		4.01
Sept. 25, 1934	{ RAINBOW { ENDEAVOUR	" "	Equilateral triangle. 30 miles..........	— —	3.40.05 3.41.00		.55
July 31, 1937	{ RANGER { ENDEAVOUR II.	" "	15 miles to windward and return. 30 miles.	— —	4.41.15 4.58.20		17.05
Aug. 2, 1937	{ RANGER { ENDEAVOUR II.	" "	Equilateral triangle. 30 miles..........	— —	3.41.33 4.00.05		18.32
Aug. 4, 1937	{ RANGER { ENDEAVOUR II.	" "	15 miles to windward and return. 30 miles.	— —	3.54.30 3.58.57		4.27
Aug. 5, 1937	{ RANGER { ENDEAVOUR II.	" "	Equilateral triangle. 30 miles..........	— —	3.07.49 3.11.26		3.37

† Built to Rating; no allowance.

RECORD OF THE AMERICA'S CUP MATCHES—*Continued*

Date	Name	Rating	Course	Allows	Elapsed Time	Corrected Time	Wins by
		Sail Area: Limits & Penalties† Int'l 12-Meter		M. s.	H. M. s.	H. M. s.	M. s.
Sept. 20, 1958	COLUMBIA ...../ SCEPTRE		Windward-leeward	—	5.13.56 / 5.21.40		7.44
Sept. 22, 1958	COLUMBIA ...../ SCEPTRE	" / "	Triangular. 24 miles	— / —	Time Limit Expired		
Sept. 24, 1958	COLUMBIA ...../ SCEPTRE	" / "	Triangular. 24 miles	— / —	3.17.43 / 3.29.25		11.42
Sept. 25, 1958	COLUMBIA ...../ SCEPTRE	" / "	Windward-leeward twice around. 24 miles	— / —	3.09.07 / 3.17.27		8.20
Sept. 26, 1958	COLUMBIA ...../ SCEPTRE	" / "	Triangular. 24 miles	— / —	3.04.12 / 3.11.04		6.52
Sept. 15, 1962	WEATHERLY ..../ GRETEL	" / "	Windward-leeward twice around. 24 miles	— / —	3.13.57 / 3.17.40		3.43
Sept. 18, 1962	GRETEL ....../ WEATHERLY ..	" / "	Triangular. 24 miles	— / —	2.46.58 / 2.47.45		00.47
Sept. 20, 1962	WEATHERLY ..../ GRETEL	" / "	Windward-leeward twice around. 24 miles	— / —	4.21.16 / 4.29.56		8.40
Sept. 22, 1962	WEATHERLY ..../ GRETEL	" / "	Triangular. 24 miles	— / —	3.22.28 / 3.22.54		00.26

† Built to Rating: no allowance.

RECORD OF THE AMERICA'S CUP MATCHES—*Continued*

Date	Name	Rating	Course	Allows	Elapsed Time	Corrected Time	Wins by
		Sail Area: Limits & Penalties†		M. s.	H. M. s.	H. M. s.	M. s.
Sept. 25, 1962	Weatherly ..	Int'l 12-Meter	Windward-leeward twice around. 24 miles	—	3.16.17		3.40
	Gretel			—	3.19.57		
Sept. 15, 1964	Constellation	"	*America's* Cup. 24.3 miles	—	3.30.41		5.34
	Sovereign	"		—	3.36.15		
Sept. 17, 1964	Constellation	"	Triangle, windward-leeward-windward ..	—	3.46.48		20.24
	Sovereign	"		—	4.17.12		
Sept. 19, 1964	Constellation	"	Triangle, windward-leeward-windward ..	—	3.38.07		6.33
	Sovereign	"		—	3.44.40		
Sept. 21, 1964	Constellation	"	Triangle, windward-leeward-windward ..	—	4.12.27		15.40
	Sovereign	"		—	4.28.07		
Sept. 12, 1967	Intrepid	"	Triangle, windward-leeward-windward ..	—	3.25.03		5.58
	Dame Pattie .	"		—	4.31.01		
Sept. 13, 1967	Intrepid	"	Triangle, windward-leeward-windward ..	—	3.29.21		3.36
	Dame Pattie .	"		—	3.32.57		
Sept. 14, 1967	Intrepid	"	Triangle, windward-leeward-windward ..	—	3.20.14		4.41
	Dame Pattie .	"		—	3.24.55		
Sept. 18, 1967	Intrepid	"	Triangle, windward-leeward-windward ..	—	3.27.39		3.35
	Dame Pattie .	"		—	3.31.14		

† Built to Rating: no allowance.

INDEX